PITT SERIES IN

RUSSIAN AND EAST
EUROPEAN STUDIES

VARIETIES OF

MARXIST HUMANISM

*Philosophical Revision
in Postwar Eastern Europe*

James H. Satterwhite

UNIVERSITY OF PITTSBURGH PRESS

Pittsburgh and London

Series in Russian and East European Studies No. 17

Published by the University of Pittsburgh Press, Pittsburgh, Pa., 15260
Copyright © 1992, University of Pittsburgh Press
All rights reserved
Eurospan, London
Manufactured in the United States of America

Library of Congress Cataloging-in-Publication Data

Satterwhite, James H.
  Varieties of marxist humanism : philosophical revision in postwar
Eastern Europe / James H. Satterwhite.
      p.   cm.—(Series in Russian and East European studies : v. 17)
  Includes bibliographical references and index.
  ISBN 0-8229-3711-5 (cl)
    1. Communist revisionism—Europe, Eastern. I. Title. II. Series.
HX518.R4S34 1992
335.43'4—dc20   92'8048
                                                                   CIP

CONTENTS

ACKNOWLEDGMENTS

I would like to express my appreciation to those included in this study who generously helped me by providing access to materials and giving of their time to answer questions. In this regard I am particularly indebted to Professor Svetozar Stojanović for all his efforts on my behalf, without which my understanding of East European Marxist humanism would be incomplete.

I would also like to express my gratitude to my wife Olwen, and to the many friends who by their encouragement saw this project through.

VARIETIES OF

MARXIST HUMANISM

INTRODUCTION

The East European Context

SINCE THE SECOND WORLD WAR, MARXISM IN
Eastern Europe has commonly been associated with its
role as the dominant or ruling ideology, a system of
thought that served to legitimize the activities of the
Communist party in any country in the process of "socialist transformation." Although this role has certainly
been one aspect of Marxism or Marxist thought in Eastern Europe—one that remained prominent until change
swept the area in 1989–90—it has by no means been the
only role Marxism played there. Marxist thought has
simultaneously served as the source of a far-reaching
critique of the ruling ideology. This second aspect of
Marxism in Eastern Europe has been appreciated only
gradually by many outside the area.

In one sense, it is not surprising that it should have
taken some time for people unfamiliar with the phenomenon to appreciate this critical function of East European
Marxist thought. After all, in the years immediately following World War II, until at least the time of Stalin's
death in 1953, a fairly monolithic ideological unity existed in most of Eastern Europe. Because of its different
development, Yugoslavia was an exception to this statement; even there, however, the rigid Marxism commonly
characterized as "Stalinism" began to lose its dominant

3

position only in 1952 and 1953.[1] Also, when a critical stance within Marxist thought began to develop in Eastern Europe, to all intents and purposes it used the same conceptual framework used by the official variant. That the substantive content of some of these concepts increasingly differed in the two cases would not be readily perceived by someone unfamiliar with the conceptual framework or with the specific social/political context.

The critical aspect of Marxist thought in Eastern Europe was the outcome of a process of searching self-examination on the part of many thinkers. They had identified with the Communist movement and its program for a better society but had been forced to radically rethink their position in response to their growing awareness of the nature of the Stalinist system. This process of self-examination differed slightly in each country, with Yugoslavia again being somewhat of an exception. Nevertheless, in every instance (Yugoslavia included) it was the question of the Stalinist reality that started these thinkers on their path of critically assessing the official ideology.

For a variety of reasons that relate to the complex interplay of social and political factors in the postwar experience of Eastern Europe, only four countries—Czechoslovakia, Poland, Hungary, and Yugoslavia—fully developed the critical use of Marxist thought as a basis for a rejection of the official ideology.[2] It is the activity of critical thinkers from these four countries that constitutes the subject of the present study.

Of interest in the present context is a specific orientation within Marxism which informed the activity of these critical thinkers. This orientation has come to be known as Marxist humanism because of its emphasis on the creative role humans play in actively shaping their reality, in opposition to the view that humans are mere objects of external forces or "laws." What this meant concretely will be carefully examined in the course of this study; for present purposes, a general overview is sufficient.

In each of the four countries, a movement developed along similar lines at roughly the same time. A basic characteristic of each movement was a return to the writings of Marx, particularly to the newly discovered "young Marx" of the *Economic and Philosophical Manuscripts.* There were several reasons for this return to Marx. One was that many wanted a fresh look as a means of breaking out of the impasse of Stalinism, which had neglected a serious study of Marx and had stressed a very deterministic approach based primarily on a selective interpretation of *Capital.* Another was that the young Marx stressed human creative activity—activity by means of which people create their reality, their world of meaning, and their social institutions. Although this creative activity takes place within the limitations of a specific social and historical context, this context still affords considerable room to maneuver. And, most important, this view of human reality offered the perspective that the process of creation was a continuous one, whereby current institutions and patterns could also be changed.

Within the context of Stalinism, this concept was extremely radical, although initially even the protagonists were not always aware *how* radical. Some of the thinkers critical of Stalinism seemed at first to believe that they were merely correcting some aberrations in a shared conceptual universe—pointing out the obvious, as it were. Also, because they used the same vocabulary official Marxism used, the radical nature of their departure was to a large extent cloaked from the view of the guardians of orthodoxy, especially in their early writings.

In the case of the three countries that remained within the "Soviet Bloc"—Poland, Czechoslovakia, and Hungary—the reaction to Stalinism came as a result of similar events. The impetus for the process was Stalin's death in early 1953. Though not a great deal changed outwardly in these countries at first, what was felt most was the disappearance of the Presence. Suddenly, Stalin was not there to oversee the course of events. Furthermore, with the succession crisis following his death, signals emanating from the Soviet Union—which guided political life in the countries of the Soviet bloc—grew weaker and were often contradictory, allowing for more leeway in intellectual life.

The result in Eastern Europe was enough change to cause some people, particularly intellectuals, to begin to reexamine their place in and their contribution to the Stalinist system and to try to come to terms with it theoretically as well. What began as faint stirrings became more pronounced after the Twentieth Soviet Party Congress and Khrushchev's speech attacking Stalin and the "cult of personality." It was suddenly much easier to be critical of what had gone on under Stalin. Although Khrushchev's intent was to consolidate his position ideologically and certainly not to undermine the system or change it in any fundamental way, the effect of his speech in Eastern Europe was nothing short of devastating. It shook the Party to its roots and opened the door to enormous changes. In Czechoslovakia, the process was contained and smoldered, only to break through the surface in the 1960s. In Poland and Hungary, the process was rapid. In Poland, the events of the "Polish October" of 1956 had a great impact, and in Hungary events led to the revolution, which was an event of incalculable import there and elsewhere in Eastern Europe. In Yugoslavia, the process of critiquing the Stalinist model as developed in the Soviet Union had begun earlier, after the Soviet-Yugoslav break in 1948; as a result, it took a slightly different course but the broad outlines were very similar.

When it became more apparent that the critique of Stalinist Marxism was more far-reaching than had been realized earlier, those engaging in this critique came to be termed *revisionists*. The term was not new, having been first applied to Eduard Bernstein at the end of the previous century, but it took on a very general meaning in postwar Eastern Europe.[3] While still referring to a "revision" of Marxist theory, the term was applied to anyone who differed from the current Party line in any given country or who identified with the allegedly wayward course of some other Communist Party in some other country. Thus, the Soviets and Chinese were fond of terming one another revisionists. And, after the Yugoslav-Soviet break, the Yugoslavs began calling the Soviets revisionists in order to contrast the Soviet approach with the Yugoslavs' claim of greater theoretical or ideological faithfulness to Marx.

To cut through the thicket that has grown up around the term *revisionism*, the expression *philosophical revisionism* is employed in the present work. The advantage of this refinement is that the expression retains the element of "revision" while clearly indicating that the revision is taking place in the realm of philosophy or theory. The term further suggests that more than a mere political deviation from the Party line is involved, that a theoretical departure of some significance is at issue. I am not suggesting that a philosophical revision of the orthodox conception of Marxist theory was not also a political event in a world where all of life was politicized—only that the stress should be on the theoretical dimension.

Furthermore, philosophy in Eastern Europe played a greater role in society than that attributed to it by some observers. This was partly due to the all-encompassing nature of Marxism as the ruling and legitimizing ideology but can also be attributed to the historical position and role of the intellectuals in these societies. It is because of this integral position of philosophy that philosophical revisionism could have had the impact it did in East European societies. Also, as one contemporary student of this phenomenon has noted: "It is not enough that the dissident intellectual think his dissident thoughts, he must also articulate them; and the manner in which those thoughts are articulated is a matter of some consequence. The dialectic of dissent thus involves a very subtle interplay between content and form, thought and structure, which is irreducible to neat and simple formulas."[4]

It is this "dialectic of dissent" that developed gradually among these thinkers, taking shape in ever more specific terms as their thought matured. It is important to note that their orientation as "Marxist humanists" was not a fortuitous one; although developed on the basis of a rereading and reevaluation of Marx, it had its roots in the search for a human alternative to the dehumanizing experience of Stalinism. Thus it was precisely this basis for the critique of Stalinism that was the most radical and the most penetrating. It was grounded in Marx's thought and yet was the very antithesis of the orthodox Marxism of the Stalinist period. As such, the critique was able to grow to encompass all areas of life rather than remaining within the confines of philosophy. Or, put another way, although the position of Marxist humanism entailed a philosophical critique and refutation of the orthodox, official ideology, of necessity (both theoretical and practical) it also moved, by the inner logic of its argument, to a critique of the social, political, and cultural dimensions of the Stalinist system.

The term *Stalinist* has been used frequently to characterize the official or orthodox position. By this is meant, however, not only the system which was extant under Stalin but also the legacy of Stalin's system, which continued far beyond his death. It can be argued that Stalinism lasted until 1956 or, in altered form, even later. Some writers apply the term *neo-Stalinist* to the system in place in the Soviet Union at least up to Gorbachev's time (and in parts of Eastern Europe until 1989). The fine points of the debate are outside the scope of this inquiry; what is at issue is the continuation of a system of party control over all facets of life, and the theoretical basis of this control in the official ideology. (Here, too, the Yugoslav situation was somewhat different, but it had certain clear parallels).

The critical thinkers, as they were referred to earlier, had in common an involvement in theoretical pursuits, whether philosophy or sociology. (In any case, such distinctions tended to blur, as sociology often was more connected with philosophy than sometimes pertains elsewhere and had a strong theoretical as well as an empirical component.) They also shared a commitment to a radical reevaluation of their theoretical background while remaining within a Marxist context, even if some later formally departed from any professed allegiance to Marxism.

To say that they remained within a Marxist context does not mean that this was a closed universe of thought. One feature of this critical, humanist Marxism was its openness to other theoretical approaches. It drew freely from existentialism and phenomenology—among others—while critically evaluating these trends at the very time it drew on them. Although Marxist humanism was labeled revisionist, it entailed far more than a mere revision of the orthodox ideology and in fact represented a radical departure from it in the name of Marx. In some sense the new approach certainly *was* revisionist, but the differences were profound. At the root lay not only a different view of human activity but underlying it a very basic epistemological split. This split came from the opposition between the humanist view that human knowledge *of* the world is a product of human activity creating meaning *in* the world, and the orthodox position (derived especially from Lenin's *Materialism and Empirio-Criticism*) that our *knowledge* of reality is a reflection of a reality that is totally external to humans, a reality "in-itself." On this basis, sufficient grounds exist for saying that the Marxist humanism that was taking shape was not only not *just* revisionist but was not even *Leninist*. Instead, it was something quite new and diametrically opposed to Marxism-Leninism, as the official orthodoxy was termed. Its newness was, ironically, in large part a result of its return to Marx as the source of inspiration.[5]

In some cases these thinkers formed a distinct group. In Hungary, a group was known as the "Budapest School" (or "Lukács School" because of their association with György Lukács). In Yugoslavia, where a number of philosophers and sociologists from different parts of the country made common cause, they came to be known as the *Praxis* group, after their journal of the same name. In the cases of Poland and Czechoslovakia, there were no such distinct groupings. A number of individuals set out to reevaluate Marxist theory critically in Poland, but they went about it in different ways. Although they were certainly aware of one another's work and shared certain broadly defined goals and assumptions, they in no sense ever constituted a group in the way the Hungarians or Yugoslavs did. In Czechoslovakia, two philosophers of quite different backgrounds and temperaments found themselves working along similar lines in their critique of orthodox thought based on humanist Marxism. In the period between 1956 and 1968, their work was mutually complementary; although not alone in their humanist orientation, they were its outstanding representatives.

What is remarkable about the phenomenon of Marxist humanism in Eastern Europe is the way in which a common identity of purpose developed among the different people involved, not only within any one country but among them all. Furthermore, beyond this identity of purpose, an almost uncanny resemblance in theoretical matters developed. Although in each country these theorists had their own history—individually and collectively—and the social historical context varied from country to country, the product in all cases was very much alike. Not only were the broad outlines similar but the use of key concepts overlapped considerably—although the stress on concepts differed from one thinker to another. The thinkers in the different countries interacted with each other and with Western European critical thinkers—the representatives of the "Frankfurt School," for example—but much of this interaction took place at a time when their basic positions had already been formulated. Still, the dialogue was genuine and managed to transcend the differences between Eastern and Western Europe in a manner that provided a leaven for further critical thought on both sides. The outcome of all of this interaction was a distinct approach within Marxism which broke new ground conceptually and had an influence that extended beyond the confines of the geographical or political context in which it arose

The aim of this study is to trace the development of Marxist humanism in Eastern Europe through a presentation of some of the key concepts as they were formulated by the various thinkers at different stages in their own intellectual growth, in the context of the historical changes that took place in each country. In addition to following the development of the approach through its various representatives, this study has as its primary purpose the task of showing the fundamental unity underlying the efforts of those from all four of these countries. (Since Yugoslav Marxist humanism has been extensively covered elsewhere, I will deal with Yugoslavia only by way of comparison in the Conclusion.) [6] This unity was neither accidental nor arrived at by some special effort. It sprang from a common purpose and a shared humanist perspective and from the fact that the logic of their critique of the orthodoxy carried them in similar directions. Given the fact that their critique took place within the framework of a humanist reevaluation and recovery of Marx, it could be expected that an essential conceptual unity would follow.

CHAPTER 1

Polish Revisionism: Critical Thinking
in Poland from 1953 to 1968

Historical Background

IN POLAND, AS IN OTHER PARTS OF EASTERN
Europe, the themes of Marxist humanism were an outgrowth of efforts on the part of many intellectuals to
come to terms with the legacy of Stalinism. Specifically,
they represent an attempt to understand what had happened to Marxism as a system of thought and to socialism as the form of social organization that, in Eastern
Europe, was the embodiment of conclusions reached in
that system of thought.

In the case of Poland, the period from 1953 to 1956 was
marked by a cautious move on the part of the government—a move to implement the new approach while
avoiding moving too fast or too far, lest its own position
be undermined. The relaxation in the political sphere was
also a result of the discrediting of the secret police and of
the past policy of extensive reliance on that force. Among
the people who had been politically active, the combination of the above factors contributed to spurring a great
deal of reflection on the reasons such an approach could
have been possible. The developing intellectual ferment
took on concrete form in the so-called discussion clubs
that sprang up over the course of 1955, beginning with

the famous "Club of the Crooked Circle" in Warsaw. These clubs became a kind of informal political assembly, where "important issues were debated and attitudes crystalized. From their sessions emerged ideas that gradually reached the populace."[1] This, then, was the background to the single most important event in the transformation taking place in Eastern Europe—Khrushchev's speech at the Twentieth Soviet Party Congress in February 1956, in which he denounced Stalin. Although the speech was delivered in a closed session, its contents nevertheless were soon widely known in Poland. The impact of Khrushchev's denunciation was devastating, although its consequences were more immediate in some parts of Eastern Europe than in others. In Poland, the intellectual ferment that had been building in intensity over the previous year was given new impetus; many Polish intellectuals felt compelled to radically rethink their previous understandings of life, which under the circumstances involved a serious reexamination of Marxism. "The void created by the destruction of Stalinism and by violent Polish attacks on Stalin himself led many of those who had previously embraced Marxism to search for some sort of individual statement of beliefs, for a self-defined statement of reference. This was particularly true of the young Marxists who now felt deceived by the past. The dogmas of the past were now to be replaced by a genuine search for the humanist values of socialism."[2]

The search for "humanist values" of socialism was not an accidental by-product of the crisis of confidence that Khrushchev's speech provoked. Rather, this search constituted an attempt to rediscover the original humanist thrust of Marx's own thought, one that had been the source of many of the Polish intellectuals' own attraction to Marxism. They were now forced to confront the ideology they had embraced so fervently as providing the liberating impetus for humankind in general and Polish society in particular. They set out to discover simultaneously what it was about the form Marxism had assumed that had led to its inhumanity, and what in Marx's own thought could form the basis for a new understanding of the humanist potential in Marxism. This dual task occupied the attention of a number of thinkers in Poland for the next several years, leading them into polemics with representatives of the old order of dogmatic Marxism. Eventually, it also led to their dismissal from academic posts and even to their emigration from the country.

Representing this search in Polish intellectual life were not only philosophers but also historians and sociologists—although, for a variety of reasons, these traditional distinctions do not fit well into the Polish reality of the period in question. The various thinkers shared not only the common goal of redefining Marxism and their own position with regard to socialist society but also certain very basic attitudes about what was important within Marxism. Within this basic understanding, different backgrounds and approaches were evident, but these complemented one another. Furthermore, institutionally, a common frame of reference was provided by the fact that in the very early part of this period they were all part of what was termed *historical materialism.*[3]

The debate that began in 1955 and carried over with greater intensity to 1956 after Khrushchev's denunciation of Stalin reached its peak in the events of October 1956. Gomułka was reinstated as the head of the party, with all the ideological shifts that implied, and it seemed to many that a major victory had been won, one that would sweep away the last vestiges of the Stalinist system from Polish life. The Soviet invasion of Hungary in November of 1956 made it very clear that, regarding the role of the Party and relations with the Soviet Union, there were certain limits beyond which no country in Eastern Europe would be permitted to go. This observation, coupled with the gradual rolling back of reform on Gomułka's part in 1957, introduced a new element into the discussion taking place within Poland. This sense was well expressed by Leszek Kołakowski in the preface to one of his early books. He says of the articles—collected in a book published in 1957 but written between January 1955 and June 1956—that they were of a "prehistoric" era and had already become anachronistic. He goes on to say of the book that

> Its *pars destruens*, the critique of a harmful tradition, was carried out on the whole from a reformist position. It was done with the hope of reforming something which may not be capable of reform. In this light, the author regards these essays as an attempt at reform from before the Great Crisis—the crisis that so revolutionized political and philosophical consciousness that hope has become doubt, although not yet hopelessness.[4]

Initially, the efforts of many thinkers were directed at liberating philosophy, as well as the social sciences and history, from the strict control of the Party and its ideological guidelines. This activity was carried on as part of the critique of the Stalinist era. Although in some sense it could be said that the critique of Stalinism provided a smoke screen for the introduction of new ideas, in another sense the fermentation process that was going on was itself part and parcel of the attempt to come to grips intellectually with the legacy of that period. It was not some unrelated agenda slipped in under the guise of this critique.

Zbigniew Jordan, a student of this period in Polish history, has said that three categories of thinkers participated in the discussions of the time. According to Jordan, "having attained the independence of thinking from political pressure, this [first] group entered completely into the ranks of the scholars in their field. Their revisionism was based on the emancipation from the previously-accepted limits; after they threw off these constraints there was nothing to differentiate them methodologically from non-Marxist specialists." The second group were those who, "in the name of preserving the internal consistency of the Marxist system of thought, wavered on the path of philosophical revisionism and then returned under the wing of the orthodoxy." The third group of thinkers was characterized by the fact that the "object of their interest was not a specific discipline, whether in the natural sciences, the humanities, or in the social sciences; their interest was also not in academic philosophy, per se, but in humanist philosophy." "Humanist philosophy" here means "the anti-scientific direction in philosophy, which is opposed to the application of those methods characteristic of the natural (or 'exact') sciences to philosophy." In this way those in this latter group "underlined the special character of the tasks and methods" of the humanities and social sciences over against the "exact" sciences.[5]

It is this latter tendency within what has been called "philosophical revisionism" that is of central concern to the present inquiry. Jordan further characterizes this approach as being concerned with "different types or families of world-views and of positions on the world and life," and "attempting to uncover their structural and typological properties, as well as their historical and social functions." This "humanist philosophy" can also be called a "philosophy of life," because it is particularly concerned with analyzing the widely varied attempts that have been made to answer the question of the sense of human life, its place in the natural world, and, finally, the relation of the individual to society or collective.[6]

Jordan singles out the philosopher Leszek Kołakowski as one who particularly exemplifies this humanist philosophy in Polish intellectual life. In fact, when one thinks of this period and of this approach, Kołakowski's contribution comes immediately to mind, and he has consequently been the focus of many studies dealing with the phenomenon of philosophical revisionism in Poland.[7] Nonetheless, Kołakowski was not alone in representing humanist philosophy, and the present study will attempt to focus on some others who in different ways can also be said to belong to this category.

Biographical Information

In the center of attention will be three names: Leszek
Kołakowski, a philosopher by training; Bronisław Baczko,
intellectual historian; and Zygmunt Bauman, a theoretical sociologist. Also deserving of mention are three
others: Tadeusz Kroński, also a philosopher; Maria (Bielińska) Hirszowicz, a sociologist; and Julian Hochfeld,
also a sociologist. As mentioned earlier, however, the different academic fields represented by these people were of
less consequence than one might imagine. The boundaries between philosophy, intellectual history, and theoretical sociology tended to blur; although the fields
contributed to differences in style and, in some cases, in
the choice of materials, their overall orientation was the
same. In the early period following Stalin's death and
Khrushchev's speech, they all were for the revitalization
of Marxism and they all were interested in rediscovering
the human dimension to history and social change.

The best known figure in postwar Polish philosophy is
probably Kołakowski. He is certainly the best known of
those representing the category of philosophical revisionism in Poland, perhaps in all of Eastern Europe. He has
written a great deal, mostly in essay form—although his
writings include several books—and many of these writings have been translated into other languages. Although
his interests range from the history of religion to a close
acquaintance with the philosophy of science, it is possible to discern a common thread throughout.

Kołakowski was expelled from the Party in 1966, after
giving a speech at Warsaw University on the tenth anni-
versary of the Polish October. The speech was highly critical of contemporary Polish political life.[8] This event
was the culmination for Kołakowski of a long process of
critical activity at the university. He and several col-
leagues were fired from their posts at Warsaw University,
and Kołakowski subsequently left the country to assume
teaching positions in Canada and the United States. He

then became a senior research fellow at All-Souls College, Oxford University.

Bronisław Baczko was born of Jewish parents in Poland in 1924. He escaped to the Soviet Union in 1939 and returned to Poland as the Germans were being driven out. He was then an officer and political commissar in the Polish Army formed in the Soviet Union that fought alongside the Red Army. Baczko studied philosophy at Warsaw University and became a professor of Marxism at the Institute for Social Sciences of the Central Committee (Instytut Nauk Społecznych przy KC PZPR). In 1956, he and others moved from this institute and the field of histoical materialism to a new location in the Polish Academy of Sciences (PAN) under the title of the Department of History of Modern Philosophy and Social Thought, which Baczko directed until 1968. Those who worked in this setting were privileged in that they had complete access to Western scholarship and periodicals, a fact that undoubtedly played a part in the formation of critical thought in many of them. Baczko was dismissed from his post at Warsaw University in 1968 and left Poland soon after, thus ending this phase of his activity.

Zygmunt Bauman graduated from Warsaw University and worked originally in the field of historical materialism, at the Institute for the Social Sciences of the Central Committee. From 1964 to 1968, he held the chair of General Sociology at Warsaw University, from which he was dismissed in 1968, at the same time Baczko and Kołakowski (along with Maria Hirszowicz and others) were dismissed. From 1968 to 1971 he was professor of sociology at Tel Aviv and Haifa Universities and, since 1971, has been professor and head of the Department of Sociology at the University of Leeds in England.

In a sense, Kroński was the forbearer of the others because he was a generation older. He studied in prewar Warsaw and at Charles University in Prague. Deported to a German labor camp during the war, he escaped and lived in France, where he was active in the French Underground. He returned to Poland after the war. His real interest in Marxism was a postwar development and an outgrowth of both his study of Hegel and his reflections on fascism as a manifestation of the crisis of Western civilization. Kroński brought Hegel to the attention of Polish Marxists immediately after the war, stressing Marx's links to Hegel and the revolutionary potential of Hegel's thought. Although he died early, in 1958, Kroński left an impression on those who studied with him—among them Kołakowski and Baczko.[9]

Julian Hochfeld was a professor of sociology at Warsaw University. He had a considerable influence on Bauman's theoretical development in the early years; his perspective on the humanization of labor pointed out the need for a sociological analysis of work as a part of the attempt to understand Marxist humanism. He was a delegate to the Polish *Sejm* and took part in events in 1957 to make it a forum for genuine debate.[10] He also attempted to mediate between Kołakowski and Adam Schaff in their debate on Marxism and philosophy.[11]

Maria (Bielińska) Hirszowicz was the other figure in the history of Polish philosophical revisionism. Like Bauman, she was influenced by Hochfeld's emphasis on the humanization of labor, and she incorporated this perspective in her sociological analysis. Among those dismissed from Warsaw University in 1968, she later went to teach at Reading University in Britain.

The Critique of the Stalinist System

All of those involved in philosophical revisionism in Poland devoted a great deal of energy in the early stages of their activity to a critique of Stalinism. This critique had a dual purpose. The first and most straightforward aim was to achieve breathing room for theoretical activity independent of Party control and to reestablish philosophy and the social sciences as legitimate fields of inquiry. The second aim of the critique was to bring about the annihilation of authoritarianism and thus enhance the possibility of human freedom.

The intellectuals involved in the critique went about their task in two ways. They attacked the bureaucratic nature of the Stalinist system, trying to allow for a more rational and human system, and they engaged in a critique of Stalinist ideology. Although the focus was different in each case, the two aspects of the critique cannot really be regarded as separate undertakings. Each aspect complemented the other, and together they proved a very effective weapon against Stalinism.

THE CRITIQUE OF BUREAUCRACY

The critique of bureaucracy and the bureaucratization of everyday life was a common tool in the battle against the legacy of Stalinism in Eastern Europe.[12] It provided the means of attacking Stalinism without calling into question the value of socialism per se. This is not to suggest that at this stage any of the critical Marxist thinkers were interested in raising this question: they were interested in overcoming "distortions," but to accomplish this task they also had to make it clear to others that their aim was to eliminate these distortions of socialism.

In a sense, therefore, these thinkers chose methods of attack that legitimated their position during the de-Stalinization period, although it is difficult to say precisely whether they did so by conscious choice or simply as a part of their general attitude. In the last analysis, there was no real difference between the two.

The most thoroughgoing critique of bureaucracy was provided by Bauman.[13] In his study of bureaucracy he attempted to differentiate between bureaucracy as "a group of people engaged professionally in management administration, the organization of other people and institu-

tions," and the meaning given in English by *red tape*
(*volakita* in Russian, *Amtschimmel* in German).[14] He
studied contrasts as a way of analyzing the distinctive
features of a bureaucracy and of determining what caused
a bureaucracy to act in terms of the second type.

A bureaucracy tends to alienate itself from society and
close itself off in a "circle of narrow interests" in inverse
proportion to the political activity and ability of those in
the society. The key to controlling bureaucracy, therefore,
is to have an active, aware, and committed public. In
practice, this translates to several concrete steps:

> The stimulation of factory and regional Party organizations
> to political activity. The achievement of worker self-
> management in the trade unions. Lastly, workers' coun-
> cils—that key to the transformation of workers into
> co-managers of their workplaces, the road to a feeling of
> responsibility for the factory, for the country and the state,
> the road to political thinking on the part of the masses. In
> addition, certain permanent rules of political life, such as
> political discussions, which would be public, open, and
> wide-ranging, and which would draw in people and accus-
> tom them to political life.[15]

Bauman adds one further criterion of immense importance, saying that a great deal of confidence in the political wisdom of the public is necessary. Even though such
wisdom might not be particularly evident at any given
moment, it would never materialize without the basic
confidence among those seeking change that it could.
Bauman was not so naive as to think that all of this program could be accomplished overnight, given the situation in Poland at the time, but he clearly indicated that
any change had to go in this direction.

PHILOSOPHY AND IDEOLOGY

The corresponding critique of ideology took form as part
of a discussion in 1956 on the nature and role of Marxist

philosophy. Most of the critical thinkers entered into this discussion, addressing different points in the debate.[16]

Baczko entered the debate by examining how Marxism should be taught at the university level. He attacked the Stalinist understanding of Marxism, accusing it of "losing—in both theory and practice—a holistic view of the complicated ties in human relations."[17] Having lost this holistic perspective, Stalinism (or "vulgar sociologism," as he calls it) could not take into account the multidimensionality of human life. It had lost sight of the complicated interaction of individual and social needs of concrete human beings, thereby contributing to an atomized view of society. This in turn led to a "bureaucratic-functionalistic" understanding of social phenomena. This line of analysis follows from Baczko's intent not only to critique Stalinism as a theory but to try to discern the social roots and consequences of occurrences during this period of history. He was concerned that real human beings and their interaction in the context of a web of relations and circumstances had been lost from view. This issue was at the center of his understanding of Marx. He accused Stalinism of "abstracting from real-life concerns in presenting a one-sided picture." To overcome this fundamental defect an analysis was necessary, in Baczko's view, of "the problems of humanism, in particular, of the problems of morality in the Marxist literature," because it was here that the distortions of "the previous era" (as Stalinism was euphemistically known) had their greatest effect.[18]

Bauman also played an active role in the debates on the state of Marxist philosophy. He linked himself explicitly with Baczko and Kołakowski in addressing the issue, joining them at the same time in a discussion on the role and form of education.[19]

Bauman wrote of Stalinism that, even without going into the cause, it was possible to see that Stalinism had destroyed the very essence of Marxism:

It ruled out social man as the starting point for philosophy, and the relationship of that man to his social-natural environment as the subject of philosophy; by the same token it strangled the deeply rooted revolutionary humanist content of Marxist philosophy.[20]

Bauman went on to stress that, under Stalinism, the perspective of nature as an object of human activity had been lost and had been replaced with a view of nature as dehumanized, having nothing to do with human reality. This change of perspective arose from the ongoing debate on whether the division of scholarship into "dialectical materialism" (dealing with the natural sciences) and "historical materialism" (the social ones) represented an adequate vision of the world.

The discussion of the content of Marxist philosophy was continued in an essay Bauman wrote in conjunction with another sociologist, Jerzy Wiatr, in which they specifically discussed the relation of contemporary sociology to Marxism.[21] They began by discussing the category of "ideology" as a "class-based, deformed reflection of social reality."[22] They went on to repeat the traditional formulations whereby the proletariat was assumed to have a privileged position in discovering the truth. The conclusions they drew from this, however, were the opposite of those reached by the traditional Marxist approach. Rather than saying that something is true because the proletariat holds it so, the position of the proletariat was to be held up to scrutiny as well, in accordance with the criteria of verification and falsification. Just because the proletariat is in the ideal social position to discern the true nature of reality does not mean that it cannot also succumb to ideology, in the sense given above.[23]

In fact, not only *could* the proletariat fall prey to ideology; in the view of these authors, it actually *did*.

This ideology . . . was formed through the petrification and canonization of certain theses which were originally scientific, but which took on an ideological character as a result of the growing divergence between what was stated in them and changing social practice. This ideology—like every other—functioned in the social sphere as a weapon for organizing mass groups of people around specified discretionary centers.[24]

The ideology took on the character of religious belief, where the tenets of the faith took precedence over any scientific rigor. Science and scholarship were in fact given the task of substantiating the claims of the ideology. More and more things became taboo subjects, and the whole ideological system underwent so many piecemeal changes that it was gradually transformed into a system of dogmas with no logical relation to one another. The net result was that all thinking took on the form of an irrational "double thinking."[25]

The consequences of this state of affairs were disastrous, according to Wiatr and Bauman. Any serious scholarship was set back years, and there was therefore no longer any real knowledge of what contemporary society was like. (This took place in a system where centralized planning was supposed to set the course for the society and economy, based on knowledge of social processes.) They called for a truly scholarly Marxist sociology, where the criteria of scholarly inquiry had to take precedence over ideological presuppositions.[26] The lack of any real knowledge of society was particularly telling for efforts to build a democratic model of socialism because almost no theoretical tools were readily available for the task.[27]

One of the themes of Wiatr and Bauman's article is shared by many writers of this period, and its best expression was in Kołakowski's essay, "Permanent vs. Transitory Aspects of Marxism."[28] The question as to what was specifically Marxist in theories of society was raised in Kołakowski's essay as part of the attempt to keep what was valuable in Marxism without making an ideology of it. The question was a recurring one, and efforts to answer it generally stressed the need for openness. The response sometimes led to the denial of any specifically

Marxist content to social theory. This was not, however, Bauman's answer; he continued to search for a satisfactory solution to the dilemma.

In addition to being sharply critical of Stalinism per se, Wiatr and Bauman singled out the social sciences in the Soviet Union during that era. They accused the Soviets—among others—of building an entire theoretical edifice to justify ignoring the issue of the contemporary relevance of the social sciences. Predictably, this essay—along with several other essays written by different people—drew a sharp rebuttal from the authoritative Soviet journal, *Voprosy Filosofii*. The authors of the articles in question were accused of being revisionists and of distorting Marxism in the guise of fighting Stalinism. The title of the rebuttal asks, "Is This Marxism?" and the article concludes, "Without a doubt, no!"[29]

The second charge leveled by *Voprosy Filosofii* is particularly interesting. It betrayed the Soviet concern that the de-Stalinization process in Eastern Europe was getting out of hand and illustrated ways in which the East Europeans were in fact using de-Stalinization as a vehicle for achieving much broader goals.

Hirszowicz echoed some of the comments made by Baczko and Bauman when she wrote that Stalinism completely destroyed any scholarly or scientific character of Marxist thought. She also said that it had "completely eliminated the humanist contents of Marxism, its moral postulates, and its ties with that which is most beautiful" in the human tradition.[30]

Hirszowicz also noted the irony that, in a society where Marxism had become the reigning ideology, people should be having to say again that Marxism can be useful in understanding social phenomena. "However much 'conformist Marxism' would seem to be a contradiction in terms, it appears that social practice can allow for any contradictions."[31] In this connection, it is no accident that a renewed interest in the concept of ideology was evident. Hirszowicz notes that any sociological inquiry must realize that "interhuman relations are in a certain sense independent of the persons acting; individuals find them when they enter a community, they form a 'given.' "[32] It is this 'givenness' that must be seen as also a human creation. Out of this problem comes the need for an examination of the concept of alienation, which Hirszowicz takes up in the context of a critique of industrial society.

Reminiscent of her article of several years earlier, the last section of the book is entitled "Ideology and Science." In this section, she examines the social character of knowledge, drawing on Mannheim in the process, as did Kołakowski in his essay on the subject.[33] She looks particularly at the way in which the issue had been treated in socialistic thought up to that time, as well as at the relation of ideology to scientific and scholarly investigation. According to Hirszowicz:

> The problem is not one of counterposing ideological attitudes with scientific positions, but rather is just the opposite. It is one of becoming aware of the structural and functional ties between the categories, theories, and methods which we make use of in the social sciences, and the perspectives and interests of specific groups.[34]

In a manner similar to many of the other reflections on ideology, Hirszowicz concludes that science does not consist of the creation of appearances; rather, it means searching for credible information that makes it possible to understand social situations and to point out effective courses of action. Her conclusion in a way is similar to a point raised in the Bauman/Wiatr essay, concerning the relationship between the perspective of the proletariat and ideology.[35] In this view, ideology can spur new insights; the ideal is to have a "progressive" ideology that would do this most or best. Even a progressive approach, however, is no guarantor of truth but must be held accountable to reality. It seems that what interests Hirszowicz here is the influence of values and attendant choice on the social sciences and the necessity for being clear in one's mind as to the values chosen.[36]

Kołakowski also addressed the issue of Marxist philosophy at some length, especially as it concerned education. As early as 1958 he dealt with the question of how Marxist philosophy should deal with other philosophical currents. The answer he gave was that Marxist philosophy should concentrate first of all on gaps in its own knowledge because Marxist philosophy's ability to effectively criticize other views is weakest in those areas where it has gaps. In this regard, dogmatism in Marxism limited the field of inquiry of this philosophy. As a result, this dogmatic Marxist criticism would search in the object of criticism for the element that would fit into the predigested and set categories of "Marxist" thought and would then cite proof texts to make its point. Anything that could not be handled in this way was not worthy of serious consideration. In contrast to this approach, Kołakowski argued for a rigorous analysis of the aspects of an opposing view that gave it its strength; on the basis of this inquiry one could then prepare a critique, thus "grounding the belief in human reason."[37] If Marxist philosophers were to take up this task and explore the questions that writers from other philosophical currents had already investigated, Marxists would be forced to expand and develop their own conceptual apparatus to the point where it would reach the boundaries of the current state of knowledge about the world.

Kołakowski is content here with a phenomenological description of the existing state of affairs in Marxist thought; he does not attempt to analyze explicitly the social roots of the phenomena described. Nonetheless, he makes it clear that not just "mistakes" were involved in the "degeneration of critical Marxist thought":

> The immediate source was the necrosis of the intellectual functions of philosophy and its reduction to a magic ritual whose task was an apologetic of the facade of socialist life. The critique of other doctrines in this situation was not intended to lead to the factual, intellectual convincing of anyone, but rather became a part of a ritual ceremonial.[38]

Although Kołakowski does not directly criticize the social reality, his "description" constitutes a damning indictment of the way reality contributed to the demise of critical thinking.

In another article written in 1955, "Fantasy and Dogmatism," Kołakowski once more takes up the question of the "style" of philosophy (to use Baczko's term). In this article the main issue is the reduction of the analysis of culture to the concept of the class struggle.[39] Kołakowski advocated the enrichment of the Marxist conceptual framework for explaining social reality, maintaining that explaining social reality is the primary task of the humanities—particularly of sociology and philosophy.

Kołakowski's view of the humanities led him to the question of education, in the sense of education in a world view. He defined the concept of "world view" to mean "the entirety of convictions which influence that behavior of a person that in his time is subject to moral evaluation by society—whether condemned or honored."[40] In the Marxist context, education should therefore ensure that the world view under formation "not only satisfied existing problems but indeed created a state of dissatisfaction; not only interpreted the horizon of those phenomena already observed, but pointed out new ones."[41] Education in this sense should enable a person to understand and perceive issues associated with his or her world view in matters of everyday life.

Kołakowski's call for philosophy and sociology to enrich the Marxist conceptual framework in order to better explain social reality and "create a state of dissatisfaction" was shared by Baczko and Bauman. Baczko called for Marxism to "free itself from mythology and go back to its authentic humanist sources" so that it would explain "the process of its own mythologization and dehumanization of reality that it affirmed in its guise as a socially functioning doctrine."[42]

Philosophy and sociology together were to provide the medium for this undertaking. Whereas Marxism had always been regarded by its proponents as being against irrationalism and as being critical, in the period of Stalinism it had gradually lost its critical edge and had itself succumbed to irrationalism.

One reason Marxist philosophy lost its critical capacity under Stalin was that it suffered from an artificial distinction between fields of academic inquiry. This approach divided all research into either "diamat" (dialectical materialism) or "histmat" (historical materialism). The former corresponded roughly to the natural sciences, the latter to the social sciences, but both categories were rigidly defined. One consequence of the Stalinist approach was that certain accepted doctrines were not up for discussion. This in turn meant that, despite claims that knowledge is always historical, philosophy under Stalinism was profoundly ahistorical.

Baczko also discussed the problem of the subject matter of philosophy and of Marxist philosophy in particular.[43] In introducing the issue, he noted that this question is often asked when quite another question, or set of questions, is really at issue—whether those who are asking are aware of this fact or not. Hence, Baczko gave the name of "crypto-problems" to the questions as to the subject matter of philosophy. Given this, what is the meaning of the question, "What is the subject matter of Marxist philosophy?" This question can have at least three possible meanings:

   a. What is the subject matter of Marxist philosophy according to the classics of Marxism?
   b. What is the subject matter of Marxist philosophy as it is practiced at present?
   c. What, according to the author [of an article on the subject], *should* be the subject matter of Marxist philosophy practiced in the future?[44]

According to Baczko, the three questions are interrelated; the answer to one depends on how the others are answered. One's sense of what the future course of Marxist philosophy should be depends on how one views the "classics" of Marxism, but this view in turn is often a function of the other two. Even attempting to answer the first question is considerably more complicated than might at first appear to be the case. What *are* the "classics"? Whom does one include in this category? Also, any attempt at answering must be of a *historical*, not *doctrinal*, nature. Even then the matter is far from simple. It can safely be said that the subject matter of Marxist philosophy was understood in different ways even in these "classics," and that different themes were stressed at different times.

The question of what the subject matter of Marxist philosophy is as presently practiced is also a matter for historical research. For purposes of argument, Baczko focuses on Marxist philosophy as it was de facto formulated in a wide range of works over the previous thirty years (that is, from 1928), even in cases where the article was not expressly addressed to this issue. It is clear from looking at examples, ranging from Stalin to Lukács and Antonio Gramsci, that there is a wide differentiation among various approaches: How does one decide what is Marxist? Again, the answer is to be determined not "administratively"—that is, by decree—but through historical analysis. There is no one "correct" answer: "Marxist philosophy develops also by means of its internal contradictions, which sometimes appear openly, and sometimes in a masked or mystified form. The measure of the maturity of Marxism at any given time is also, among other things, the degree to which it is a theory of the internal contradictions of its own development."[45]

With regard to the future form of Marxist philosophy, the issue of importance is again whether only one given approach is to be considered Marxist or whether different solutions and subjects of research can coexist, even though mutually contradictory. Also, Baczko stresses that the matter of *political* relevance or commitment of philosophy is a separate issue from its philosophical relevance or importance. Certainly it is not right to ask if

Marxist philosophy will lose its distinctive character if it is not politically involved. There is no doubt that Marxism, in its interest in human freedom, has a political aspect and that this aspect has a strong influence on the formation of a Marxist understanding of the rationalization and humanization of human relations. But this does not mean that any and every political action is useful. Political involvement is sometimes achieved at the cost of theoretical understanding. The potential for conflict is inherent in the very nature of the activity, where sometimes immediate action is required that cannot wait for theoretical reflection.

The question of political involvement of philosophy was very important and was faced by philosophers all over Eastern Europe. At issue was not simply whether philosophy or philosophers should take sides politically or become involved in activity other than just their philosophizing. When this question came up in the East European context, the issue was primarily whether philosophy and philosophers should serve the party or whether there was room for philosophical activity not directly in service to the party. It is this question that Baczko addressed implicitly. Certainly it is not service to the party that differentiates Marxist philosophy from non-Marxist, and the task of comparison is not served by comparing some ideal state of Marxist thought to other philosophical trends similarly approached. The task of philosophy, its new "style," should be to restore to Marxism its revolutionary and critical nature.

All of this brings Baczko to his second point of emphasis: the necessity for a comprehensive analysis of both the history of Marxist thought and what he calls the "sociology of Marxism." In this term Baczko includes two areas: first, the study of how Marxism developed and spread as a system of thought, and second, the sociological analysis of the formation of a particularly Marxist style of thinking in philosophy and the ways in which it changed.[46] Also included is the need for an analysis of the

sociological conditions under Stalinism that contributed
to the "disintegration" of Marxist thought. The particular style of thinking in Stalinism that characterized
the disintegration "was formed under certain specific
social conditions and fulfilled certain functions; the atomization of philosophy reflected and sanctioned the processes of atomization specific to that society itself."[47] In
Baczko's view, there is no hope for any further development in Marxism unless this sociological and historical
analysis of the Stalinist period is carried out, leading to
an understanding of the dynamics of that era.

SOCIOLOGICAL ANALYSIS

It was Bauman who gave most thought to how sociology
was to contribute to the demythologization of Marxism,
although Hirszowicz also addressed this concern.[48] From
1956 on, the issue occupied Bauman in different ways.
First, he was battling against the irrational character of
Stalinism, fighting for a place for rational analysis and
scholarship in general. In addition, he was engaged in trying to carve out a place for sociology in the process of social planning and in social life generally. He was also
involved in attempting to define the particular attributes
of Marxism in sociology and in stating how these were to
be understood in light of other currents within contemporary sociology.[49]

Bauman outlined what he regarded as the central characteristics of Marxist sociology. Some of the characteristics that differentiate this sociology from other disciplines
within the humanities are knowledge about:

   a. different types of social wholes and their structures.
   b. the social conditioning of the lives of individuals.
   c. the way in which history is created by people and groups
      of people.

On the other hand, Marxist sociology integrates all of
the humanities in that it deals with:

a. the general characteristics of human life as social life.

b. the connection between the economic, political, and
ideological spheres of social life; and, more generally, between all of the areas of human historical practice which,
taken apart, are the subject matter of the various special-
ized disciplines.[50]

Bauman went on to write more on the question of sociology, this time on the need for a sociology of political
parties, which he saw as part of the need to make Marxist
sociology equal to the task of becoming relevant for contemporary life.[51] Bauman called for an analysis of the
structural factors that not only allowed Stalinism to
emerge and cause the "degeneration" of Marxism but
also prevented any effective opposition from within the
Communist movement.

An analysis of the structural principles of the Party and
their practical functioning can give an answer to the question as to the causes of the Stalinist deformation only when
done together with an investigation of the economic transformations which took place, as well as of the type of ownership which replaced private property.[52]

Among the effects of this "deformation" was the total
atomization of the working class, making it politically
passive and depriving it of any sense of collective identity. This atomization took place more easily because
most workers were newly uprooted from a peasant background and had not had much opportunity for forging a
new identity.

Bauman regards the sociological analysis of political
parties as necessary not only for the sake of reviving
sociology but also for creating a theoretical basis for a
system of democratic self-management. This is a continuation of a theme introduced in the article coauthored
with Wiatr. Bauman's interest in the sociology of political parties lies in discovering what specifically about
the Party in socialism was distorted, as well as what

potential such an analysis might have for enhancing the democratic process.

According to Bauman, at the commencement of an analysis of political parties, questions must be asked in two key areas: the relation of parties to social stratification and the differences between the function of parties in a multiparty system and those in a one-party system. One of the dangers inherent in a one-party system, according to Bauman, is found in the merging, for all practical purposes, of the party and governmental apparatus. When this happens, democracy—intraparty as well as general—is threatened.

In reference to contemporary capitalist societies, Bauman writes of the atomization of society and the monopolization of political decision making by a self-perpetuating and inflexible elite. He could as well have written these comments in reference to socialist societies and, in fact, does come close to doing so in places. Another problem raised in connection with this issue of atomization is that of the distribution of political power among the various levels within a party. Where does the control actually lie, and what does this location of control say about the democratic character of a party?

Central to any analysis of political parties is the issue of their impact on political life, the extent of their activity in society. Here the range is from totalitarian parties, which totally eliminate any distinction between public and private life, to "limited" parties, which are concerned only with the voting behavior of their adherents.[53] The different types of political parties reflect different understandings or visions of the nature of social ties, and this is the key issue behind the question of their spheres of activity. When this fact is properly understood, one can then more clearly see the features in a political party that are conducive to the formation of a different sort of system than the one under critique.

After his discussion of political parties, Bauman's next step was an examination of political elites. As the basis for his analysis, he used Vilfredo Pareto's work on the subject.[54] Although there is little direct mention of the socialist context in this article, its relevance is clear even without the links Bauman introduced in his concluding remarks.

After looking at the question of elites from a variety of perspectives, Bauman makes a case for the relevance of a theory of elites for socialist societies by noting that the problem transcends class structure. He warns that to ignore this fact makes it impossible to see, let alone analyze, the dynamics of the development of socialist society. This blindness in turn means that any systematic understanding of socialist democracy is rendered impossible. The key problem is the issue of *ruling*, in the sense of the "ruling elite." What does the term mean? For the concept of a ruling elite to have relevance for the socialist setting, according to Bauman, it can be understood in one of two ways. The first sense in which *rule*, or *ruling*, can be understood is that of "the sum of the organizational, planning, and implementation measures essential to any large organizations, regardless of its structure." The second sense of this concept is "the realization by force of the interests of one group accompanied by the violation of the interests of other groups in the same society."[55] In Bauman's view, both sets of attributes can exist in a given setting, though the ideal is when only the first set is present. This ideal he identifies with the vision present in the ideals of socialism. When the concept of elite is separated from the concept of class and the ideal attributes and function of elites in a socialist society are characterized, an elite theory can become "an unusually valuable instrument for understanding the contemporary world."[56]

In a later work, *Towards a Critical Sociology*, Bauman continues the task he set himself much earlier—defining the role of sociology in contemporary society. He is still interested in the relation of Marxism to sociology, although now in a manner quite different from his earlier writings on this subject. The critique of positivism is carried further and expanded, but it too has a character different from that found earlier. The later critique is further reaching and deeper, and it springs even more from an imminent critique that transcends the bounds of the perspective analyzed. Bauman also criticizes existentialism and phenomenology for not providing real alternatives to positivism. In his attempt to transcend these perspectives, Bauman draws on Marx through the mediation of the Frankfurt School, particularly Habermas, and seeks to arrive at a new concept of "critical sociology," based on emancipatory reason.

THE CRITIQUE OF RELIGION AS A METAPHORICAL CRITIQUE OF STALINISM

One further aspect of the critique of Stalinism was the use of religious metaphors as a disguised attack on Stalinist institutions. Kołakowski excelled at this because of his background as a critic of religion and the Catholic Church. "The mutual debt between the anti-Stalinist movement and Kołakowski's work is manifested in the importance that the association Communism/Christian Religion gained in his thought. From 1955 onwards his polemical essays against Catholicism were more and more penetrated by a double edge which also cut through the 'Stalinist sect'."[57]

One can already see the development of the implicit comparison between Catholicism and Stalinism in 1956 in the essay "Catholicism and Humanism." "Catholicism" stands for a mental and social situation in which "the religious person accepts oneself as the instrument of designs beyond human reach—the moral judgement is founded on obedience, the intellect accepts authority as the ultimate [criterion] for truth. . . . 'Humanism', in turn, recognizes only 'human beings' as the source, the carrier and the end of values."[58] Also, in the humanist view, any content of thought is subject to verification, understanding, and, above all, revision. Only in this way can human dignity be affirmed and maintained. Thus, for Kołakowski, "the unmasking of the 'Gods' became complementary to the affirmation of 'human freedom' as the central subject of philosophy, and that, in turn, became dependent on the possibility of a political annihilation of authoritarianism."[59]

The issue that occupied him from this time on was that of the relationship between freedom and institutional control—particularly in the context of a revolutionary movement. This was the theme that led Kołakowski to his study of seventeenth-century Dutch anticonfessional movements, a study that resulted in the publication of a book on the subject in 1965 under the title *Religious Consciousness and Ecclesiastical Ties*.[60] What attracted him to these movements was that they were attempting to "realize Christian values without conforming to the rules of ecclesiastical organization. They sought a religious practice which would be free from the 'visible' constraints attached to Church membership, such as credo, rituals, sacraments, institutional sacerdoce, etc. They tried to form a Christian community that would not be a church."[61]

Some of the issues most important to Kołakowski in his study of the anticonfessional movements were those of the relationship between orthodoxy and heresy and between orthodoxy and reform, as well as the issues of democracy, tolerance, and human freedom. All these issues had obvious relevance for his critique of Stalinism, but the examination of the nature of orthodoxy is a theme that runs throughout the book. This is, of course, the central issue in an examination of anticonfessional movements, since by their very nature these movements were attempting to avoid constituting themselves as a new orthodoxy. Each in its own way identified the link between confession or creed and the formation of orthodoxy, and each tried to avoid this trap. Kołakowski saw that "the concept of orthodoxy has meaning only in relation to

organized communities, that is, communities which—
among other things—have a stratum of organizers, specifically a priestly caste. Orthodoxy is the ideology of this
stratum, it gives it its *raison d'être*, which is to guard the
orthodoxy. Whenever a heresy achieves organized form, it
in turn becomes the orthodoxy, and gains strength by battling heresies of its own, and this process of burgeoning
reproduction can continue indefinitely."[62] In another
sense, however, orthodoxy is as much a function of heresy as heresy is of orthodoxy. Kołakowski called it a problem of the chicken and the egg. "If the concept of heresy
makes no sense until it is looked at relative to an orthodoxy, in the same way one could say that an orthodoxy
'comes into being', constitutes itself, as a function of
heresy."[63] He went on to observe that the very existence
of an orthodoxy is connected to the existence of an organization and of authority. Any criticism of this authority,
however slight, is a criticism of the whole—whether
meant this way or not—because it threatens the central
feature of any orthodoxy, its claim to be the sole bearer
of truth.[64]

One consequence of this which Kołakowski cited, using an example from one of the seventeenth-century figures he studied, is that those in the (religious) orthodoxy
are prone to

> rule the faithful with the aid of fear rather than learning.
> They keep people in darkness and ignorance, and beat things
> into their heads which they themselves do not understand.
> They usurp control over the civilian authorities, and want
> to use the political institutions to persecute those who do
> not accept their rule. They condemn an honest life—one
> lived in accordance with one's conscience and with the law
> of the land—as an example of a cult of worldliness, and do
> the same with any aspiration for peace among people. Any
> attempt to use reason as a guide they regard as atheism.[65]

The problem that arises from this description of the
nature of orthodoxy is that of reform. The need for reform
is clear, but the real issue involved here is not simply

whether reform is possible. Any reform movement is by definition heretical to the orthodoxy, which will obviously do whatever it can to prevent serious reform from taking place. As was noted above, any attempt at reform, however limited, calls the whole of the existing structure into question. Because of this particular characteristic of reform, however, a strange dynamic is brought into play:

> The organic difficulty of every partial reform . . . [is] that for any reform to be carried out effectively requires that the brakes be put on almost from the very beginning. The chain reaction which causes any critique of the entire orthodoxy to destroy the whole edifice when only part of it was shaken must be held back. . . . If it is therefore necessary to set a limit to the reform from the outset, if in tearing down the original orthodoxy the attempt is made to determine the limits within which it is sacred, then from the beginning the task of negation must simultaneously be a task of construction . . . that is, the simultaneous declaration of a new orthodoxy. In other words, any partial reform can only be successful by adopting an orthodoxy at the same time, or, [it] can only be carried to completion when it becomes conservative and when it ceases to be reform. It comes into being by ceasing to be itself.[66]

This then was the central dilemma Kołakowski identified from his study of the seventeenth-century anticonfessional movements. The "annihilation of authoritarianism," which he so clearly sought, risked the possibility of becoming just like its predecessor. In 1957 Kołakowski had written of "the hope of reforming something which may not be capable of reform." As his thought developed, however,

> he did not relinquish his former assumptions on the radical opposition between freedom and institutional control, but the additional reflection on the repressive function of political institutionalization led him to redefine that opposition as an internal antinomy of the revolutionary movement. It was in that respect that the "utopian" nature of the left was most pertinent, for, as Kołakowski had it, the left wanted

more than power: the libertarian left wanted to eliminate
political power as such. It existed in the paradoxical position
of a political movement that could not accept the institutional implications of holding power without losing its raison d'être. In other words, the "left" could not sustain a
legal system.[67]

FREEDOM, VALUES, AND MORAL CHOICE

Of the themes that emerged from the critique of Stalinism to occupy a central place in the conceptual framework of these critical thinkers, the most prominent was
that of freedom. But freedom can be understood only in
reference to other key ideas, such as alienation, community, and human creative activity (or *praxis*). All of these
concepts are bound up with a specific understanding of
human nature (or "human essence").

The theme of freedom is taken up in the most comprehensive manner by Kołakowski.[68] He compares the
concept of freedom found in Hobbes and Spinoza and
then analyzes the meaning of the concept for Marxism.
Here he says that "historical progress is identical with
the widening of the scale of real freedom of a society—
that is, the scale of its control over the conditions of its
own life."[69] Humans are understood as social beings, and
freedom as spoken of here means the overcoming of alienation. In the traditional Marxist approach to this subject,
however, Kołakowski sees a tendency toward oversimplification. This oversimplification results from the belief
that the political emancipation of the working class has
eliminated alienation. The assumption implicit in this
sort of identification is that any possibility of conflict between individual interests and general social interests
is excluded.[70]

This simplistic assumption produces one of the main
problems for Marxist theories of freedom: the relation
of individual interests to social interests in a socialist
setting. An observation Kołakowski made earlier, with

reference to the Catholic concept of freedom, fits well
here. To be free in this view meant to be faithful to the
Church—or to every secular authority sanctioned by the
Church—that is, voluntary submission to the authorities. Stated metaphorically, "the expression of individual
freedom for man was the confessional, while the expression of his social freedom was the institution of the
police."[71]

To fail to take seriously the problem of the relation of
individual interests to social interests in a socialist setting was to risk identifying individual interests with social interests, which in turn were identified with the
interests of those in power. The only way out of this dilemma was to see the problem as a function of the degree
of democratization of public life. The greater the degree of
democratization, the less likely it is that individual and
social interests will conflict. This in turn means that an
individual's freedom to choose his or her own fate "can be
extended to the maximum degree possible—not over
against the interests of society, that is, the interests of
other people, but in unity with them."[72]

Here Kołakowski returns to the original definition of
the Marxist concept of freedom set forth in this article,
"Istota i Istnenie w Pojęciu Wolności." Social development—historical progress—in all its dimensions grows
out of the tension between individual aspirations and the
possibilities in a given society for their satisfaction—or,
from the lack of freedom, in a Marxist sense. The key to
understanding this approach lies in realizing that human
progress is possible because the satisfaction of existing
needs continually gives rise to new needs. The implication is that the process of freedom is not a one-time oc-
currence (such as a successful socialist revolution) but is
rather ongoing and open-ended, with new aspects being
created in the process.[73]

The theme of freedom as the control over one's choice
in a social context is continued in the discussion of the
interrelation between one's world view and everyday

life.[74] As was seen earlier, the connection was a very important one in the sphere of education. In this later article, the emphasis is on the question of the meaning of life. Kołakowski asks what we mean when we ask that question. In answering, he focuses on several themes that appeared in other articles: the need to be open to change, to be critical. The meaning of life is tied to human activity:

> The consciousness of active coexistence with historical reality accompanies every authentic, and thus every free human creativity—political, artistic, scientific, that of everyday life, and every other kind. Every value, every passion that gives meaning to life gives it through the sense of participation in creating the rhythm of history.[75]

Kołakowski sees freedom as closely linked with the concept of moral responsibility. Freedom as the freedom to define one's own existence in a social context necessarily means determining what is right, or at least the best course of action in any given circumstance. As Kołakowski puts it:

> History is not merely a remote, indifferent force like the gods of Epicurus, but a series of situations that we are concretely engaged in independently of our will. If this involvement is a voluntary act of the individual, then it is also a moral act, at least in the sense that some values accepted in other circumstances come to the fore here as decisive factors.[76]

Elsewhere he quotes an account of God speaking to Adam after the Creation, where God tells Adam: " 'You alone have freedom of growth, intensification of your essence; you have in you seeds full of life.' In other words, the condition of human indeterminacy is not only exceptional in the universe but is also the source of what is particularly human, the reason for the unique value of the human being. Indeterminacy, freedom, value: three words which in the human world have the same meaning."[77] How values are chosen, accepted, and applied becomes the question for Kołakowski, especially in the socialist context. There the problem became acute as a consequence of Stalinism. Stalinism involved what Kołakowski calls the "problem of the single alternative," where "every criticism . . . would amount, objectively, to an automatic adherence to the reactionary camp."[78] This phenomenon fosters two kinds of responses in particular: one is total commitment to the cause, the other is escapism. Escapism can be seen as "the ideology of renouncing choice [and] results from the confrontation of two social facts: the ideological consciousness of the anti-Stalinist left on the one hand, and a reality that bars this consciousness from asserting itself in social life on the other."[79] The other common alternative, total commitment, or dedication, results from the belief in some sort of historical necessity or inevitability. Neither response is adequate and overcoming the dilemma presented by Stalinism is the most urgent task. The escapist withdraws because no alternative means of preserving values seems apparent, whereas the one who is dedicated denies the values in practice. For:

> Moral duty is the conviction, perpetuated in a given social setting, that certain types of values are ends in themselves, not just means to an end, and others, in and of themselves, are anti-ends, that is to say, proscribed. If historical necessity is seen as an unlimited process without a defined final stage, or if an ultimate goal is attributed to it that has not yet been attained but constitutes merely a promise for the future, and if at the same time moral judgements are subordinated to the realization of historical necessity—then there is nothing at all in daily life that can be an end in itself. In other words, moral values in the strictest sense cease to exist.[80]

Here, Kołakowski forcefully stresses the theme of the value dimension of life. To live in history involves moral choice; even the escapist cannot avoid this, because escapism entails only an illusion that commitment is being avoided. In pursuing this theme, Kołakowski looks at the derivation of value and concludes that the world of values is rooted in the "material conditions of social life."

There are many possibilities for the choice of values: by its very nature moral choice is a social phenomenon. As such, it becomes a part of the historical process and can influence its outcome. In fact, any social setting calls forth certain value judgments in the form of duty, and the specific features of duty in this sense spring from the needs of that society. This is what is meant by the statement that values are "rooted in the material conditions of social life."[81]

It is possible to counterpose other values to those prevalent in a given society; this is the social function of utopias. Utopias are necessary as a means of presenting alternative visions of human reality. A distinction can nonetheless be made between utopias that have some social relevance and those which are "utopian" (in the popular sense). The distinction, however, is not whether the alternative vision is immediately realizable; by its very nature it must point far beyond the existing reality. There is always some point, though, where utopian thought no longer makes contact with any potentialities latent or implicit in the given reality, and at that point that thought loses its relevance. If the alternative visions do strike a responsive chord somewhere in the society, they spring out of the real issues of that society and are hence not "utopian" in the pejorative sense.

The question of moral choice applies equally to the evaluation of political choices, all the more so where life has become totally politicized. "Each choice we make arises from a combination of the values we affirm . . . and of *knowledge* about the probabilities of their being realized in specific conditions."[82] The goal in social life is to provide the conditions that will allow for and encourage alternative visions of human reality and knowledge about probable outcomes of moral choices. For us to know the probable outcomes of moral choices, every possible facet must be examined to see if anything can call it into question. The society must be structured in such a way that this feature is built in, which is what Kołakowski was working toward by calling for democratization as the structural component of choice.

As a reality and as a recurring possibility, Stalinism represented the antithesis of the possibility of moral choice. It regarded itself as an "end in itself, and thus autonomous of the social forces that engineered it. . . . What Stalinism implies in the life of Communist parties is not that they are so badly organized that they do not allow for the control of the party masses over the authorities; it means that the *social function of the party* is to render impossible a change in this type of organization."[83] Although the above lines were written as a critique of Stalinism, they were equally a warning against a return to Stalinist principles after the "Polish October." These principles had begun to reassert themselves more every day, although certainly not on the scale of the Stalinist era.

In his discussion of the roots of escapism, Kołakowski used the term, *anti-Stalinist Left.* Used in passing, the term is the subject of a penetrating analysis in "The Concept of the Left," an essay he wrote a few months before "Responsibility and History," also in 1957.[84] This analysis can also be said to mark a change in Kołakowski's own approach after November 1956. "Before, Kołakowski was positioned to confront the 'enemy' on behalf of total reform, now he was involved in an internal dispute among reformers. Before, his ideas were meant to rally the Communist movement as a whole, now he found himself to be a spokesman for a wing of the movement, which he called the 'left'."[85]

It is clear in this essay that Kołakowski had a grasp of the political realities in post-October Poland and was not as much given to exhortation as in his earlier writing. Still, as he himself pointed out in a number of places, "political realism" can mean several things, and it certainly does not mean giving up a utopian perspective, relinquishing an alternative vision of human society in the name of what is given. Furthermore, moral values are not utopian in a political system but must be understood as being a part of its condition. In the case of socialism, which expressly identifies with certain human values, its intellectual and moral values are not "luxurious ornaments of this activity, but the conditions of its existence. . . . A communist movement that subordinates its ideology to immediate tactics is destined for degeneration and defeat. It can exist only with the support of the power and repressive capacity of the state."[86] Part of the function of a utopian perspective is to provide the basis for a critical perspective, and in this sense Kołakowski freely admits to being utopian—but not in the sense of a perspective cut off from "reality."

In "The Concept of the Left," Kołakowski introduces the term *leftist socialism* to designate the contrast between the critical perspective that he identifies with the "left" (and with which socialism as a whole traditionally was identified). This distinction is necessary because "a communist movement whose sole form of existence is sheer tactics and which permits the loss of its original intellectual and moral premises ceases to be a leftist movement."[87]

Baczko entered the discussion of freedom through his reflections on the task of philosophy. Specifically, he examined the relationship between freedom and necessity. He understood Marx on the question of freedom to be referring to the concept of a "socialist context," in which freedom would consist of "universally developed individuals, whose social relations are their own joint relations, and are subjected to their common control."[88] The version of the relation between freedom and necessity in Stalinism, Baczko argues, too often tended to stress only necessity, where freedom meant conscious conforming to the objective laws governing existence. Left out of the picture was the awareness that, in a socialist society: "freedom in the various aspects of social life—socialist democratization of social life as the political form of the process of the liberation of man and of the many-sided development of his activity—is a necessary objective condition in order for the laws to be used consciously."[89] The consequence of this omission of the active, human side of the formula was that it gave rise to a bureaucratic system that grew up as an alien force lurking over people, limiting their growth and their freedom and taking on the character of something inevitable.

In an article, "Hegel, Marx, and the Problems of Alienation," Baczko returned in a different way to the theme of Hegel and freedom that is found in the work of Kroński.[90] The occasion for the article was a review of the book by the French Hegelian, Hyppolite, *Études sur Marx et Hegel*, published in Paris in 1956. Again here Baczko stressed that reality should be understood "not in its relation to 'abstract, isolated concepts,' but rather from the perspective of a 'system of knowledge'." Like Kroński, he was adamant that Hegel is not an apologist for reality as given, "only the process of historical development— understood by Hegel as a process of consciousness, as a process of the realization of the idea of freedom through its alienated forms—is real. Only the unity of the substantial and of appearance, arrived at in the complex dialectic of this process is 'true reality'."[91] Like Kroński, Baczko placed the emphasis here on the development of freedom as true reality; he went on to examine the nature of the "alienated forms" of this reality through a confrontation of Hyppolite with György Lukács' reading of Hegel. Baczko accused Hyppolite of an ahistorical understanding of the problem of alienation, in contrast to that of Lukács (which Baczko held was consistent with that found in Marx's *Economic and Philosophical Manuscripts*). Baczko noted, however, that Hyppolite hit upon an aspect of Marx which was of great importance: that *Capital* takes up the theme of alienation where the *Economic and*

Philosophical Manuscripts left off. "To the extent that in the *Economic and Philosophical Manuscripts* Marx showed how the alienation of social man takes place in history, and how capital becomes the product of this alienation, then in *Capital* this very product of alienation becomes the point of departure for the analysis."[92] Hyppolite grasped Marx's efforts to understand the "concrete historical" meaning and content of alienation; he showed that, according to Marx's understanding, "man is the creator of his own history," and that in creating this history he transforms reality. Thus Baczko used Hyppolite's insight to point out what he regards as the central feature of Marxism, that "at the base of the Marxian conception of society lies the understanding of the free, integral complete development of every individual."[93]

In the essay, "Marx and the Idea of the Universality of Man," the theme of human creative activity finds fullest expression. Baczko quotes Marx from the *Economic and Philosophical Manuscripts*, where he writes that "the whole character of a species—its species character—is contained in the character of its life-activity; and free, conscious activity is man's species character."[94] Developing this idea further, Baczko again examines the historical nature of this life activity. "Man creates himself as a universal being by living and acting in history. . . . History is, at the same time a fact, a reality that man encounters, and a set of problems to be unravelled, a field of man's activity, of human *praxis*."[95] Baczko further writes that: "Man is a being who, on the basis of his activity, grasps the world of nature and the world of his own history as a totality that is for him a meaningful structure."[96] Meaning is not discovered but created "by the way in which humans relate to the world." Man transforms things into objects of his needs, gives them human meaning, and endows them with values. . . . The universality of man is based on the fact that he applies to the world his specific, human standards of values."[97] Again, the twin concepts of need and value come to the fore.

Baczko stresses that "need" does not mean simply "biological need," but includes what he calls "spiritual needs," those "connected with man's striving towards a comprehension of the world, toward self-affirmation, etc."[98] These "spiritual needs" are those that, following Marx, Baczko characterizes as specifically human. It is through the medium of needs that humans first confront their environment. They have needs that must be satisfied, and the environment provides the means for doing so. For Rousseau, this first step in satisfying needs forges the initial link in the chain that makes up the social order. At some point along the way, needs become independent of the person—they are no longer the person's doing but are imposed by society. They function as an element of their own reality, change and grow spontaneously, and are entangled in a net of ever more complicated interpersonal relations.[99] Examining the process by which this takes place is therefore a means of understanding how alienation comes about. This exercise also allows one to distinguish between authentic needs and "false" needs, those fostered by an alienated society.

These human needs especially manifest themselves in the need humans have for other humans, with whom they can have personal relations as human relations. Marx refers to this as the "plenitude of human need," where—in contrast to the understanding of plenitude or wealth as the collection and possession of objects and goods—this "plenitude of human need" means "the fact that man 'needs a complex of human manifestations of life, and [his] self realization exists as an inner necessity, a *need.*'"[100] Humans create their own meaning and authenticity in history in dealing with the concrete challenges and problems faced by each individual each moment. But mass inauthenticity is also possible, understood as the "depersonalization of human existence, of interhuman relations, and of the individual's relation to himself."[101] This possibility is a function of what Marx calls alienation. "The reign of alienation means the materialization of man, the degradation of man to the status of a thing, and the rule over him of things, relations, and institutions created by him."[102]

It was Baczko who examined the meaning of alienation most closely, especially as understood by Marx and Rousseau. Alienation is the core theme around which Baczko organizes his study of both Marx and Rousseau.

Where there is alienation, it is understood in reference to an ideal situation in which alienation does not exist or is overcome. For Rousseau, alienation is tied up with the world of appearances, in contrast to the authentic world. According to Baczko:

> The distinction between "to be" and "to appear to be" is found somehow at the center of Rousseau's entire conception. Connected to it is . . . the search for the sources and mechanisms from which the world of appearances, and of man's apparent existence, is formed.[103]

By the very act of positing the duality, Rousseau posits the possibility of its being overcome. In Baczko's understanding, this is done in two ways. First, according to Rousseau, to reveal inauthenticity is simultaneously to unmask it. The other method is more complex, although similar. In any vision of the world where a distinction is made between "appearance" and "authenticity," with existing reality characterized as "appearance," an appeal to some ideal is always implicit in the characterization. Not only is an appeal to some ideal always present, the very act of making the distinction between "appearance" and "authenticity" helps to create that ideal. "Authenticity" is always bound up with a utopia, or even with many utopias. These utopias can be already clearly formulated and definite, or they can be only partially so. "Utopia" here is understood in the sense of going beyond the given reality in the name of a set of values counterposed to it in whose name the given reality is held to be "apparent."[104]

The "world of appearances," the alienated world, is a world in which the fundamental bonds are those of private interests. It is a world where interaction takes place between isolated individuals operating according to their own perception of their interest. Contrary to the prevalent view, this *modus operandi* does not lead to social harmony, according to Rousseau, but to competition, the crossing of private interests and social chaos. It destroys the person.[105]

Individuals are caught in a "net of opaque, impenetrable relations—all of these threads accumulate, and symbolize the feeling of a threat to one's own freedom, and the loss of one's individuality."[106] Part of this sense of "opaque" relations (used here in contrast to "transparent," which is the ideal as posited by Rousseau) is a sense of distorted communication. Words no longer serve authentic communication but rather falsify relations among people. In fact, all authentic communication between people is made impossible in this "world of appearances." Part of what is needed to overcome the alienated world is to have the kind of communication between humans that would eliminate appearances and restore authentic bonds to them.[107]

In contrast to the world of appearances, authentic reality is characterized by Rousseau as the state of nature. The state of nature, "in providing a model of a different situation of man in the world, at the same time makes it possible [for man] to achieve some distance from that dimension of his own 'I' which is 'appearance,' a 'mask'. . . . It makes it possible for him to locate himself 'outside' of the culture which . . . [he] unknowingly and without reflection recognizes as his 'own'."[108] The state of nature thus provides an image in which human nature, "natural man," exists as a set of possibilities. Potentially, humans are creatures of reason and beings who are free, for they have the freedom of moral choice. But the question Rousseau asked was how and why these potentialities, unrealized possibilities, were turned to their opposite during the process of socialization. This process thus becomes one of internal contradictions:

In the same way, human nature—seen from the perspective of the results of the socialization process—is shown as
a set of human possibilities not realized in society, at least
not in the present society. But, in the same way again, it
is shown as the negation of the existing state of affairs,
and as the continual possibility of going beyond this existing state.[109]

The subject of socialization opens up two other facets
of Rousseau's thought that are important for Baczko:
those of everyday life and history. History, in this understanding, "possesses its own dynamic and tragedy. It is
rich in internal contradictions and tensions. It creates
varied chances; it is the terrain of human creativity, of
man's self-realization, but also of the loss of his own
humanity."[110] History is not a mere assemblage of facts or
events but is rather the area in which is located the world
that for modern man constitutes his own *given* world, the
world of his everyday life. Natural man does not need to
reflect on history or the meaning of history; it is only social man to whom history assumed significance, for it is
here that he finds that which separated him from his own
self.[111] The "world of appearances" is the world of history, although history is also where the possibilities of
overcoming this world are found. "Everyday life" is the
world of givens, and it is here that human existence is
played out. For Rousseau and his age, as for Baczko, all
problems of philosophy were ultimately reducible to problems of the meaning of everyday life.[112]

Kołakowski similarly tries to understand the person
as part of the permanent dialog with the "socially unified
world." In this dialog:

> The activity of creative expression, an activity which re-
> alizes the person—as well as the opposite activity, that
> which consists of the appropriation, by the person of the
> world as already modified by their own expressive work—
> constitute two opposite processes where each brings about
> the other.[113]

Several consequences emerge from this interpretation of the person: one is the possibility of analyzing social reality in terms of whether it enhances the person or is destructive of the process of authentic development. Included is the question of interpersonal communication, in which authentic communication presupposes an understanding of persons as irreplaceable, as ends in themselves.[114] This understanding in turn implies a certain vision of human community that would make authentic communication possible. Kołakowski is very close here to Baczko's exposition of Rousseau; Bauman has an understanding of community that is quite close to these others. In his view:

> Liberalism saw the community as a major obstacle on the way to individual freedom and understood the body politic as the only desirable form of supra-individual integration on the new societal level, with citizenship as the only integrating link; while socialism aimed at the reconstruction of a community-type integration on the societal level.[115]

One of the possibilities inherent in the concept of human nature advanced by Rousseau is that of being or becoming an individual. This is in a sense a normative concept; someone who identifies with the "world of appearances" and cannot distinguish between appearance and reality is not an individual. A true individual is characterized by intellectual autonomy—his or her reason is not controlled by misconceptions. The true individual is also autonomous morally, in that he or she judges self, others, and things themselves in terms of their "true" value, rather than values ascribed to them.[116] Being an individual entails being free from the world of appearances; in fact, "to be oneself means to be free, and the roads of liberation from alienation are the roads of freedom."[117] To be an individual, however, to "be oneself," means the same thing as to exist in community. "Community" refers to a common moral order shared by all those living in it, in contrast to the atomized, depersonalized society of the alienated world.[118]

The concept of a moral order was central to Enlightenment thinkers, including Rousseau. It had its place beside two other key concepts, "nature" and "reason." "[The concept] 'moral order' rises above the opposition between 'nature' and 'culture'; it is meant to express the existence of a continuity between the world of nature, which is a given for man, and the world which is created by man himself."[119] It can be seen that the three concepts do indeed have a central position in Rousseau's thought. Baczko points out that they have further dimensions beyond those sketched here: they fill out the vision Rousseau had of the world. One other observation is in order regarding the concept of "moral order":

> Finally, 'moral order' was not only a metaphysical-moral concept, but also a *political* one—it served for reflection on the relations of man to man, on the human social community. It was a political concept in the sense that it encompassed the imperative of the conscious participation of the individual—especially the enlightened individual—in the formation of social reality. It also provided the basis for considering that reality as one which was created by people themselves. 'Moral order' was a concept which was involved in politics because in metaphysical determinations it based values in the very ontological structure of reality that fell into conflict with the existing social relations, and turned against them.[120]

In his analysis of Rousseau through the themes of solitude and community, Baczko accomplished two things simultaneously. One was to provide a penetrating analysis of Rousseau's thought and to bring out the continuity from Rousseau through Hegel to Marx. The other was to use the study of Rousseau to examine certain key concepts, concepts that had immediate relevance for the task of the theoretical renewal of Marxism in which Baczko was engaged. "Alienation," the "world of appearances," "needs," "individual and community" were concepts that he used in other contexts and that were shared in one form or another by many of his contemporaries. The key focus for this analysis, however, is the human role in creating social reality—its potential for overcoming alienation as well as the way in which it fostered alienation. The view of human activity as creative expression is also stressed by Kołakowski in a comparison of Hegel, Marx, and Husserl, showing that the three share one crucial element:

> the conviction . . . that a non-actualized essence of man . . . is given in such a manner that it imposes on history, so to speak, the necessity of its actualization. If history is a successive realization of the essence of humanity, if its progress must result in the coincidence of essence and existence, then that essence cannot be the product of history: and it is history, on the contrary, which becomes intelligible and understandable *by reference* to it.[121]

Ultimately, this understanding involves a choice of values, Kołakowski acknowledges, but this choice is unavoidable. "Without it history remains eternally obscure. With it, history becomes significant by virtue of the imposed intelligibility of which we are the authors, fully aware that we are and that we believe it to be real despite everything."[122]

What Kołakowski calls the "non-actualized essence of man" is analogous to Rousseau's concept of "human nature" used by Baczko. Underlying Bauman's work is a similar view of human nature as defined by human creative activity in the world. This activity creates the conditions of social life and makes for what is distinctly "human" in the world. "All of the objects and norms of behavior created by people together form an *artificial environment* for man; artificial because it does not exist independent of human collective historical activity, and is not a product of nature in some prehuman sense, but is in fact created by successive generations of people. This artificial environment, in which human life takes place, is called culture."[123] Bauman draws on Kołakowski's

concept of the "expressive personality," but he develops
the theme in his own way.

The Question of Knowledge

To understand the human environment requires, in Bauman's view, a holistic approach. This approach is opposed
to the quantified approach to atomized individuals characteristic of positivist approaches to human reality, and it
is opposed to the economic determinism that adherents
and critics alike identified with Marxism.

The holistic approach looks at the active role played
by humans in "making sense" of their world:

> The whole is something more than the sum of its parts; the
> whole is a certain social system, and a system is primarily a
> relatively lasting arrangement of connections between the
> elements of the whole.[124]

Within this structure it is possible to view items from
several points of view—some connections with structure
of a phenomenon have a "genetic sense": they create the
phenomenon and influence the form it takes. Other connections in turn have a "functional sense"; through
them, a phenomenon influences the condition of other elements of the greater whole, as well as influencing
changes in the other elements.[125]

The holistic approach to the study of human reality,
the study of its structural aspects, opens the way for an
understanding of alienation. Human reality is created by
human activity; by understanding the structural interaction of the different elements in the whole it becomes
possible to recover sight of the human origins of reality
when this perspective is lost.[126] Bauman also says that
"what is left if one takes away the general physiological,
biological attributes of the human organism, that which
is generally referred to by the term 'man,' is the product of
human collective activity . . . the product of society." By
this latter he means "the product of the artificial envi-

ronment of relations, conflicts, and their materialized expressions created by humans."[127]

Bauman holds that human knowledge in general, and knowledge about society in particular, can be understood only by regarding knowledge as an organic element of human historical activity—rather than as a detached sphere, ruled by autonomous laws.[128] Bauman continues his polemic against the mechanistic view of the world held by some Marxists, and he again emphasizes human activity in history. In Bauman's view, history is a collection of possibilities, from which a choice must be made. "We know reality only in connection with man," he writes, "and inasmuch as man is a 'historical becoming,' then knowledge and reality are also 'becoming,' and objectivity is also 'becoming'."[129]

Kołakowski undertook the most far-reaching analysis of the epistemological roots of the belief in "historical necessity." In so doing he simultaneously pointed out the crucial epistemological differences between the mechanistic approach to Marxism and that stressing human creative activity. This analysis had enormous implications for Polish revisionism, and was characteristic of all of East European "philosophical revisionism."[130]

In examining the question of epistemology, Kołakowski focused on the distinction between the young Marx, primarily the *Economic and Philosophical Manuscripts of 1844*, and the views of Engels and Lenin. He also looked at the pragmatist view of knowledge as a way of introducing another perspective for purposes of comparison. (Engels and Lenin both held, despite certain differences, that "the development of man's conceptual apparatus . . . [was] an effort to copy ever more faithfully the external world, which was regarded as a pre-existing model.")

According to both, human cognition, thought incapable of absolute and ultimate mastery of its object, approaches mastery by constant and progressive evolution. Its limitless striving for perfection is intended to make it more similar to reality, to make it imitate better the external world's properties and relations, which in themselves are independent of this effort and exist beyond the realm of human knowledge.[131]

This view, formulated within Marxism by Engels and then by Lenin in more extreme form, formed the basis for the theory of knowledge that was held by most Marxists and that was commonly identified as the Marxist view. This theory of knowledge had certain practical and political implications when used in the Marxist context. Without going into a detailed analysis of these implications, one can say that they had certain consequences, both for the way in which the Party was defined and for the view of historical necessity. To counter those features of Marxism that had reached an extreme form under Stalin, thinkers such as Kołakowski tried to redefine Marxism. An essential part of this task of redefinition, or "revision," was to reach a new understanding of Marx's epistemology; this was necessary because the theory of knowledge understood in the new light was only a part of a general understanding of the place and role of man in the world. The new understanding can be characterized as follows:

> Active contact with the opposition of nature creates at one and the same time conceptive man and nature as his object. No epistemological absolute exists, either as reality in itself which "is reflected" in consciousness, or as a sense impression, or a *cogito*, or innate categories of the mind, or pure nonpsychic phenomena. The only accessible world that exists is the needless conflict between social man's needs and the natural environment as the possible means of satisfying them.[132]

Several features of this approach call for further elaboration. First, cognition is not something that every person must do over from the beginning, but rather:

> There exists a reality that is common to all people and that remains forever in a state of incipience, a reality in which the phenomenon of creativity certainly occurs but in which

a certain constant is retained that corresponds to what we can call "human nature" or else to that totality of human properties, biological needs, and social relations which can rightfully be termed immutable.[133]

This constant assumes the place of background to the "creative activities and later deformations attendant upon all the mutable components of history; epochs, social classes, political situations, national sentiments."[134] According to Kołakowski, this background becomes in a sense a "given" for people, and they are unable to see that it is a human creation. Put another way, the world of things "out there" is one shaped by categories of human cognition, but it appears to be removed from these categories as something "in itself." In contrast, there is the realm of "practical positions and preferences," the "sum of values each of us tends to prefer over others. It is evident that this world of values is not created automatically by the world of things which is common to almost everyone and in which habits common to the whole species are involved."[135] Kołakowski concludes by stressing once again that:

> Man as a cognitive being is only part of man as a whole; that part is constantly involved in a process of progressive autonomization, nevertheless it cannot be understood otherwise than as a function of a continuing dialog between human needs and their objects. This dialog, called work, is created by both the human species and the external world, which thus becomes accessible to man only in its humanized form.[136]

Not only the opposition to the "classical definition of truth," Marxist and otherwise, is noteworthy in this exposition. Certain themes found here were also stressed by Baczko and are found in others as well: needs as the mediating element between humans and the world, alienation and the possibility of overcoming it, and the idea of the "humanizing" of the world. These themes had a value in the political and theoretical battle then being fought in Poland, but they also transcended this context by the way in which they contributed to a new understanding of Marx in general.

COGNITION, WORK, AND PRAXIS

In another context, Kołakowski takes up two themes that he stressed in his discussion on epistemology.[137] The first is that "man as a cognitive being is only part of man as a whole," and the second is the dialog with nature in the form of work. It should be emphasized that "work" refers not to the activity of making a living but to its primary characteristic of creative interaction with nature in satisfying human needs. If work is understood only in the sense of "making a living" then it is destructive of the person. "The formation of the person takes place simultaneously with the person's imposing his own form on circumstances; the person and his situation are not mutually reducible, but come into being through a permanent dialog of the expression which forms the circumstances with the circumstances acting on the person."[138] This "dialog of expression" is a social event, not something accomplished by isolated individuals. "Being a person takes place as a social fact through interpersonal communication, and only as a result of this does it become a fact for the person's own consciousness. . . . The circumstances in which individuals enter into relations with one another are not external to the person, but are rather appropriated as a component part of their individuality."[139]

Given this view, that persons realize themselves in free activity which is by nature social, then "work" in this sense must be the focus of any inquiry into the distortion of persons and their knowledge. In Marx's understanding, the division of labor was a key factor in the distortion of human capabilities, but behind this concept is the issue of the social conditions in which the person is formed. When the conditions that deform the person are eliminated, then the "many-sided development" of the individual can take place. Individuals become "species beings" by realizing themselves in their creative activity.

For Baczko as well as for Kołakowski, the development of an authentic existence and the creation of meaning define individuality. Consequently, he calls any situation that prevents this creative activity of self-definition "the constraint of individuality." Baczko also elaborates on the humanization of work as part of the human "emancipation from the social forces of alienation." The humanization of work means "the overcoming of the division of labor," and "the humanization of the technical-productive and institutional forms of work by the maximum approximation of the process of work to instinctive, spontaneous work." On the other hand, "Marx stressed the fact that for the individual the idea of the universality of man is inseparable from the *time free from labor,* which the individual disposes of as a sphere of his own free cultural choices."[140]

Hirszowicz and Hochfeld were the ones who dealt most with the issue of the humanization of work as part of a more general study of the sociopolitical structure. Hirszowicz focused on the relationship of work to the human "species being," human essence. In work, humans create and recreate their essence, and in the process they create the forms of society in which they participate.[141]

Hochfeld approached the issue of the *humanization* of labor by examining it in the context of the *alienation* of labor, which in turn opened up the possibility of examining the specific features of Polish society that contributed to that alienation. In this discussion, he is close to Baczko's analysis of alienation but develops it further as it relates to work. Hochfeld asks the following questions: "How do the conditions and limits of the liberation of work from the shackles of alienation appear today? The perspectives for the humanization of labor? The possibilities for the affirmation of the human person through work?"[142]

In attempting to answer these questions, Hochfeld proposes two models, which he regards as complementary. The first model is Marx's vision of the complete liberation of work from total alienation. The second is an amalgam of particular characteristics of the reform program which have as their aim the improvement of the material, cultural, and political situation of work for people.[143] Marx's vision of liberation from alienation comes, Hochfeld points out, from his theory of human nature, the "species being" of humans. This concept of human nature is bound up with the understanding of humans as *homo faber*, beings who create their specific nature, their "species being" through conscious, purposeful work. "The result of this form of species life which is specific to humans is the origin and development of an artificial environment, in some sense of man's own creations."[144] According to this conception, this work activity has the potential for affirming the human person as specifically human rather than the potential for reducing the person to the level of animal life by being confined to mere physical reproduction. Hochfeld is close to Kołakowski here, but is interested in examining work in the interrelation of both of its aspects—human creative activity and making a living.

Marx's own understanding differentiated among three aspects of the alienation of work activity, according to Hochfeld.[145] First, there is the alienation of the product of work. Second, there is the alienation of the work activity itself, and, third, there is the alienation of the human essence by virtue of the fact that work fails to affirm what is specifically human and instead degrades it.

Hochfeld sees two separate approaches in Marx's view of alienation. One deals with restoring to work its unalienated, life-affirming character; the other, as Hochfeld perceives it, holds that the "kingdom of freedom" lies outside work activity altogether, in the sphere of leisure time.[146] The latter of these two approaches appears to Hochfeld to be one that is closer and easier to realize: a vision of the gradual curtailment of the sphere of necessary labor, and a corresponding vision of another sphere of free and creative public activity, modeled in some ways on the Greek *polis*.[147]

Having outlined Marx's understanding of alienation in some of its complexity, Hochfeld then asks whether this understanding—formed in the last century, under different social conditions—has any relevance for the present. In his view it does, for several reasons. The first is that the increasing mechanization and automation of the work process in the modern era actually fosters alienation as much as, if not more than, the brutal work conditions characteristic of the early Industrial Revolution. Another reason is attendant on the first—the increasing distance between those who make decisions and those who are responsible for executing them. Yet another aspect of this relevance is in the phenomenon of mass culture, the mass society. As Hochfeld puts it: "The culture of 'mass society' is the 'inverse fulfillment' of dreams of not only the 'real kingdom of freedom,' but even of freedom within the limits of the 'kingdom of necessity'."[148]

Hochfeld concludes that in developed industrial societies, Marx's vision of the liberation of work from alienation performs the function of exposing the alienating character of these societies. In addition to this, the vision Marx described has the virtue of showing that there are many serious problems yet to be solved, especially the central one of restoring direct ties between humans.[149] In this latter case, Hochfeld warns that there is a danger that an illusion of affirmation of the person and of direct ties can be created, which is often what the rubric of "human relations" in the workplace really means. He goes on to say that:

> At any given time only certain limited programs of reform are capable of realization—coming out of circumstances, possibilities, the specific makeup of social and political forces; dependent on the state of knowledge, the illusions of those involved, even on conscious mystification by

manipulators and those who empower them. But these programs can be subjected to constant inspection and verification in practice, broadly construed, in economic, cultural and political life; they can be changed and perfected; they can increasingly embrace the sphere of the affirmation of the person of those working.[150]

It is precisely here that Marx's holistic vision finds its place, according to Hochfeld. It serves as a guiding perspective for reform, providing the means of exposing those concrete features that hinder the process. Reform without this overall revolutionary perspective will lose sight of its own reason for being, whereas a revolutionary critique that demands total change without engaging in real, concrete, possible reforms—however limited—is barren and has little in common with the ideal of the humanization of work.[151] Hochfeld compared two concepts of socialism: that inspired by the British experience, and that which came to being in Russia with the revolution there in 1917. Hochfeld characterizes the first as reformist, which he took to mean that "the socialist goal is identical with the continuous movement of economic, political, legal and cultural reforms; and secondly, that the possibility of such reforms is inherent in the technical and economic tendencies of the development of modern industrial society, as well as in the democratic mechanism of political institutions."[152] The second concept of socialism held that "social ownership of the means of production is the basis of the socialist system," and that this "requires the gaining of lasting power by the working-class party."[153]

In the context of this dichotomy, Hochfeld maintained—contrary to official Marxist dogma—that it would be a mistake to dismiss out of hand the relevance of the reformist concept of socialism for the highly developed countries. He went on to discuss the problem of democratization, drawing on Rosa Luxemburg's writing on the Russian revolution and tying her writing to contemporary concerns. He spoke of the contradiction between "the positive effects of reforms and industrialization" and "the destructive results of dictatorship," between the "humanist tradition of Marxism" and the "radically anti-humanist forms of policy."[154] In this connection, Hochfeld noted that a movement for greater democratization was under way in Eastern Europe after the death of Stalin, "accompanied, and powerfully promoted, by an intellectual movement which subjects each canon and each dogma to revision and criticism" and "animates all spheres of political, economic and cultural life."[155]

In the same vein, Hirszowicz examined the question of social organization in both capitalist and socialist societies. In the latter case, she wrote, "the assertion that progress in socialism means the formation of new types of social self-management and the increasing involvement of more people in the governing process is worthy of a more detailed analysis than has so far been done."[156] Whatever new forms of self-management exist in socialist societies, she noted, are still experimental, and what is of particular interest for a theoretician is to look at alternative models of rule. What is also quite interesting is to see what hinders the development of new forms and new models, and to examine the influence different facets of society exert on the way in which these alternative models are actualized.[157]

Hochfeld provided an inspiration for the sociological approach to the humanist potential of Marxism through his inquiry into the humanization of work. It should be understood, however, that in their study of the sociopolitical structure Hochfeld and Bauman (and Hirszowicz) were merely concentrating their endeavors and were by no means devaluing philosophical anthropology. On the contrary, the perspective of philosophical anthropology is very much with them, and it lies at the root of their analysis of the sociopolitical reality, as is evident in Hochfeld's use of Marx's concept of "species being."

By the same token, although Kołakowski and Baczko are better known for exploring the philosophical concepts underlying this critique of social and political forms, they did not limit themselves to this dimension. They were also active in criticizing specific aspects of society which they regarded as antithetical to the humanist ideal. It must also be remembered that the activity of the revisionists was not confined to theory. They were all involved in trying, wherever possible, to influence the course of events in Poland. The political and intellectual change that followed Stalin's death and Khrushchev's speech of 1956 provided the original impetus for this action. These revisionists continued to work for change until they were no longer able to do so within Poland, although at least Kołakowski is still very active in Polish affairs while living abroad.

THE SOCIAL ROLE OF THE CRITICAL INTELLECTUALS

To stress this active role, however, is to risk forgetting that the reason the revisionists were able to have such an impact on Polish life was because theory was not isolated from practice but was instead an integral part of it. The theoretical work and personal activity of these critical thinkers were closely connected; together, these individuals influenced much of the critical activity that followed.

They influenced the official Marxism by compelling it to come to terms, however reluctantly, with the humanist perspective. They influenced later attempts at social reform, particularly through the emphasis on the humanization of labor and the search for models of worker self-management adequate to the task. Most important, though, their vision of human reality left its impact on later critical activity.

Not surprisingly, these critical intellectuals also engaged in reflection on the social role of intellectuals and the nature of their activity. In an early essay, Kołakowski examined the expectation that intellectuals should serve the Party, and he returned to the theme later, after leaving Poland. This second essay was a meditation on the social role of intellectuals and their attraction to irrationalism.[158] For Kołakowski here, echoing his work of six years earlier,

> [The most important function of intellectuals] is to maintain and to convey the accumulated stock of human spiritual culture as common stock; in other words, their work is meaningful only in terms of the assumption that despite all struggles and conflicts the human species participates in essentially the same intellectual structure, and that all the world's conflicts do not destroy the continuity and unity of human intellectual effort.[159]

Hirszowicz reflected on the social function of intellectuals in the socialist system (and, by implication, elsewhere) in a book published after her departure from Poland.[160] She made an observation there that speaks for all of those involved in philosophical revisionism:

> Here also begin the differences between those people who regard their intellectual creativity on the same basis as that on which they would bake rolls in a bakery or paint an apartment according to the wishes of a client, and those for whom intellectual creativity is an expression of a certain inner need, and who apply autonomous standards to it.[161]

This "inner need" is precisely what characterized the representatives of philosophical revisionism in Poland. From the beginning, they felt personally compelled to work through the legacy of Marx's thought and their own place with reference to it. This need caused them to develop their own thought and to become increasingly more severe in their criticism of the Polish political reality.

Throughout the work of Bauman, for instance, one can see the passionate defense of the vision of the development of a Marxist sociology and an expanded role for it within socialism. He hoped—as did all the others—that an increasingly rational ability to plan for social change and a move toward greater democracy and humanization within the society would result. In one sense, 1968 represented a defeat for these hopes in Poland, but the concrete steps that Bauman proposed for controlling the bureaucracy in 1957 had an influence in Polish life even beyond the setback of 1968.

The critical intellectual activity of these thinkers did not stop when they left Poland, but it did take different directions. Baczko ended up in Switzerland, where his later work dealt primarily with Rousseau.[162] Hirszowicz, in England, was harsh in her analysis of socialism and chose to further study issues related to the workplace.

After his departure from Poland, a new theme emerged in Kołakowski's work, to accompany the themes of human freedom and creative activity. He began to question whether something about Marx's theory did not lend itself to appropriation by Stalinism. The question as posed is new only in the way it was asked. Kołakowski no longer asked "What went wrong?" or counterposed some "authentic" Marxism to its deformation in Stalinism. Rather, he asked whether something in the way Marx framed his questions led to the subsequent deformations. In many ways, this shift was the logical extension of Kołakowski's position of early 1957. At that time, Kołakowski wrote in the preface to a collection of earlier writings that the critique they embodied "was done with the hope of reforming something that . . . may not be capable of reform."[163]

One commentator, George Kline, has posited at least two stages in Kołakowski's development: a revisionist phase and a postrevisionist phase, with the latter leading into a non-Marxist phase. According to Kline, Kołakowski was influenced in the first phase particularly by Kant and contemporary existentialists (mainly Sartre), as was evident in his treatment of the problems of individual freedom and responsibility. The postrevisionist writings seem to have been equally influenced by Spinoza,

Kant, Hegel, Marx, Dilthey, Mannheim, Husserl, Sartre, Heidegger, and Camus.[164] Kołakowski himself has acknowledged that he no longer considers himself a Marxist, and his history of Marxism ends on a highly critical note.

Of the representatives of philosophical revisionism in Poland, only Bauman continued to maintain and develop his interest in Marxism after leaving Poland. Particularly in one book written since his departure, one can see an effort to come to terms with the socialist system and ideas and, in a way similar to Kołakowski's efforts in *Main Currents of Marxism*, to come to terms with his own past. The parallel to Kołakowski becomes more interesting if one considers the very different conclusions the two men reached.

Bauman took up the question of utopias and their social function in a way similar to that of both Baczko and Kołakowski, and he proceeded to analyze the characteristics of the specifically socialist utopia. He examined the historical development of socialism and tried to understand the "socialist experiment" in the Soviet Union. His interest there lay in how the socialist vision developed and was transformed under the dual pressure of the negative model in the Soviet reality and the changes within capitalism over approximately the last one hundred years. He wrote of socialism that:

> The socialist utopia has brought contemporary society as far as possible while active within the framework circumscribed by what has come to be known as the industrial society. The next step, if there is one, will lead into the great unknown ... And this is perhaps the major cause of the present strength and present weakness of socialism. Its traditional tenets now acquired a powerful foothold in social reality itself and socialism is no longer forced to argue from the purely utopian position. But ... socialism has to begin again from the roots, from a reanalysis of essential and unquestioned values on which reality is grounded ... The present crisis is therefore deeper than anyone has experienced in the history of modern socialism.[165]

Bauman saw the frontier of this unknown as being in the sphere of culture and felt that the critical focus of the "reanalysis" he spoke of should be located there. In his history of Marxism, Kołakowski saw the same crisis, but, when confronted with what appeared to be a cul-de-sac, he decided that Marxism had nothing more to offer, that it was in fact "the greatest fantasy of our time." In contrast, Bauman pointed beyond the cul-de-sac, although acknowledging that the way is uncharted and that "vast, unexplored expanses" stretch ahead.

It is clear that the Polish revisionists have undergone a process of change from 1956–57 to the present. Although Kołakowski uses the term *revisionist* in a relatively narrow sense in his history of Marxism, it can be argued that he and the others have never stopped being revisionists. It is certainly possible to argue that the boundaries encompassed by that concept go considerably further in Kołakowski's case than either he or Kline have assumed. Nevertheless, it is also possible to state that revisionism is something that seeks to revise Marxism-Leninism and that the emerging Marxist humanism went far beyond that point.[166] However the case is argued, all of these critical Polish thinkers made a significant contribution to East European philosophical revisionism, and they went on to pose some key questions for contemporary interpreters of the Marxist tradition as well.

CHAPTER 2

The Budapest School

The Historical Context

HUNGARY EXPERIENCED A PARTICULARLY IN-
tensive period of social coercion during the Stalinist period; extensive purges affected all parts of society and
many people were confined to internment camps. The result was that a great deal of hostility accumulated under
the surface toward the Stalinists, whose rule was person-
ified in the Party general secretary, Mátyás Rákosi. In
the period after Stalin's death in March 1953, some of
this opposition toward Rákosi rose to the surface. There
was peasant unrest that spring in response to the harsh
grain requisitions imposed under a system of forced industrialization and campaigns against "kulaks," and discontent spread throughout the society. These events
coincided with the advent of new policies in the Soviet
Union, associated with Georgi Malenkov and his "New
Course." The New Course represented a move away from
heavy industry and toward an increased emphasis on
light industry and consumer goods.[1] The impact of this
change in Eastern Europe varied, but a common feature
was that it implicitly undermined the Stalinist leadership
in these countries.

In the case of Hungary, Rákosi was pressured by the Soviet leaders to follow the Soviet example and institute changes. As a consequence, he was forced to appoint as premier Imre Nagy, a person who had consistently advocated policies that resembled those of the New Course. Nagy's appointment marked a decisive turning point for Hungary, even though the immediate results were rather indecisive because Rákosi remained head of the Party and, in this capacity, worked to obstruct any changes proposed by Nagy. Still, Nagy's appointment had immense symbolic value in Hungary, "for it created a conception of an alternative economic and political policy within the existing framework."[2]

This alternative policy was at first primarily economic in nature, although it also entailed a relaxation of political tensions. The strategy had a built-in problem, however. Economic problems were so deeply rooted that any effort at reform entailed severe criticism of the way things had been done, so severe that it also implicitly called the whole system into question.[3] In a speech before Parliament on July 4, 1953, Nagy promised such things as an emphasis on light industry and food production, a slowing of the process of collectivization, and even the possible dissolution of collective farms. He stressed the need for changes in the labor code and for greater relaxation in intellectual life and in policies toward religion. He also called for the elimination of camps for political prisoners and a reduced role for the police. All these measures would contribute to the emergence of greater democracy in Hungary.[4] The problem came when these moves were hamstrung by Rákosi. A situation of dual power existed, with the Soviet Union supporting both sides but supporting neither decisively. This situation caused a great deal of uncertainty and undermined the morale of the society; it was one of the factors that contributed to the upheaval of 1956.[5]

In February 1955, Malenkov's New Course was repudiated in the Soviet Union, and Malenkov himself was forced out of his position as premier. As a result, Rákosi was able to overturn Nagy's policies, and in April 1955 Nagy was stripped of all his posts. Nevertheless, it proved impossible to turn back the clock in Hungary. Nagy's ouster caused many of his disillusioned supporters, who had seen in him a promise of reform, to bitterly oppose Rákosi.[6] In October 1955, the writers' union issued a memorandum of protest against "crude administrative interference in literary affairs." The main literary magazines came under the control of Communist opposition writers, and the rest of the media was increasingly sympathetic to new ideas. Opposition also coalesced in the discussion clubs, the most famous of which was the Petöfi Circle—an ongoing series of gatherings of intellectuals aimed at the revival of critical theoretical issues.[7]

After the Twentieth Soviet Party Congress and its policy of de-Stalinization, Rákosi's position had once again become untenable, but once again halfway measures were chosen. In a situation that satisfied no one, opposition grew until it culminated in the outbreak of October 1956 known as the Hungarian revolution. The central issue of the revolution was how to create a coherent new style of Communism along more specifically Hungarian lines.[8] On the face of it, this quest failed. Nagy's "National Communism" was suppressed and János Kádár came to power, ostensibly pursuing a policy of setting back the clock. Still, under the appearance of returning to the status quo ante, Kádár did the unexpected. In late 1961, after Party control had been reestablished, Kádár embarked on a program of liberalization. This policy was aided by the renewed emphasis on de-Stalinization at the Twenty-second Soviet Party Congress. Kádár wanted to effect a reconciliation between the government and the people, especially the intellectuals. Achieving this goal was made more feasible by a number of factors, among them the fact that the intellectuals, historically the bearers of the national consciousness, were now more ready to compromise. As they in turn found that they benefited from this new attitude, the political situation became more and more relaxed.[9] After about 1963, another shift in thinking occurred: the Party began to place more emphasis on economic solutions to social and political problems, thus deemphasizing political or "administrative" approaches.[10] The New Economic Mechanism (NEM)—a far-reaching economic reform plan—was approved in 1966 and implemented in 1968.

The Members of the Budapest School

This was the context within which the critical intellectuals attempted to develop a new understanding of Marxism in response to both the developments in Hungary and the need for a theoretical alternative to Stalinism. They found one such alternative in the philosophy of Marxist humanism, which manifested itself primarily through a group of scholars known as the "Budapest School," associated with György Lukács. Indeed, this association played so prominent a role that the group was also known as the "Lukács School." The principal members of the group were Ágnes Heller, Ferenc Fehér, György Márkus, Mihály Vajda, Maria Márkus and András Hegedüs. Of these, the first four were most closely associated with Lukács.[11]

Ágnes Heller studied under Lukács when he taught aesthetics at the University of Budapest. She received her doctorate in 1955, in philosophy. Subsequent to that time, she edited the *Hungarian Philosophical Journal*, taught high school, and, in 1963, was made a research associate of the Sociology Research Group of the Hungarian Academy of Science. She had been expelled from the Party in 1956 after the Hungarian "revolution" and was never readmitted. In 1968 she, György Márkus, and three other Hungarian philosophers attending the Korčula Summer School in Yugoslavia joined in issuing to the press a statement "condemning the [Soviet] military intervention in Czechoslovakia and pointing out the disastrous effect of the military intervention on the theoretical and practical development of Marxism."[12] She and several other members of the Budapest School (including Hegedüs and Vajda) lost their jobs in 1972–73 when they "refused to acknowledge the 'correctness of the Party line' in the controversy over the interpretation of official Marxist ideological tenets as contrasted with the 'Lukácsist' interpretation."[13] From 1973 to 1977, Heller and the others lived on the royalties from works published abroad. In 1977, when the Budapest School was dispersed, Heller accepted a teaching position in Australia, along with her husband, Ferenc Fehér. They now both teach at the New School for Social Research in New York.

György Márkus was not a student of Lukács's but studied philosophy in Moscow, graduating in 1957. He later became a close associate of Lukács and was employed as a research associate at the Institute of Philosophy of the Hungarian Academy of Sciences; he also taught at the University of Budapest for some time. He was expelled from the party for his part in the Korčula statement protesting the Soviet invasion of Czechoslovakia and has been teaching abroad since the mid-1970s. Everyone in the group has lived abroad except Hegedüs, but Mihály Vajda has since returned to Hungary where he is once again teaching philosophy at the University of Debrecen.

Ferenc Fehér is most noted for his writings in aesthetics and literary criticism, as well as in political philosophy. Mihály Vajda is a philosopher, and Maria Márkus and András Hegedüs are sociologists. Vajda was an associate of Lukács for a time at Budapest University and worked in the Institute of Philosophy. Although he is best known for his work on fascism and his study of phenomenology, he contributed to the critique of socialism as well. Hegedüs and Maria Márkus were members of the Sociology Research Group, which Hegedüs directed for a time. He was replaced as director in 1968, following the protest by some members of the Budapest School against the Soviet invasion of Czechoslovakia and as a result of the general ideological tightening that was Hungary's response to Czechoslovak events. Hegedüs had served as premier of Hungary under the Stalinist Communist Party Secretary Rákosi in 1955 and 1956, during the latter's attempt to discredit the Nagy line in Hungarian politics. At that time Hegedüs was still identified with the Stalinist position. Following the Hungarian revolution, however, he was no longer a part of political life and, after much reflection on the pre-1956 events, he broke with his dogmatist past. He then became interested in the sociological study of the socialist society in Hungary.

The Philosophical Agenda

There is a fundamental underlying unity to the work of the various members of the Budapest School. They are all concerned with elaborating the conditions necessary for the creation of a humane society and with the analysis of contemporary reality necessary to this task. In this effort, they can be said to be following Lukács's dictate to the effect that the revival of Marxism requires a methodological return to Marx, and at the same time, a "forward move towards Marxist interpretation of contemporary phenomena" for an understanding of reality.[14] Lukács profoundly influenced the activities and thought of the group and in some ways even set their tasks for them. This can be seen in the way in which they refer to him and in how they deal with themes he set out. Nevertheless, for the most part, they all moved beyond him in the development of their own perspective.[15] They subjected his ideas to criticism and moved beyond them in their own theoretical development.

The members of the Budapest School were faced with the necessity of responding to a situation in which the traditional approach to—or within—Marxism had lost much of its credibility or theoretical coherence. This traditional approach still viewed the proletariat as the motor force that, by virtue of its position in the capitalist system of production, would overthrow and transcend that very system. As early as the "revisionism" of Eduard Bernstein, a number of problems had been noted with that view—most notably, the perception that the position of the proletariat was not progressively worsening, as Marx's original prediction held it would. This phenomenon became marked in the latter half of the twentieth century, especially in the United States and Western Europe, where the working class had achieved a quite comfortable position in terms of material well-being, as a result of the successes of the trade union movement.

These events served to bring to the surface questions as to whether the proletariat could still be regarded as the agent of radical change it had been assumed to be. Thus, the search began for some group that could be regarded as having assumed this role by virtue of its position in the total structure of the capitalist economic system. Some argued that such an approach was no longer fruitful, given the far-reaching differences between the type of system prevailing and that characteristic of nineteenth-century, laissez-faire capitalism. These critics suggested other means of analyzing the prospects for overcoming the present system.

Another issue members of the Budapest School faced was the recognition of the problematic nature of the Soviet attempt to transcend capitalism by using Marx's theories. Many people questioned the validity of the Soviet claim to fully represent the embodiment of Marx's vision of the future society. These misgivings provided a fresh impetus for reexamining Marx himself, in search of another way of understanding him which would avoid the pitfalls demonstrably present in the Soviet reality.

The personal and theoretical development of those associated with the Budapest School took place slowly and over an extended period of time. The process began in 1953, after the death of Stalin and the initiation of Malenkov's New Course once again opened up the possibility of different approaches to socialism. From 1953 to 1956, a gradual change took place, with a dramatic moment following Khrushchev's speech at the Twentieth Soviet Party Congress. Heller described the process well, referring to her own experience:

> Allegedly, I was a good Communist because I identified totally with a system which suffered only for improper execution. Still, I often asked myself whether my dissatisfaction was the result of my shortsightedness as a "bourgeois individualist." Instead of thinking things out, I ignored my conscience and relativized my indignation. Thus, the period between 1953 and 1956 was a period of enlightenment—a process of "emancipation from self-incurred tutelage."[16]

Heller goes on to say that after March 1956, she and others had "come of age" and that they committed themselves to reason as opposed to "faith." After March 1956, they had freedom of thought, but this freedom was manifest more in the political than in the theoretical sphere. The emphasis on theoretical development resulted from several different stimuli. One was participation in discussions of the Petöfi Circle. Another was the writing of the *Aesthetics* by Lukács, which was begun in 1956, and a third was the participation by Heller and others in the Berlin Conference on freedom. This conference, organized by the East German Academy of Sciences in March 1956, was also attended by Leszek Kołakowski and Tadeusz Kroński from Poland.[17]

The significance of the Berlin Conference cannot be overlooked. According to Heller, it had a threefold influence. First, it provided a context in which philosophers from all over Eastern Europe could meet one another and discover common concerns—often for the first time, as such contact had been severely restricted before that time. Second, the theme of the conference, freedom, was the central problem facing these intellectuals in their own development, and the variety of approaches represented at the conference demonstrated that many different understandings of Marxism were possible. Third, the conference held out the hope of even more dialog in the future. This hope was not fulfilled for many years, but as a hope it provided encouragement for the participants in their own activities.[18]

The period between the Twentieth Soviet Party Congress and the Hungarian revolution was one of intense activity and great change on the part of many in the Budapest School. The Soviet intervention that put down the revolution evoked a despairing reaction from Heller and others, although this despair was mitigated by Khrushchev's proposed reforms and the Twenty-second Soviet Party Conference. Only after these reforms failed to get off the ground did they begin to realize how difficult reform in Eastern Europe was.

From the revolution of 1956 until 1964 the predominant mood was still one of despair and bitterness, coupled with a feeling of being "trapped." The situation changed in 1964, after a discussion on alienation provided a means of dealing with these feelings. It was in the early 1960s that the Budapest School was formally constituted, and in the mid-to-late 1960s members of the group participated in the Korčula Summer School—hosted by the Yugoslav *Praxis* group.

Heller speaks of the period from 1965 to 1968 as "marked by increasing philosophical depth":

> During this time we endeavored to found a "positive" philosophy based on a new reading of Marx and, in so doing, we participated in an international renaissance of Marxism as a pluralistic theory. This period was also a time of new illusions engendered by our active, but at the same time critical participation in the reform movement. Our goal was to transform economic reforms into social reforms.[19]

The year 1968 was a time of contrasts for the group, beginning with optimism and ending with disillusionment after the Soviet invasion of Czechoslovakia. In 1972 strict ideological control was reinstituted in Hungary, and this year marked the beginning of the end for the Budapest School.

The crisis of legitimacy of many traditional Marxist categories and of the Soviet model made it imperative that some way of approaching the problem of social change be found. This was particularly true because the "class" approach, stressing the proletariat, seemed almost of its own accord to lead into the Soviet model. The position Lukács elaborated in his book *History and Class Consciousness* provided a good example of that type of argumentation.

The major problem perceived in Lukács's presentation was that if the proletariat did not exhibit the characteristics attributed to it according to this view, then it fell to those conscious, aware members at the forefront of the movement for change to act on behalf of the class as a whole. The problem with this view was that it provided justification for the leading role of the Party—with all that entailed—in the Soviet Union and Eastern Europe. (Lukács himself was not an apologist for the Party, but the logic of his argument led in that direction.)

The Budapest School group followed Lukács, however, in attempting to overcome the strict historical determinism that had existed within Marxism. This attempt took the form of placing more emphasis on the *activity* of humans in striving to create better conditions and to transcend the existing social and economic system. In this regard, they were a part of the tradition of what has been termed the "philosophy of praxis" within Marxism. Praxis, or human activity, has been interpreted in different ways, but a common feature is the stress on human activity as the subject or motivating force in social change. This stress is in opposition to the view that humans are merely the objects of historical laws that operate regardless of human activity.

To deal with the problem raised by Lukács's emphasis on the proletariat, the Budapest School thinkers were forced to find a different theoretical category within Marxism, a category that could also provide a critical perspective on contemporary reality. The category they chose was that of "needs" and the role needs play in society.

A THEME OF HUMAN ESSENCE AND NEEDS

The person who explored the theme of needs most thoroughly in the group was Ágnes Heller. She analyzed the concept of need in Marx's writings and, on the basis of this analysis, came up with an original approach to the theory of need. This theory, which underlay the work of all the members of the Budapest School, is closely connected with the Marxian concept of human essence elaborated by György Márkus. The two concepts, need and human essence, are closely intertwined in the works of the Budapest School. In a sense, however, the question of human essence is the prior one; the theory of need has within it a normative concept of human essence. For this reason Márkus's presentation of the theme of human essence in Marx should be examined prior to an analysis of Heller's theory of need. Heller's work, however, is clearly central to the theoretical activity of the Budapest School, and as such forms the center of the present study. The concepts she develops will be examined at length in order to provide the basics for understanding the conceptual basis for the activity of the entire School.

The work in which Márkus dealt with Marx's concept of human essence was *Marxism and Anthropology*.[20] In it, he attempts to show both how this concept appears in Marx and the importance it holds for an understanding of Marx—and, by extension, for current Marxist efforts to understand human development. Márkus also shows how the concept plays a normative role in both the critique of the given reality and the description of the ideal society that is sought as an alternative to present systems.

> According to Márkus, in Marx's conception, man is a universal, social, and conscious natural being. . . . On the basis

of both early and late Marxian texts he shows that the concept of human essence implies a conception of life-activity, i.e., *work* in the general, anthropological sense, that mediates natural surroundings by transforming, humanizing, socializing external nature and human nature itself, by objectifying human needs, capabilities, skills and norms, and by (self-) transforming each human generation on the foundation of what is already objectified.[21]

This definition of human essence focuses on the species rather than on the individual because, "for Marx, the 'human essence' lies precisely in the 'essence' or inner unity of the total social development of humanity.[22] It is *not* some sort of collection or amalgam of traits or qualities found in every person throughout time—especially not some sort of independent substance that is almost given a life of its own, separate from the concrete actions of actual human beings in time. The immediate value of this way of approaching the matter is that a difference can be made between the development of possibilities on the level of the species and the actual ability of individuals to appropriate the possibilities for themselves.

This kind of distinction is implicit in the dual quality of work: on one level, work is simply the "necessary precondition of human life, that is the material exchange between man and nature," but work is also "a free self-activity in which man forms and appropriates his own capacities."[23] Thus it can happen that, for individuals, work becomes merely this "necessary precondition." But it can still be said that—on the whole—some sort of progress or development is taking place as the result of this activity, insofar as the widening of possibilities takes place generally.

This view is not, as sometimes happens, an apology for existing conditions or a praise of technological development. Rather, it provides the basis for the critique of those social orders where the gap exists between the individual and society, or between abstract possibilities and their realization. This gap, or split, is what is understood as alienation; it can be expressed as the "separation and op-position of man's essence and existence." At the same time, the effort to transcend this state of affairs entails the "creation of the conditions for a historical development which ends the inverse relationship between the wealth and many-sidedness of society and the passivity, limita-tion, and one-dimensionality of single individuals."[24]

History is the record of the widening of human possi-bilities through human work as human "self-activity," but this "self-activity" becomes restricted as a conse-quence of the division of labor at the same time that this very phenomenon in the modern era allows for a virtual explosion in the widening of human possibilities in the abstract. "In examining the historical origins and neces-sity of alienation Marx, in *The German Ideology*, de-scribes it as an aspect and determinant of the whole process of history, just as it is defined by the emergence and persistence of the naturally-given (naturwuchsig) *di-vision of labor* and of *private property*."[25]

Márkus implicitly ties in the concept of "human es-sence" with that of needs when he writes:

> But precisely because human practical activity, work—in contradistinction to animal activity—'reproduces the whole of nature' and since '. . . man knows how to produce in ac-cordance with the standard of every species, and knows how to apply everywhere the inherent standard to the object,' so not only through the subjective prism of his needs is man capable of knowing reality, but also, since *these needs them-selves are universal* in their tendencies, objectively, accord-ing to the 'inherent standard' of the object.[26]

When he speaks of the conception of "human es-sence" (as "work, the self-formative and self-actualizing free and universal activity of men") as part of the "pro-letariat's "revolutionary praxis," in the form of theory, Márkus is in some respects closer to the Lukács of *His-tory and Class Consciousness* than is Heller. But Márkus does not limit his conception of revolutionary praxis to the activity of the proletariat.[27] His discussion of the problem of transcending current conditions does something Heller (and Vajda, elsewhere) was careful to avoid: it attributes the possibility of social transformation to the "*interests* of certain large groups and classes of men." In contrast, Heller was at pains to show that it was on the basis of *needs*, not *interests*, that transformation (or transcendence) could take place.[28] In her book *The Theory of Need in Marx*, Ágnes Heller set out to explore Marx's use of the concept of need and to try to go beyond Marx in following through on some of the issues raised in her analysis.[29] Heller was not the first or the only person attempting to use the category of needs within the framework of Marxist thought. The problem with other attempts was that they tried to

> merely adapt the Marxian theory of need and class to contemporary conditions. Instead of seriously re-examining the original theory of need and its relation to the theory of class, they uncritically sought to reproduce Marx's method of theorizing and to find a new revolutionary subject with new radical needs. . . . By considering the theory of need *independently* of the theory of class, [Heller] takes the first crucial step toward a reevaluation of the class theory on theoretical rather than on historical grounds. Any classificatory analysis of needs presupposes a *philosophically-elaborated value concept of need*, which alone can provide the basis for an evaluation of needs. Accordingly, she systematically unfolds the relation of the theory of need to the normatively-based philosophy of history as the unifying thread of Marx's project.[30]

In Heller's own words, the role that a theory of need plays in the reformulation of Marxist theory can be seen as follows:

> For Marx, the precondition of "human" wealth is . . . the basis for the free development of all the capacities and senses of the human being, the free and many-sided activity of every individual. Need as a category of value is none other than the need for this kind of wealth.[31]

The key phrases are those that refer to the "free development of all the capacities and senses of the human being, the free and many-sided activity of every individual." The analysis of these concepts, or this concept, points to an understanding of the possibilities and potential for radical social change and at the same time provides a vision of the goal of such change. The normative concept within this vision draws on elements and characteristics already present, but in using it, Heller attempts to understand what prevents the realization of these features and to develop a means of overcoming impediments. It is a philosophy of "praxis" because the concepts of "free development" and "free activity" clearly stress the role of humans acting as the subject of social and historical change. Also, the free development of *individuals* is stressed; this provides one of the central themes in all of Heller's work, where the discrepancy between the development of *social* wealth and *individual* wealth is stressed. Here, *wealth* does not refer only—or even primarily—to material wealth, for to do so would simply restate the old thesis of increasing poverty, whether it be that of the proletariat or not. Rather, the discrepancy is seen as one of capabilities as well. "Whilst the individual, subordinated to the division of labour, remains poor (in the broadest sense of the word) there is a parallel enrichment of the species. The highest level of enrichment reached so far, i.e., capitalism, is also the peak of individual impoverishment."[32]

THE THEORY OF VALUE

In *The Theory of Need in Marx*, Heller carries on her earlier work on value: "Towards a Marxist Theory of Value." The two overlap to a large extent; in a sense, the work on value is primary but it introduces the concept of need as well. "Need" is a *value* category, as was seen before, and is always seen as a function of true human wealth. In this context, "value" as a concept must be clarified before "need," as a category of value, can be examined properly. It was not until the modern era that the concept of value became problematic—before that time, values were considered as "givens" in one sense or another. "Their 'givenness' became questionable in bourgeois philosophy, beginning with certain tendencies in the Renaissance. The fixed hierarchy of values disintegrated along with the 'naturally-given' community as the measure of the objectivity of values."[33]

According to Heller, all attempts to deal with the newly problematic relativity of values end up facing three problems, which are related to each other, and a fourth problem that is common to the first three.[34] The first problem is the following: *Is value a primary category that cannot be derived from anything else?* Is it a category of existence? Attempts to resolve this problem led to a separation of value from existence or experience, inasmuch as values could not be *derived* from experience. The second problem has to do with the problem of validity and value realization: *Are values valid even if never practiced or realized?* Is there a validity of values underlying *all* value judgments or is this validity relative? The third problem, in Heller's view, is most cogently expressed by Max Weber: "(a) is a value-free social science possible? (b) should we strive for such a science? (c) can man clarify those values with which he 'enters' into an investigation of society? (d) is he able to regard his values as relative? And is this desirable? (e) can science decide in the choice of values? and can science convince those with different value premises?"[35] From these questions Weber draws the conclusion that ultimate values are outside the purview of science. Nonetheless, before any action or investigation can be undertaken, Weber believes the following questions must be addressed: (1) What are the basic value axioms? (2) What are the consequences for the evaluation of facts in their light? (3) What are the practical consequences that are, or would be, an outgrowth of these axioms? The fourth problem, common to all of the above, is the following: "Are values objective or subjective in nature?" Heller's answer to Weber is not only that social science cannot be value-free but that value presuppositions should be put out "on the table" prior to entering into the investigation of society. In addition, although the primary *value-axioms* are not relative, the *concrete* values are *always* relative and must be re-examined at any given time to assess their faithfulness to the value axioms. Furthermore, social theory's ability to sway anyone depends on the degree to which a theory expresses the problems the person being swayed is concerned with, and the degree to which the theory seems to incorporate within its structure an adequate resolution. "A theory that can shape its value-choice into a coherent world view, and can comprehend the dynamic of social totality, is far more able to convince than a theory that cannot do so, on the basis of the same value commitments."[36]

Heller considers it necessary to clarify the value-premises of Marxism. She believes that the above-mentioned problems in a theory of value can be resolved within a Marxist framework, but that previous attempts to deal with the issue of value from within Marxism must first be dealt with because some of these attempts were influenced by the very tendencies they were trying to avoid or overcome. As Heller puts it, "the positivist and historicist distortion of the Marxian concept of value began with Engels' reinterpretation of the Marxian concept of base and superstructure in *Anti-Duhring*."[37] Marx's understanding of these two concepts was that the "social life process," otherwise known as the "mode" or "relations" of production, constituted the foundation of all social life, all societies. Although this foundation manifests itself in what Marx termed the superstructure, the two have to be understood as being part of a structural unity. In no sense can it be said that a cause-and-effect relationship exists between the two.

It was Engels who transformed the interaction to one of cause and effect—base to superstructure. Although he tried to mitigate the effects of this understanding by introducing the concept of "reciprocity," Engels still did not give up this approach. He also went on to add something further: "since ideologies and value preferences are 'agencies' for the expression of social conflicts, he took the Marxian claim that *social existence is manifested* in the superstructure and transformed it so that *interests* (primarily class interests) became the factors constituting values. Thus, Engels rehabilitated one of the favorite theories of derivation of the bourgeois enlightenment: the 'theory of utility'—the only modification being that he derived value preferences from social classes rather than from individual interests."[38]

Engels's formulation became the one most adhered to by Marxists until it was challenged by several new reformulations. These (represented by Karl Korsch, György Lukács, and Antonio Gramsci) were critical of the above formula, and they also brought the concept of alienation to the fore again by stressing that Marxism involved *conscious* value choice, rather than seeing values as simply the result of economic development. But, according to Heller, if the only available criteria for determining values are to be found in the interests or the value choices of the proletariat, the problem then becomes one of differentiating between the values of earlier ages that have been conditioned by their relations or mode of production, and the supposedly absolute values of the proletariat. The problem was not solved by claiming that the proletariat was in a position to know 'objective truth' because of its place in the scheme of things.

All this discussion brings Heller to the crux of the matter: the ongoing necessity of critiquing the "empirical derivation of values still dominant in Marxist theory."[39] In this approach, values are derived from either interests or needs. But value, as a "universal category of social ontology," cannot be derived from interests, because by their very nature interests are particular—they manifest "the realization of the goals of certain groups, classes, and individuals *against other groups, classes, and individuals. . . . There is no interest without opposition of interests.*[40] Hence, interest is something which, by definition, is only in class, or alienated society, and cannot serve as the basis for a universal value formulation. Need is not limited in the same way that interest is; it is equally a "category of social ontology," in the same sense that value is. But need is always a desire for "something," an "object of need." "Needs create the objects, the types of activity, and the relationships necessary for their satisfaction, and the latter in turn generate new needs. Social production, objectifications, and relations create the 'sphere of possibility' which determines the movement of needs."[41] Values cannot be *derived* from needs because this 'sphere of possibility' always comes between the two; needs are dynamic and changing. Also, in no sense can value be derived from what are called "social needs"—either these are at root individual needs, or they are part of what *determines* "social needs," defined as "the factors necessary for social reproduction," and therefore cannot be *derived* from them. Thus we are led to the heart of the matter: Values cannot be empirically derived. This does not mean that it is impossible to speak of value in a Marxian sense, for

> Marx, in fact, did have a fundamental universal value axiom from which all his values and value judgments can be axiologically derived. This ontologically primary, and empirically underivable category is *abundance (Reichtum)*. What is 'abundance?' *It is the many-sided unfolding of the essential power of the species.* Thus we obtain the first value axiom: value is whatever helps the enrichment of the powers of the species; and the second value axiom: the highest value is *the ability of individuals* to appropriate the abundance of the species.[42]

These are the value assumptions that underlie Heller's attempt to develop a Marxist philosophy of value and a philosophy of needs. The two, value and needs, are inextricably interwoven in her work, and the analysis of each shares many features with the other. "Species-being," or mans' essential powers (*Gattungswesen*), consists of "sociality, work (production, and objectification in general), freedom, consciousness, and universality," and these essential powers are the "potentialities with which man enters history."[43] These powers are not "given," once and for all. They must be developed; they must "unfold."

This process takes place in essentially three ways, through which natural limitations are overcome. The first way is represented by the "conscious development of production." Contrary to the usual sense in which this concept is understood in the capitalist social and economic system, here it refers to something more than production to expand capital accumulation. "Production for its own sake," in Marx, "means nothing but the development of human productive forces, in other words, the development of the richness of human nature as an end in itself."[44]

> This is both the premise and the motive force of the abundance of use values, which is at once "the discovery, the creation and the satisfaction of those new needs which arise from society itself; the culture of all the characteristics of social man, and the production of this man who represents the highest possible abundance of needs, since he is rich in properties and relationships."[45]

The second part of this process, or second way, has to do with replacing the "naturalness" of society by "purely social relationships"—something that is a characteristic feature only of the modern era. The third way is the individual side of what in the second way is social: the needs of the *individual* become more human—that is to say, they become "more free, more conscious, more social and more universal."[46]

Thus human essence, or "species-being," *is* the fundamental category and value assumption for Marx, and the category or concept of "needs" is an integral part of it. In the analysis of value and of needs, several facets of the argument can be seen as being present already in the brief sections outlined above. In addition to the "essential powers" being the subject of much of the discussion, several other terms that have been used here suggest themes that will become crucial later in the examination. These are, for example, "the *discovery,* the *creation* and the *satisfaction* of those new needs which arise from society itself," and "rich in *properties* and *relationships.*" The *discovery* of new needs is central because it plays a part in the defetishizing process of the overcoming of existent social relations; the discovery of *new* needs implicitly puts *old* needs in a new light. New needs of one kind or another are constantly being created by the production process. Although all of them do not stand in a critical relationship to old needs (rather, many simply take their place alongside the old), the discovery and creation of new needs potentially can play a critical role. When linked to the question of the satisfaction of needs—old and new—there is even greater potential for constructive use of the concepts of the discovery and creation of new needs. This is evident in the observation that "to be able to subsist as a 'social formation,' capitalism had to have, within its structure of need, certain needs that were not satisfiable internally."[47] The two aspects of the abundance of needs, richness of properties and richness of relationships, refer to the dual set of qualities essential to the fully developed individual. The inseparability of individual properties and relationships is a very important point in Heller's analysis—there is no fully-developed individual outside of community. This theme will be developed further at a later point; richness of relationships not only presupposes "community," but predicates community of a certain type as well.

In the discussion of value and need, one feature that plays a prominent role is that of the object, in the sense of "objectification." It was noted earlier that needs are always found within a given "sphere of possibility" and always in relation to some object. "The orientation of needs toward objects also points to the *active* character of needs. Needs are simultaneously passions and capacities (the passion and capacity to appropriate the object) and thus *capacities are themselves needs.* The capacity for objective activity is thus one of the greatest needs of man."[48]

Objects and objective activity have a value dimension as well as being related to the ongoing dynamic of needs. Values, or choices of values, take place immediately through what Heller calls "in-itself species objectification"—objects, customs, language. Objects have value in relation to customs, which are among the most complicated of value systems. Language figures in all value choices. In addition to the category of "in-itself" objectifications, which are more or less "given" features of any society and, as such, form the background for life in society, there exist "systems of criteria." These, the more conscious objectifications, express certain preferences with regard to possible values in the form of capabilities, conduct, and so forth. They include "ideal objectifications," "abstract norms," and *"for-itself* species objectifications." The first term refers to virtues or pure value concepts, the second to the type of ideal objectification by which given values can be compared with other values in providing for choice, and the third to such objectifications as art and philosophy.[49]

The last category mentioned, "for-itself species objectifications," is very important. The value aspect of the objectifications that man creates is important because it is in relation to these value aspects that the *individual* (*individuum*) is formed, in contrast to the isolated man in society (*Einzelwesen*). This is a very crucial distinction: the "single man" or isolated man is someone who simply accepts the "given" value hierarchy spontaneously, whereas the "individual" consciously chooses to create a different system of values.[50] The "individual," as posited here, is analogous to the "man rich in needs" who occupies such a central place in the theory of need.

In a certain sense, the "individual," or man "rich in needs," is a future-oriented concept, an ideal type, based on a certain concept of human nature and a vision of the ideal future society. At the same time, however, the concept cannot be only a utopian vision, for if it were it would have little value in the present, apart from its function as a norm contraposed to the present. To bear fruit, the concept and vision of human essence and future society must in some sense correspond to actually existing needs. Thus, the task is to try to show in what way this concept of human nature is borne out and how the normative vision of the future that springs from this concept relates to actually pertaining conditions. Another part of this task is showing how these pertaining conditions contain within themselves the elements of that future—otherwise it would be sheer fancy to talk of them. The concept of needs provides for this sort of analysis. When needs are viewed in light of Marx's understanding of human nature, it becomes possible to show the conditions that favor and the conditions that impede the development of the kinds of needs that most fully express this essential character.

NEEDS AND ALIENATION

In this regard, it is necessary to understand what is—in terms of this frame of reference—most important as far as needs are concerned. Heller says, following Marx, that "the highest object of human need is the other person. In other words: the measure in which man has become the highest object of need for other men determines the level of humanization of human needs."[51] It then becomes possible to contrast any given historical era or social formation, including the present, with this conception of "human needs." If "the main end of man is other men," then when this priority is no longer present, man's needs are alienated. "Alienation changes this main end into means, and man becomes for other [men] a mere means: a means toward the satisfaction of his own private ends of his greed."[52] This is particularly the case under present circumstances, in the capitalist socioeconomic system.

This same system, however, created the possibility for the development of "human needs"; it must be carefully examined to see what it is about the capitalist socioeconomic system that simultaneously creates and alienates these needs.

Heller separates Marx's discussion of the alienation of needs into four sets of problematics, which she will use as an organizing principle for her own attempt to develop a philosophy of needs: the means-end relation, quality and quantity, impoverishment (reduction), and interests.[53]

Some of the salient features of the means-end problem were discussed above; man is turned from an end into a means. This has two aspects to it. First, one might expect that social production would, almost by definition, go toward satisfying social needs. This is not the case under conditions of capitalist production, however, because production for social needs is not the goal here. Production is oriented toward increasing and expanding capital, and the satisfaction of needs (on the market) is the way in which this increase and expansion takes place. The other side of the coin is that the same dynamic holds for social relations as for economic transactions: "When alienation assumes its extreme form (in capitalism) authentic community disappears, because the commodity relation becomes the sole pseudo-'community'; social ends and content (and social togetherness) become means to the private ends of private persons."[54]

Yet another facet of the problem is that needs themselves become means—they are manipulated so that new needs are constantly being created; these needs are meant to serve only the end of profitability, through the plethora of objects designed to elicit these needs. The consequence is that, whereas individuals may believe they used satisfying their own needs, they are in reality being used. Also, needs that do not serve the purpose of profitability are ignored, including the need for *human* development if it conflicts, for example, with the needs of commodity production. One cannot, therefore, speak of

individual freedom either in this case, when the needs
are so shaped and determined in advance. Although the
individual may also accumulate more goods and develop
needs for yet more things, this does not make an individual "rich in needs." On the contrary, this accumulation
represents an impoverishment in terms of his or her all-
round development.

This last point leads into the set of problems considered under the heading of quality and quantity. At issue
is the need for possession, which in principle has no
quantitative limit and which is contrasted to the need for
enjoyment of an object, per se, and to a rounded development of needs and their objects. The medium for the need
for possession is money. Money epitomizes quantity and
expresses wealth in a purely quantitative sense. As such,
it is the opposite of qualitative, human wealth, the "richness of needs," which is the mark of an *authentic development.* This qualitative wealth (or the possibility of its
existence) is ironically, however, a product of the very
quantification represented by money. This is illustrated
by the following statement from Marx:

> When the aim of labour is not a particular product standing
> in a particular relation to the particular needs of the indi-
> vidual, but money, wealth in its general form, then, firstly,
> the individual's industriousness knows no bounds; it is in-
> different to its particularity, and takes on every form which
> serves the purpose; it is ingenious in the creation of new ob-
> jects for a social need, etc.[55]

Still, once the conditions of general wealth that are
necessary for further qualitative development have been
created, money has the effect of "restricting" quality,
quantifying qualitative needs, and causing those not
susceptible to quantification to slowly die. Furthermore,
it can even quantify that which is intrinsically non-
quantifiable and change qualitative needs into quantitative ones, which are their very antithesis.[56] Contrasted
to this depiction is the portrait of the future society,
which will be in keeping with the human character of

needs. This contrast is expressed well in the famous lines written by Marx in his *Economic and Philosophic Manuscripts of 1844:*

> Assume man to be man and his relationship to the world to be a human one: then you can exchange love only for love, trust for trust, etc. To enjoy art, you must be an artistically cultivated person; to exercise influence over other people, you must be a person with a stimulating and encouraging effect on other people. Every one of your relations to man and to nature must be a specific expression, corresponding to the object of your will, of your real individual life.[57]

Following on the quantification of needs comes the impoverishment of needs and capacities and the attendant reduction or homogenization of needs; everything comes down to the need for possession. This need "to have" can relate to the need for *more* and *more*, as in money or goods, or in another sense, to the person who "may only have enough to want to live, and may only want to live in order to have that."[58]

The next and final of these sets of problems is that of interests. In this section, for the first time in this particular examination of related problematics, Heller engages in an implicit critique of socialist society as well as of capitalist. Although at the outset in the analysis of interest, the focus is still on capitalism, this focus shifts further along. First, though, two concepts, "utility" and "interest," must be clarified, according to Heller. They did not always have the essentially identical meanings now ascribed to them; "utility" meant something of value for humans, a good. It had to do with what Heller refers to as "categories of value orientation": "good-bad" was the primary category and under it could come a whole range of secondary and even tertiary categories. "These categories 'direct' our socially-regulated, optional and imperative preferences, . . . [and] indicate what is to be chosen or avoided."[59] In the present era, however, the concepts of interest and utility have been merged, and utility has come to mean interest. Interest can refer to individual interest or general interest; at root, however, they are the same: "general" interest is merely an aggregate term.

This particular problem was discussed by Heller in "Towards a Marxist Theory of Value," and was mentioned earlier in this study, when it was seen that value could not be derived from interest and that general interest was merely the flip side of the coin to individual interest. That discussion of values and interests is repeated later in "Towards a Marxist Theory of Values," but it is carried further there because the context is broader. The "general interest" can be seen as an "alienated power resulting from the struggle between private interests, and thwarting the ends and aims of individual human beings."[60] Although specific reference was made in this section to "the world of commodity exchange," and hence more specifically to capitalist society, the "general interest" standing over against individual interests can also be seen as a feature of socialist society. In fact, that this was also an insight of Heller's can be seen as a feature of socialist society. In fact, that this was also an insight of Heller's can be seen in another context. [61] The critique of the concept of "class interest," and the situating of this concept within the broader critique of the trade union movement—as being a struggle for rewards *within* the structure of capitalism rather than aiming at *transcending* capitalism—is in itself a critique of a dominant category of thought within socialist societies.

Mihály Vajda also dealt with the question of interests in a discussion on the interrelationships among the three concepts of "law, ethics and interest."[62] In this essay, he criticizes attempts to deduce ethics from the principle of interest—individual or class. Vajda tries to show that for a proletarian, "class-interest" by no means coincides with "individual interest"; the individual's *interest* is to "increase his own property," not to overthrow the system. Therefore, any class solidarity can be possible only on an entirely different basis, where it is "not the product of the proletariat's class interest, but rather of the proletariat's possibility as such not to reduce or transform their own needs to interests."[63]

If the proletariat is unable to avoid reducing or transforming its needs to interests, a situation results wherein the individual proletarian can be accused of acting against his own interests:

> [If] individual proletarian interest and class interest coincide and have the same orientation, which constitutes the possibility of a class ethics, and of surpassing the dichotomy between selfish interest and pure ethics, it should follow that, if a proletarian does not by his own action contribute to the construction of this bridge, he comes into conflict not only with his class interest, but with his own individual interest as well.[64]

The consequences of the conflict between individual interest and class interest can be seen clearly in Eastern Europe, where the proletariats "create for themselves a legal order by means of which [they] compel . . . individual members, the proletarians, to act in accordance with their class interests. The proletariat then exercises dictatorship against itself."[65]

SOCIAL NEEDS AND RADICAL NEEDS

The critique is continued by Heller in *The Theory of Need in Marx*, in the section devoted to the discussion of "social need." Again, this concept appeared earlier, during her discussion of social need as it related to the attempt to derive value empirically from society or social categories. "Social need" is sometimes identified with "general interest," and it is on this point that the critique implicit in Heller's discussion of that latter topic is made more explicit. She criticizes Marxist perspectives that mistakenly make this identification and brings out the consequences of such an approach. These consequences are political, or "practical," as well as theoretical; they involve the subordination of individual needs to social needs, which later, in disguised form, come to mean the needs of the dominant strata.

If social needs are really individual needs but specific individual needs are not "social" needs, then the individual needs cannot be "genuine" or real. "From this conception there follows a distinction between 'recognized' and 'unrecognized' needs," with the same problem resulting of who is to decide which needs are "genuine" or not.[66] As a solution to this problem, the concept "radical needs" was used by Marx and adopted by Heller. "Radical needs" are the same as the "human needs" discussed earlier; this concept will be explored in greater detail at a later point. Here, Heller analyzes the concept of social needs further and discovers a variety of meanings. The term can refer to "socially-produced" needs in a broad sense, or to "the needs of 'socially-developed humanity.'" In both cases, the needs are of individuals.

Another sense of the term "social needs" is that of "the average needs for material goods in a society or class," which translates to demand. Demand can be effective or ineffective, but in neither case does this definition of "social need" refer to "real" social need, as Heller puts it. "True social needs represent actual, thoroughly-conscious needs, whilst the 'social needs' that are presented on the market indicate the possibilities of satisfying true social needs in a given society."[67] This statement refers to material needs only in the context of the definition of social needs used here. Nonmaterial needs viewed in this light are the epitome of alienation, the "quantification of the unquantifiable." Yet one more sense of the concept "social needs" is that in which the needs are such that they can be satisfied only socially, generally through institutions created for that purpose. In this latter sense, the concept of social needs leads into the discussion of "radical needs."

"Radical needs" were mentioned previously as being the "human" needs, the needs that have as their object the "species-being" of humanity. It is not enough, however, merely to posit "radical needs" and refrain from examining how they are already present in society. It is not a question of "ought," in the sense that these are needs that "ought" to develop or "should" be found, but needs that can be discerned in the actual structure of present society. Heller writes that Marx confronted this problem in two ways: the first was to make the subject of the "ought" into a collective; the second was to posit the problem in terms of causal necessity.

> The Ought itself is *collective*, because at the maximum point of capitalist alienation it stimulates certain needs among the masses ... ;these are the radical needs which embody this Ought and which by their very nature, tend to transcend capitalism—and precisely in the direction of communism.[68]

The second way Marx confronted the problem involved the theory that the inherent dynamic of the economy would of necessity effect this transition. These two approaches can be seen more clearly when viewed as part of the dynamics of social structure. This theme also came up with the discussion of the question of value derivation, where Marx's understanding of social structure, or formation, was contrasted with Engels' more mechanistic portrayal. For Marx, "every social formation is a total whole, a unity of structures coherently linked to each other and constructed interdependently. There is no causal relationship between these structures (no one of them is the 'cause' or the 'consequence' of another); they are only able to function as parts of an interdependent arrangement."[69]

Such an understanding allows for the "grounding" of the "ought" in the way mentioned. If society is this whole, this social formation, it can be looked at in terms of the way it is structured. If this view is taken, it becomes possible to see, according to Heller, that part of the structure of capitalism involves the presence of a concomitant structure of need. This structure of need which is characteristic of capitalism in turn depends on the presence of certain kinds of needs that are necessary to its continued functioning but that cannot be satisfied within the given structure. Those whose needs are of this radical character are those who embody the "ought."

In Heller's view, Marx's own thought contains a fundamental contradiction: between the idea of the transformation of society by those whose radical needs drive them to transcend the given structure and the view that capitalism "brings about its own negation with the necessity of a natural process."[70] She finds a paradox in Marx's thesis of the impoverishment of the proletariat because elements of both means of dealing with the problem are evident in it. In the approach focusing on the development of radical needs, as opposed to that of necessity or natural law, one finds a contradictory development within capitalism. Rather than this being the contradiction between "forces of production" and "relations of production," however, it involves another sort of contradiction—one that is characteristic of advanced *commodity* production, which is what capitalism represents. This feature of the commodity provides an insight into its character; it is a special product, inasmuch as it has a dual nature and function. It represents *use value*, as a good or products, and at the same time represents *exchange value*, because it was produced to be exchanged for something else. Thus, already in the commodity one can see a tension that is reproduced on the social level as well. "In the production of commodities, human relations assume the form of relations between things; social existence becomes fetishized in 'the thing' [*zu Dinglichem fetischisiert*]."[71]

Heller's statement refers to the fact that people no longer realize that what they are so assiduously exchanging represents their own activity and is an expression of their own selves. "Social relations fetishized in 'the thing' confront individual human beings in the form of economic laws—laws of nature, as it were."[72] What is

produced bears no relation to the needs of the person producing the commodity but is produced only to be exchanged. The rules of exchange tend to assume a life of
their own, and thus appear as "laws of nature." To Heller,
then, it is the overcoming of this situation as a conscious
project, based on a realization of the true character of capitalism, that will effect radical social change; this realization is brought about by the growth and development of
"radical needs"—not by a "law of necessity."

For Heller, the specific aspects of the contradictory nature of capitalism are freedom and necessity, necessity
and chance, teleology and causality, and, following from
these, social wealth and social impoverishment.[73] The
first antinomy, freedom and necessity, refers to the fact
that the apparent freedom of the commodity-producer
and the wage-laborer are both subject to the "quasi-
natural necessity of the economy," operating above them,
so to speak. The antinomy of necessity and chance relates
to another part of the same phenomenon—the "quasi-
natural necessity" referred to above appears in a chance
way, where "production and need meet on the market in
the form of supply or demand." It also appears in the tension between the fact that, although people's role in life is
"accidental," in the sense that it is not determined by
birth, it is nevertheless fixed by the structure of society
in a different way, through the division of labor.

Causality and teleology are seen as an antinomy in
capitalism, where "everyone sets out to realize his own
individual ends but the result is something completely
different from what the individual wanted to achieve,"
because the laws of capitalist economic life operate in a
way that alters the individual goals. The antinomy of
wealth and poverty is especially important because it refers to the dichotomy between the wealth of society as a
whole and the way in which this wealth is achieved at the
expense of individuals in capitalism. These antinomies
are embedded in the structure of capitalism and are part
of its very nature. They cannot be ignored in an analysis

of the workings of the capitalist system, but they do point to a resolution. This resolution is to be found in the "development of the human species," the "development of the richness of human nature as an end in itself."[74]

In looking at the two ways in which Marx addressed the problem of transition or social change, Heller asks if "the development of the human species" means the same thing as "centralization of the means of production" or "socialization of labour." She answers her own question by stating that it clearly does not: "the 'development of the human species' is a much broader concept than the others; and, it is not, of course, a mere consequence [of the others]."[75] Although both this question and its answer fall within the framework of Marx's writings themselves, the answer to the question has definite implications for the socialist systems, for whom the concepts of "centralization" and "socialization" are central tenets of dogma. This dogma, of course, is by no means limited to socialist societies—it is shared by much of present-day Marxist thinking and, as such, is the subject of the critique.

The "development of the human species" means for people to *actualize* their human potential, which means the development of radical needs and their satisfaction. According to Marx, this would take place through the "revolutionary struggle of the collective subject (the working class), having become such by virtue of its radical needs and revolutionary practice."[76]

Marx's belief that the working class was to be the bearer of radical needs resulted from his understanding of the way these needs are formed. For him, the workers become the revolutionary subject because the needs are created in the labor process. The contradictions within the system are brought home to the workers when they realize that the way they are structured into society is antithetical to their own development as persons. Labor is what creates radical needs because "surplus labour (performed for its own sake) becomes need; or because of the increase in free time, which gives rise to radical needs (and to the need for still more free time); or because of the need for universality, which, having arisen in the form of mass production, cannot be satisfied within capitalism."[77]

> Free time becomes a radical need when it conflicts with the system of capitalist production; universality becomes one because its dynamic moves it beyond the universality created by capitalism (in contrast to earlier systems). The universality of capitalism is one-sided and is in fact limited by the structure of capitalism itself. People become interchangeable parts in production, but this is not the universality of full human development. The realization on the part of the workers of their situation is the simple consciousness of alienation, the recognition that the social relations are alienated: from this there follows (or this constitutes the base for) the need to overcome alienation, to overturn the alienated social and productive relations in a revolutionary way, and to create general social and productive relations which are not alienated.[78]

Marx says that "to be radical is to grasp things by the root, but for man the root is man himself. . . . Theory is actualized in a people only in so far as it actualizes their needs. A deep-going revolution can only be a revolution in basic needs."[79] Marx saw the radical needs growing out of the contradictions inherent in the structure of capitalism, formed by the labor process. Thus he saw the working class as the ones who embodied these needs and would go on to realize them by overthrowing capitalism. Since "radical needs" are *human* needs, not just needs representative of a particular group, this action by the workers would represent true human emancipation.

This is the classic formulation of Marxist theory, springing from Marx himself. Heller, however, attempts to get behind this way of expressing things to find out what in Marx's theory was more basic yet. She states that, even if the foregoing is true—even if the workers' freeing themselves means the simultaneous freeing of humankind—it still does not follow automatically that it is the working class that is the embodiment of radical needs or even that the working class *wants* to free itself. She saw Marx as determining that it was the "radical needs" that would lead beyond capitalism and then, for reasons outlined above, ascribing those needs to the workers.

It is important to realize that Heller is neither calling Marx into question here nor attempting to undermine his theory. Rather, she is attempting to validate it in its truest sense. "It does not detract from Marx's greatness that the bearers of these radical needs today are not, or rather, not exclusively, the working class. Marx could only construct radical needs where he saw some possibilities for their development."[80] According to Heller, when viewed from the perspective of radical needs, the question of who is to change the existing order does not necessarily have as its answer the proletariat, because the analysis can be taken to a deeper level. A theory of radical need must assess the ways in which these needs are produced and whether this process is limited to the arena of labor. Or,- another approach would be to broaden the understanding of that activity to include more than "wage-labor."

Heller sees that, for Marx, the radicalism of theory is measured "in terms of the way it attributes value (i.e., its value-premise): theory is radical to the extent that man (human wealth) represents the highest value."[81] Once again, Heller's value premise plays a crucial role; by tying it to radical needs, however, she shows that the value premise is in a sense grounded in reality.

> This standard of value, which is a consequence of a historical decision, is at the same time objective, since it immediately applies to human history and all its phases the standard of *human* society, i.e., the viewpoint of the species. However, this objectivity is only conditional: it presupposes the realizability and realization of communism.[82]

The "overthrow," or transcendence, of the capitalist system therefore presupposes a process whereby the future, "communist," society develops out of the present.

THE CONTEXT OF NEEDS: NEEDS TO AN END

So far, there has been much discussion about needs, radical and otherwise, but little has been said about the context—that needs always exist within a *system* or
structure of needs. "Production, the relations of production, social relations and systems of needs are, as we
know, different aspects of a single formation, in which
each is a precondition of the other. The structure of needs
is an organic structure inherent in the total social
formation."[83] It is the "radical needs" that are not satisfiable within the capitalist system of needs which lead to
the transcendence of this system, and these institute a
new system of needs. This radically different new system
is referred to variously as "communism" or "the society
of associated producers." As a social system, this "society
of associated producers" is comprehensible only in relation to the new system of needs; at the same time, this
new system of needs can be clearly understood only in
reference to this new society.

Heller devotes a great deal of attention to the relationship between "material" and "non-material" needs
within the new system, as this subject has a large bearing
on the character of the society. In this subject, a prominent part is played by the analysis of work, the extent to
which work enters in the creative development of humankind, and the relation of this to free time (or leisure
time). Work must be creative work, but there must also
be leisure time for personal development. "The clear
common interest of every member of society, apart from
the satisfaction of necessary needs (which, as we have
seen, still play a subordinate role in the structure of
needs), will be the reduction of labor time." Every individual thus "represents the species, and the species is represented in each individual. The needs of 'socialised'
human beings determine production—and this means
that the human species itself makes the decisions."[84]

In this new system, the question of "objectivation" (or
"objectification") retains its importance because "needs"

always have "objects" as their reference. In this connection, the reduction of labor time and the creation of leisure time become all the more important. Leisure time is "time for genuinely human, high-level activities—free activities," wherein it will be possible to create the objectivations "for-themselves," those which "conform to the species," the need for which is the "true human need of the members of the 'society of associated producers'."[85]

The same theme is taken up by András Hegedüs and Maria Márkus in an essay entitled "Free Time and the Division of Labour." They examine in that essay the question of whether Marx's "realm of freedom" should be understood to mean only free time—time outside of work—or whether it must by definition also include work.[86]

Needs for objectivation (objectification) for themselves can be needs for art, for instance, or they can be needs for "human integration," community. In all cases, however, these needs are qualitative, and "needs to an end."

> The centre of organization of life is represented by those activities and human relationships which conform with the species for itself. The needs directed towards these (qualitative needs as ends) will become man's primary needs, they will constitute his unique individuality and will limit needs for material goods. It is in this way that the personality that is 'deep' and rich in needs will be constituted.[87]

ART AND PHILOSOPHY The significance of these "for-itself" (or "for-themselves") objectivations (objectifications) is also examined in the context of the discussion of value. Two of the most important of these are art and philosophy because both have as their common principle the organizing of reality according to value choices, and at the same time both give expression to the social existence surrounding their creation. Different ages have different systems or hierarchies, and when we from one era approach art from another era, we always do so in terms of the awareness of similarity and difference. We "enjoy" most and find most "meaningful" those works of art where the values expressed resemble our own.

> We enjoy works of art and philosophy, but, of course, what creates value is the value hierarchy expressed in them. Our own situation decides not only whether or not we can accept the values of a work of art, but also *what* we accept within it: we can accept only what the objective value hierarchy in the work 'poses' for us. To the extent that we consider the behavior of Richard III paradigmatic we are no longer accepting any part of Shakespeare's values.[88]

Because they express value hierarchies in this way, art and philosophy can serve a critical function by counterposing these value choices of other eras to those of the present. They also provide a sense of the continuity of humankind by enabling those in later ages to understand the values of earlier eras. In a work of art, "value is realized, it becomes a self-closed perfect form, an autonomous, and evocative world, when the will-to-value—the value world and value hierarchy manifested by the individual—is constituted from the level of the species being." "A work of art has aesthetic value only when the *will-to-value and the realization of value, the individual and the creation*, become a homogeneous unity." A work of art's ability to outlast its own era depends on "the richness of that age (within the given social possibilities)," or, put in a different way, on "the extent a work is constituted from the level of the species being."[89] Thus, for Heller, the possibility arises of evaluating a work of art by its homogeneity and individuality and the unity it expresses of individual and creation.

The critical function of art, mentioned earlier, comes to the fore even more when art is understood in this way. Not only are values expressed in the art of one age counterposed to the values of another age, but values closer to the "species-being"—the human potential—are contrasted to values of an age in which this human potential is not as fully realized. For example, "under developed capitalism depiction from the level of the species demands a critical attitude toward the alienation of given reality. As a result, the leading epic art form of this period is the novel."[90]

Ferenc Fehér's essay, entitled "Is the Novel Problematic? A Contribution to the Theory of the Novel," discusses this theme at length.[91] The last part of the title has a double meaning, for it refers to both the theory of the novel in the general sense and to Lukács's *The Theory of the Novel*, of which it is a critique.[92]

The major emphasis in Fehér's essay is twofold: to compare and contrast the epic art form of the classical era with the novel as the epic art form of the modern period (as Lukács did in his book), and to throw new light on the issue through a critique of Lukács's position. The position held by Lukács in *The Theory of the Novel* was, according to Fehér, "that the age of the epic and its artistic production are of a higher order and greater value than capitalism and its epic, the novel." Fehér set out to refute this contention. First, though, to give a sense of the problem, he reconstructs Lukács's argument in its main points. For Lukács,

> the age of the epic is characterized by its 'self-certainty'; *life and essence are identical notions*. Similarly, the epic universe is homogeneous in the sense that the relations and creations of man are just as substantial as his personality. On the other hand, the form of the novel is the expression of a transcendental homelessness. The novel is the epic of a time for which totality (and therefore, the dominant homogeneity of the world, as well as human substantiality, and the substantial relation between man and his products) has become only a problem and an aspiration.[93]

In his analysis of the novel, and the contrast between it and the epic form of the classical age, Fehér grounds his approach in general philosophical themes shared with other members of the Budapest School. Most important among these concepts is the concept of human essence as "dynamic historic potentiality given from the beginnings of human society," and the conviction that the "realized domain of human essence is enriched" by "every evolutionary sequence that develops the power of the species as the foundation of values . . . even if it be through the liquidation of earlier [types of society and their products] which could rightly have been considered as prefigurations of realized human essence (realized at least *within* a limited sphere)."[94]

Fehér considers the modern age, the age of bourgeois society, as doing just that: of developing the powers of the species (though in a one-sided manner) while at the same time doing away with earlier forms of human social development. Thus, his analysis takes on a dual task: showing how the novel is the preeminent art form of this modern age, expressing the age most clearly, and showing how the novel points beyond itself—and thus beyond the age—toward an art form that will succeed it and will be an expression of the society that is evolving to succeed the present one.[95] In this analysis, Fehér touches on a theme discussed at length by Heller—everyday life—and tries to analyze its place in the novel.[96]

Another part of Fehér's analysis lies in the discussion of the defetishizing function or role of art (following Lukács's *Aesthetics*) as part of the question, "What can man make of himself?"[97] He writes that, "the question nevertheless remains open in every novel that is a work of art: is the universal context that finally takes shape the result of the free self-determination of the characters or of the bad objectivity of the natural laws of the fetishized world?"[98] In answering the problem Lukács posed, Fehér ends by once again contrasting the classical epic with the modern—he writes that

> there is a certain 'dumbness', something profoundly narrow in the unreflecting, harmonious and passive way in which an Achilles, a Hector, a Siegfried live their strictly limited existence. It is precisely the ethical questions that are lacking, the feeling that man is a moral problem to himself, and perhaps an enigma to be solved. On the contrary,

the novel, in its very form, unveils the major ethical tension of human life, the 'lack of time', the fact that our existence has an end and that we therefore have to use the temporal process that has been given to us in such a way as to lose neither the fulfillment of the moment nor the totality of higher human development.[99]

A close reading of Fehér's essay will show that he is doing within his analysis of the novel what Heller and Márkus did in their works—trying to show how human possibilities are both enriched and limited through the development of modern society, and how the preconditions of the transcendence of this society are formed and evident in the present structure. Fehér attempts to show how this process is evident not only in the themes or content of the novel but in the very structure of the novel as an art form. The genre sprang from a society where earlier, seemingly natural forms of community were replaced by purely social forms. This new form of society was expressed in a new art form. Characteristic of both the earlier society and its representative form of art was that it was "dominated by the duality of the self and the external world." "The novel is born in a society without community; the structure of its world is not communal."[100]

Out of this duality comes the possibility of freedom of action for the individual in society and in both the novel that was not present in earlier societies and the art forms that are most representative of their dynamics. This possibility of freedom thus illustrates the "higher level of emancipation" achieved by the new social form and art form, in contrast with previous social formations. The novel as an art form explores various aspects of this freedom. One of these aspects is orientation toward the future, with the corresponding activity whereby the individual, the "hero" of the novel, "constitutes his own world." Another aspect is "the flexible and dynamically changing character of the system of values." Yet one more aspect is the theme of "self-education" and "self-realization," a theme exemplified by the *Bildungsroman*.[101]

The novel expresses in its form the essential features of the society from which it springs. By contrasting the novel to earlier dominant art forms, one can see the differences between the types of societies that gave birth to these different forms of art. By the same token, the novel points to the limitations of the present social forms and thereby points beyond them toward their transformation. "The novel imparts to the reader the knowledge of the maximum possibilities of humanization of which this society is capable, [and] clearly shows the limits to which humanization can go. This is both the essence of its structure and its functional mission."[102]

Values constitute the object of philosophy, as they do in art, and, like art, philosophy gives expression to an age. It has already been noted that philosophy has the potential of counterposing value choices of another time to those of the present. In her discussion of philosophy, Heller tends to speak of it as social theory or social science; one reason for this can be found in the description or definition just mentioned.

Philosophy has the additional feature of being oriented toward truth, or seeking to discover truth. Heller writes: "The social sciences [philosophy], in a sense, make their own truths. They decide over their own truth by contributing to the realization of their values through the intensity of their chosen values, and through recognizing—on the basis of this value commitment—the real forces of the social dynamic, the real possibilities which they can 'latch onto'."[103]

In the above formulation one can see the reply to the questions posed by Max Weber. Social science (or philosophy, in this sense) is the "theory of social totality," within which it is possible to interpret and evaluate assorted facts. As such, theory always has within it, implicitly or explicitly, a value commitment or choice. This is a modern phenomenon, as was seen earlier in the discussion of Heller's approach to values: There was no real sense of alternatives. To deny that there is a choice of values in every theory is to accept what is given and to engage in apologetics. There *can* be no "value-free" social science, or philosophy.

> The truth content of a social theory depends on how *radically* it manifests the conflicts of classes, strata, and integrations, how *significant* these conflicts are, and what kind of value contents they manifest. Furthermore, this truth content depends on how and whether the *totality conception* of a social theory can order the facts and the relationships of social reality, on whether the theory can uncover the objective possibility (*dynamics*) or impossibility of carrying out conflicts to the end within the given social reality and its alternatives, and whether the theory can become active in the realization of its own perspectives.[104]

Heller chose to stress the "social theory" aspect of philosophy as a reaction against the "metaphysical world views" of bourgeois philosophy, and she describes Marx's work in this light.[105] Also, the task of philosophy—viewed as social theory—is the "grasping of the social totality, defetishization, the uncovering of existing alternatives, and the unification of the forces of the chosen alternative."[106] This task is one that each age must confront anew—no one age can do the work for another, and certainly not "once and for all."

Hegedüs and Maria Márkus echo this theme when writing on the task of sociology in the socialist countries. They state that sociology should attempt to "draw up a model of society realistic enough to endow men with a wider possibility of choice between the available alternatives; by this very fact it contributes to the real humanization of social relations." Sociology should also compare "existing institutions and social relations with the chosen hypothesis of development . . . [and] attempt to study them in their movement, in their contradictions, in their transformations, in the context of the consciously-chosen perspective."[107]

The discussion of needs as the fundamental category for the analysis of social reality is not confined to Heller's writing alone, although she elaborated the theory of need most thoroughly. The concept of need and the contrast between "radical" needs and nonradical needs provide a central axis for the critique of the Hungarian reality and socialist societies in general. This use of the concept is evident in essays by Hegedüs and Maria Márkus, and those of Ferenc Fehér. In an essay entitled "The Role of Values in the Long-Range Planning of Distribution and Consumption," Hegedüs and Maria Márkus deal with a problem that frequently arises in planning: predictions tend to extrapolate from "an existing structure, with exciting proportions and tendencies, and the method of extrapolation does not take into account the possibility that these might be significantly changed by human action—action whose course is not predetermined by some sort of general laws, but is the result of conscious choices of values."[108] They point out the dichotomy between planning for economic growth alone versus planning for "the humanization of social life," and they propose a way of working to combine the two elements.[109]

Underlying this discussion is the premise that the "humanization of social life" can take place only after people's "basic needs" are satisfied—and Hegedüs and Maria Márkus point out that in Hungary today this is not yet accomplished. In this context, they address the problem of the extent to which the direction of change of needs in society can—or should—be influenced.

NEEDS AND SOCIAL CHANGE   In addition to the various factors that influence change indirectly, or "naturally," other ways of *attempting* to change needs are possible, among them "the conscious and deliberate forming of the system of values, and direct advertising for certain goods."[110] Maria Márkus and Hegedüs seem to think that both of these means are in principle suitable, though they criticize the reliance on the second that was evident in Hungary.

They do see, however, that for new (human) needs to emerge, a change must take place in the "sphere of human activity." This change would entail a democratization of the work process, among other things, for "one cannot implant the sort of values in people which are irrelevant to their everyday life, that is, values which have no importance in their everyday activity."[111] This last line shows the concern for the transformation of everyday life on the basis of the "radical needs" posited by Heller. The concession to the state of a role indirectly influencing values, however, raises problems of a sort dealt with by Fehér in his essay, "The Dictatorship Over Needs."[112]

In this essay, Fehér examines the problematic area of needs with reference to the framework of socialist societies in Eastern Europe. He attempts to explain the nature of these societies by looking at the way in which they deal with human needs. He contrasts the socialist societies with capitalist societies on the basis of what Heller calls the "structure of needs," the total social context of needs. The socialist societies are "political societies," where "state and society become one under the exclusive direction of the state," and they are also "ideological societies." In contrast, in capitalist societies constitutions are "*subsequent* summaries of *prior* developments (mostly of an earlier and gradual growth of civil society), not *projections* for the future."[113]

According to Fehér, the socialist societies are characterized by certain basic claims, which are set up as guiding principles. Although Fehér disputes the validity of these claims, he nonetheless tries to show the way in which these societies use the claims as constitutive principles of the ideological system.

These societies use the claims for legitimation purposes, based on their apparent validity, and Fehér tries to point out the ways in which the reality contradicts this apparent validity. The "ideological society of the dictatorship over needs," as he refers to it, has three fundamental principles: "the *abolition of exploitation*, a *rationality* guiding social life (and superior to capitalist market rationality), and *the leading role of the planning elite*—the depository of 'public welfare' and the embodiment of working-class rule."[114]

This system reflects an attempt to set up a "guaranteed society," a society in which "dysfunctions resulting from people's 'empirical frailty' are ruled out." This society is thus based fundamentally on "a voluntaristic conception of freedom and on a deep anthropological pessimism."[115] As such, it has a number of basic features:

1. All of society is transformed into a conglomerate of wage-laborers . . . [This is an] effort to approach people at their very core: at the level of working activity, at the crossroads of work time and free time, and of the needs originating from and related to both.
2. Once labor-power is fully subjected to the planning elite, the state can authoritatively define what human needs in general may be and what structure they may assume in order to fulfill the system's goals.
3. Workers within the dictatorship over needs are completely deprived of any opportunity to articulate their needs for freedom.
4. All social objectifications must be planned out . . . in such a way that they fully fit in the authoritative determination of the system of human needs. . . . Planning is the ultimate principle of rationality . . . and amounts to grasping social rationality at the head of the needs of people, to declaring despotically that these needs are nonexistent, and to substituting for them the theoretical prescriptions of the planning elite.[116]

Fehér goes on to show the concrete forms these aspects take and to discuss some of the problems inherent in such a system, especially in terms of the ongoing problem of legitimation. He ends by demonstrating that although people are homogenized and their basic needs are catered to gratuitously—freeing them of the responsibilities and risks of the "truly individual life"—this condition is accompanied by the "utter demoralization of labor power," where "one of man's greatest capacities, that of doing meaningful work, is squandered."[117]

Fehér suggests that the market is a medium for overcoming the system of "dictatorship over needs" on the basis of several factors that accompany stress on the market. Any emphasis on the market involves the technocracy, as the bearer of "goal-rationality." For Fehér, the question of "goal-rationality" is an alternative to a discussion of "value-rationality," in which the basic values of the system would be openly debated. Because he regards this kind of debate as impossible under the prevailing circumstances, the drive for "goal-rationality" is another means to similar ends.

> The attempt to create "authentic market relations" does several things: In the first place, it entails a commitment to certain civil liberties—the most important being the freedom of productive agents to dispose of their own labor power as they see fit. In addition, attempts to introduce authentic market relations sharpen the contradictions between technocracy and workers (as in Hungary in 1969), and unmask the legend of a homogeneous society by exposing at least part of its actual structure and dynamic. Finally . . . the option for an authentic market embodies the radical philosophical idea that a truly emancipatory movement towards socialism can only be based on the acknowledgement and free articulation and debate of the totality of existing needs. Thus, pragmatic goal rationality is a corrective principle in the interests of rationalism after the debacle and excesses of "designing" hyperrationality.[118]

This emphasis on the market is only part of what Fehér sees as a revolt against the "dictatorship over needs" in the name of rationalism. "Having inextricably bound its fate (with Marx) to rationalism, socialism must seek to transcend the phase of a totalizing hyper-rationalism that has turned into irrationality."[119]

One feature of the market which Fehér stresses, the freedom to dispose of labor power, brings out a fact about Eastern Europe that Heller mentions in the context of an assessment of the task of intellectuals there. She holds that "the greatest concern of Eastern Europe was and remains the liberation of civil society and the guaranteeing of civil liberties."[120] This "liberation of civil society" is the precondition for any attempt to transform the society into one based on "radical needs," but in and of itself it means only returning to the level of formal democracy characteristic of Western societies. As a result, to focus on this task alone has, according to Heller, an additional consequence for intellectual endeavors. To identify primarily with Eastern Europe on this level carries with it the danger of "the acceptance of a liberal or even conservative way of thought, or the complete renunciation of philosophy."[121]

COMMUNITY AND EVERYDAY LIFE   Another of the fundamental objectivations of need, as mentioned earlier, is *community*, understood here in a specific sense, as a "human integration." In Heller's view, the question of community is one of the most important questions of the modern age. As subject-matter, "community" is closely tied to the subject of "everyday life"; the two are interrelated.[122] "Integrations" are many and varied: nation, class, stratum are some—but community is conceived of as a *human* integration. The distinction is one of value—"human" communities represent those values that help to realize the human potential. As such, they must be of a certain type. The type of community under discussion here is a *chosen* community, rather than a *natural* community that a person is born into.

The possibility of this type of community came into being only with the more or less complete dissolution of pre-existing "natural" communities. In either case, a community is defined as "a structured, organized group-unity, with a relatively homogeneous value-order, with which the individual is necessarily affiliated."[123] "Necessarily" can mean by birth or by choice. In the case of choice, Heller sees "two rational motives for choosing a community: 1) The objective value-content of the community, that is, its potentialities for developing the human essence, and 2) the degree to which it enables a man to develop his individuality. The first criterion, however, always has primacy over the second."[124]

"Community" is not the same as "group," per se, nor is it synonomous with "society." The problem of community is one that has assumed greater importance the further the modern age progresses. Although the possibility of individuality was a function of the rise of modern, bourgeois society, which dissolved the previous natural communities, it was that same society that made the individual's actions and relationships so fetishized, seemingly removed from personal control. The theme appearing here is the same that was seen earlier, where capitalism is shown to have made possible the growth of human wealth on one hand, while severely curtailing it on the other by virtue of its very structure.

Although the problem of community is one which has assumed greater importance in more recent years, this fact does not mean that there is a general desire for community. On the contrary, community is something that is extraordinarily difficult to achieve in this age. This difficulty results partly from the philosophy of individualism, wherein the *absence* of community is the positive value, and partly from the nature of modern, "manipulated 'mass-society'."[125] However, a considerable ground swell is evident, in which people are at least becoming conscious of the need "to transform the existing structure of needs," to substitute qualitative for quantitative needs; thus, they are becoming more aware of the need for community.[126]

The question of community is closely tied in with that of "everyday life" and specifically with the possibility of the transformation of everyday life.

> Everyday life is the sum total of those activities which express the continual possibility of societal reproduction by individual acts of self-propagation. There is an everyday life

in *every society:* without it there is no society. Accordingly, every man, whatever his position within the division of labor in his society, has an everyday life.[127]

Some of the characteristics of everyday life are that:

the human subject in everyday life treats his environment as 'ready-made,' 'given' that he spontaneously adopts the whole systems of customs and techniques proper to this environment; that his behavior is pragmatically patterned.[128]

The question any concept of revolution must therefore face is what to do with everyday life. Heller writes that it is absurd to imagine that there could be a society—present or future—without an everyday life and that it is equally absurd to hold that *all* activities in everyday life can be transformed into activities of the sort that are directly reflective of species-being. Rather, what is at stake is to ascertain what can be done with everyday life' so as to render it more conducive to the realization of a human society. And here a distinction is introduced, between two types of person in society, or two approaches to everyday life—between the *"particular,* alienated man," and the *"Individual."* These two types are reminiscent of the contrast between the individual and the "isolated man." The "particular" person is one who is completely caught up in the patterns of everyday life, who "spontaneously identifies himself with every convention and requirement of the system which makes his (or her) mere self-preservation possible, and renders life free of conflict and 'convenient'."[129] In contrast, the Individual keeps a distance between self and everyday life and attempts to live consciously as a "species being." Consequently, "the Individual,

precisely because he has a conscious relationship to his specificity is capable of ordering *even* his everyday life on the basis of this conscious relationship, though, naturally, within the limits of particular circumstances and possibilities. The Individual is a man who 'synthesizes' the factual uniqueness of his individuality and the universality of his species within himself."[130]

Individuality thus is the outcome of a process by which the world is *created*, or structured, rather than treated as a given other. The Individual remains a part of everyday life but has a relationship to it quite different from that of the "particular" person. This difference is to be found specifically in the Individual's ability to "discern within the ready-made structures of everyday life those factors and demands which hinder his species regarding development, which have become mere formalities, or which conceal efforts and interests of negative value," and on this basis order this life.[131] This distancing and ordering activity takes place on the basis of an awareness of human values (or the values of "species-being") and of the way in which these values are manifested in society and social creations ("objectifications"), combined with an ability and commitment to change and restructure elements of everyday life in accordance with this awareness.

The subject of community takes on paramount importance at this juncture, as the synthesis of the "uniqueness of individuality" and the "universality of (one's) species" is really possible only within a community. Either a person lives in a community—a freely chosen community, because part of Individuality, or becoming an individual, entails the *choice* of community—or a community of some sort is present in theory where no actual community is possible. Community is the "sudden creation of immediate human relationships within the world of mediation . . . , the re-structuring of reality *in such a way that we are able in the process to order our own lives in their totality in a manner of human beings.*"[132]

"Particular" persons are incapable of creating community because this process of creating involves a perspective on everyday life that they are incapable of having as long as they are immersed in the categories of that life. Understood in this way, the creation of community is a revolutionary activity—it is, in a sense, the primary revolutionary activity that must take place if political and economic changes are to have any significance. This is

true because this activity involves "the creation of new patterns of life and new structures of needs which would penetrate and influence the whole scope of human activity from everyday life up to the most complicated human 'generic' activities (Gattungsaktivitaten)."[133]

Creation of community, or the choosing of a *human* community, is revolutionary for both contemporary capitalist systems and socialist systems; in both instances, it involves the critique or defetishization of given structures and the attempt to restructure along the lines of human values. Capitalist societies require total restructuring, whereas socialist societies as they currently exist have to be restructured in a different, but equally thoroughgoing, way, to allow for the possibility of socialist democracy:

> Socialist society, *qua socialist*, simply cannot function without communities which have as their goal the transformation of reality and themselves. The active Marxist revolutionaries within socialist society must plan the creation of those institutions which not only safeguard the individuals' right to freedom (even bourgeois democracies do that), but, far beyond that, create the possibility that the activity of the whole of society be built upon the activity of communities based on direct human relationships.[134]

Maria Márkus and Hegedüs also write on the subject of community in their essay, "Community and Individuality." The difference between them and Heller on this point is that they relate their work to a survey of Hungarian working conditions as they involve this problem. In this regard, they criticize some assumptions of the Hungarian system of production that, by denying workers a say in their working conditions, approaches the problems of management from the standpoint of a modified "Taylorism."[135]

In their criticism of the system of production, Maria Márkus and Hegedüs make a connection between community and self-management. They state that, as a result of social atomization, "ways in which man can express and develop his personality must generally be looked for in the world of work, not only as part of his working activity, but also in the field of self-management and social control that goes with it."[136] The development of personality presupposes for them the presence of social groups functioning as communities, which serve "to link everyday activities of individuals and larger social units," thereby at least partially overcoming "particularity." The social units they chose to examine were work-related.[137]

Here the distinction that Hegedüs and Márkus make between the "particular" person and the fully-developed person is the same that Heller made in her discussion of the "Individual." They thus make the quest for community simultaneously an attempt to introduce some measure of control into the working conditions. Heller herself returns to this point, when in her retrospective commentary on Eastern Europe and the activities of the Budapest School she stresses the connection between community and work organization. There, she says that

> Units of self-administration, such as production or housing collectives, may be organized as communities. Within these communities persons are trained to participate in social discourse. A pluralistic democracy, with all its institutions, can to a certain extent be protected against bureaucratization and alienation only if the entire population has been educated in communal discussions and decisions.[138]

RENAISSANCE MAN

In addition to the works already mentioned, one other work by Heller is particularly important in regard to the themes discussed so far. That book is *Renaissance Man*, and in it Heller attempts to discover the origin of many of the ideas that are central to the Budapest School. It was in the Renaissance that the modern conception of life was formed. Heller rediscovers those concepts and interprets them in a way that brings out their relevance for the kind of rethinking of Marx in which she is engaged and that sheds light on contemporary society in a new way. She is most interested in the dynamic concept of man, of human activity, which grew out of that period. Within this dynamic understanding of human nature are several themes that appear in her other works—versatility, or "many-sidedness"; the development and expansion of needs as social needs; and the concept of human nature as something created or forged by human activity from nature itself. The Renaissance was also important for Heller because it created the modern conception of society and social life as a category in and of itself, separate from that of state.

Although *Renaissance Man* is a work of history, it is explicitly an inquiry into the roots of the modern world as well. In fact, history as a subject figures in this work of history, giving a sense of a hall of mirrors. Heller writes that "the Renaissance was the first era which chose for itself a past," and she sees that this act was "a sign of liberation from the bonds of feudal or communal life; those peoples who still live[d] within the bounds of these communities receive[d] their past ready-made and given, in the form of myth."[139] The choice of a past, or pasts, with which an affinity was felt, was a function of a "sense of social distinctiveness," which in turn was dependent on the emergence of modern social relations. It was this emergence that ushered in the possibility of a social philosophy. After this:

> To be a philosopher means two things above all: to create a vision of the world which illuminates its objective contents more comprehensively and more profoundly than before, and at the same time to incorporate in social and ethical attitudes the practical consequences of that new vision.[140]

It was the Renaissance rediscovery of Stoicism and Epicurianism, according to Heller, that was very important to the dynamic concept of human nature. The Stoics and Epicurians were notable for the way in which they reconciled the difference between philosophers and ordinary

people—thus grounding philosophy in everyday life—
seeing that the meaning of life for all lies in the way in
which meaning is given to life and to the world. This
view was commonly held by Stoics and Epicurians, who
did not see the question of meaning as "only" a philosophical matter. In this view of things, nature was threefold: "nature proper, the *macrocosm*, independent of all
human will and striving; social nature, an outgrowth of
the actions of men; and finally individual nature, which
every human being at all times has to contend with—nature as *general*, as *particular* and as *individual*."[141]

Most important for the new conception of *human*
nature was the twofold understanding of human emancipation in terms of *self-development* as freedom and
self-realization as being at the heart of human activity. Common to all of this was the view that man "must
live according to his *own* nature," which meant that
man must attempt to harmonize that in him which is
"universally human," with that which is peculiar to
himself alone.[142]

This demand is reminiscent of the discussion of the
"Individual" as one who is able to achieve a synthesis between uniqueness and universality, and Heller in fact
takes up the question of everyday life in this context as
well. All thought in the Renaissance was more closely
tied to everyday life and its categories; at the same time,
everyday life in itself was the subject of thought.[143] The
synthesis described, however, is one that is actively arrived at—self-knowledge comes about through activity.
In the section entitled, "What Is Man Capable Of," Heller
writes of the notion of freedom as the existence of alternatives, or free will. On this basis, the essential forces of
humans could develop and people could become aware of
them. These forces are the following:

1. The capacity and exercise of *creativity* (work, art, science, technique);
2. *self-creation*—including the development of [their] ethical substance and self-awareness

3. *versatility*
4. *dissatisfaction (insatiability)*
5. as a manifestation of the latter, *limitlessness* with respect to knowledge, creation and the satisfaction of needs.[144]

The Budapest School: An Assessment

From this brief overview of *Renaissance Man*, it is possible to see how interrelated it is with the themes discussed by the Budapest School. The same problems that are examined from the vantage point of their historical emergence are analyzed philosophically elsewhere. The two approaches serve to complement and enrich one another, and the picture of human activity that results is a tapestry woven of many threads.

Some authors, commenting on the activities of the Budapest School as representing the "Hungarian radical left," have chosen to identify Hegedüs and Maria Márkus as the main representatives of the social critique of the school. Serge Frankel and Daniel Martin, for example, argue that although the Budapest School was originally concerned primarily with philosophy, a later emphasis on sociology as social critique became more pronounced.[145]

Insofar as Hegedüs and Márkus have done most of the *sociological* analysis of socialist society, there is some truth to the statement that they are the leaders of the "social critique"; but to say this is also to foster a certain misapprehension as to their role in this "social critique." It is misleading to introduce too great a dichotomy between philosophy and sociology and to identify only the latter with social critique. A work of a philosophical nature is equally a critique of socialist society and ideology, although it generally is not as concrete as some of the sociological writing dealing specifically with socialist (especially Hungarian) societies. In addition, the sociology rests on premises that were worked out theoretically in the philosophy, a fact Frankel and Martin acknowledge.[146]

Hegedüs and Márkus themselves note this fact when they say their approach is "intimately bound up with the 'socio-ontological' tendency in Marxist philosophy." They continue by saying that "whereas the main function of philosophy is to determine and justify the values chosen, the task of sociology is to undertake sociological analysis of different concrete solutions on this basis and to foresee the social consequences of the different variations."[147]

Both Márkus and Hegedüs did well at this self-imposed task. Their studies of the Hungarian social realities were penetrating, and their critique was based—both implicitly and explicitly—on the value choices worked out philosophically by some of the others, primarily Heller. In this regard, their work was an integral part of the activity of the Budapest School.

There were, however, differences between Márkus and Hegedüs in their analyses, although they operate from the same premises. Hegedüs does not carry his critique of existing conditions nearly as far as the critiques of Maria Márkus and others. This feature has been noted in a number of contexts by reviewers of their works, and by Ágnes Heller herself in one assessment.[148]

The work of the Budapest School was of great significance for both the Hungarian reality and the development of Marxist theory generally. Through their philosophical and sociological critique of Hungarian society and of the official ideology, the Budapest School had an impact on other thinkers and spurred the development of critical thought there. Their success can be measured in part by government reactions; in 1973 they were harshly attacked by name, with specific references to some of their writings.[149] This attack was only the culmination of a long history, going back at least to 1956. It was, however, indicative of how sensitive the Party was to the position of those in the Budapest School. Although part of the attack was directed at the sociological work of Maria Márkus and Hegedüs, Heller and Vajda were also the focus of criticism.

It was to be expected that the Party would react to studies critical of the Hungarian "socialist transformation," especially those based on empirical findings, as were those of Hegedüs and Márkus. The Party reacted just as strongly, however, to the theoretical works by Heller and Vajda, which called into question the "socialist" nature of Hungarian society and the sole right of the Party to claim to be Marxist.

Ultimately the members of the Budapest School were denied the right to work in their field and the right to publish in Hungary. Most of them eventually chose to go into exile. Their exile was in several ways the logical outcome of the development of the group and their interaction with Hungarian society. As time went on, their position was clearly becoming more and more radical, which brought them into increasing conflict with the defenders of the orthodoxy. But exile was also the logical outcome of the increasing orientation to Western issues, which Heller described in her assessment of the group's activities.[150]

Revisionism did not immediately carry the Budapest School beyond Marxism, as it did Kołakowski, for example. But it carried them—both figuratively and literally—beyond the bounds of Eastern Europe.[151] Their contribution cannot be measured only by Eastern European standards, however. Their work has made an impact on Marxist thought generally. This is especially true of Ágnes Heller. Her work on the theory of need signifies a major theoretical breakthrough for Marxist social analysis. It draws on Marx but goes beyond him in attempting to assess the contemporary relevance of his conceptual framework. Heller's work is parallel to that of several of her contemporaries, but her approach is original in many of its essential features.

Taken together, the critiques of the Budapest School form a coherent whole and provide a rounded picture of life in our time—how it developed as it has and where it could go in the direction of a more human social order. As

Heller writes of Marx, so we could say of the Budapest School: they establish a "norm against which we can measure the reality and value of our ideas, and with which we can determine the limitedness of our actions."[152]

CHAPTER 3

Czechoslovakia: The Philosophical
Background of the Prague Spring

The Historical Setting

THE YEAR 1956 WAS OF PARTICULAR IMPORTANCE
in Czechoslovakia, as it was in all the countries of Eastern Europe. Stalin had died three years earlier, and in
1956 Khrushchev came out at the Twentieth Soviet Party
Congress with his denunciations of Stalin and Stalinism.
This had the effect of giving further momentum to a
trend that had begun in part at the death of Stalin—that
of disorientation and of the questioning of basic assumptions about life. Khrushchev's speeches sent a shock wave
rippling throughout Eastern Europe, undermining the
trust of many people in what they had been led to believe
about the world. Compared with the way it registered in
Poland or Hungary, this shock was less immediately felt
or seen in Czechoslovakia; but even there, it eroded the
foundations of the Stalinist order. This erosion first revealed itself in the questioning that arose in regard to
many of the manifestations of the Stalinist era.

This erosion of the most basically believed values was
accompanied by an undercurrent of searching for new,
more authentic values. In Czechoslovakia, this search
was not manifested outwardly, as it was in Poland or

Hungary, but began quietly. It took the form of a desire to gain more flexibility in everyday endeavors. This meant less control by the Party over the details of everyday work and over the first, tentative attempts to redefine social life. The search was, of necessity, cautious because the Party still retained firm control in Czechoslovakia and was anxious not to participate in the "de-Stalinization" campaign any more than it had to, lest it destroy its own authority in the process. The Party resisted any and all questioning of its position and was extremely reluctant to give up any part of its prerogatives in any sphere. In fact, the reaction to the events of 1956 in Hungary and Poland was to make Party leaders in Czechoslovakia still more resistant to change and less inclined to implement any new policies related to the de-Stalinization process set off by Khrushchev's speeches. The Czech Communist Party newspaper, *Rudé Právo*, even ran an editorial on January 29, 1957, saying that "the ambiguous word 'de-Stalinization' stands only for the idea of weakening and giving way to the forces of reaction."[1] In November 1957, Antonin Novotny, who had been head of the Party since 1953, assumed the post of president as well, thus further consolidating power and resistance to change within the Party.

Nonetheless, the shock wave had done its damage, and the questioning process that had begun could not be halted. The years 1956–68 witnessed a revival of creative activity in all spheres of life in Czechoslovakia, most notably in the sphere of art and culture. Art was breaking away from the hitherto prevailing theory of "socialist realism," in which it was expected to serve an edifying function, and was beginning to explore new modes of creativity. The guidelines of "socialist realism" were being more and more loosely interpreted under pressure from artists who, uncomfortable with the strict style that had been required of them, wanted to be free to create as they chose. Part of this discontent focused on the demand made by socialist realism that art play a socially edifying role in building up the character of the new socialist man and in furthering the progress of socialist society. As early as 1956 and 1957, a series of debates on philosophy and culture took place in the newspaper *Literární noviny*; two philosophers, Karel Kosík and Ivan Sviták, played a prominent role in these debates. The articles, which attracted a good deal of public attention, were instrumental in raising public awareness of some of the questions being asked in intellectual circles and in bringing some of the issues of the day out into the open.[2] At the Second Congress of Czechoslovak Writers in April 1956, voices were already heard protesting the Stalinist cultural policies in Czechoslovakia.[3]

The event that most undermined belief in the Communist Party and in the system as a whole as it was then constituted was the series of revelations in 1963 that the Slánsky trials were not what they had been represented to be.[4] In the legal profession, these revelations about the trials prompted a rethinking of the problem of the nature and role of law in a socialist society, whereas demands were heard from the philosophers for more room in which to carry on their activity.[5] One commentator has said that "1963 was the most important year in Czechoslovakia between 1948 and 1968; it was a year in which all the political, ideological, intellectual, and economic problems suddenly escalated and escaped the control of Novotny's regime."[6]

The first open challenge to the Novotny regime came from the congress of the Slovak Writers' Union in Bratislava on April 22, 1963. This challenge resulted partly from the fact that the Slovaks had suffered disproportionately under Stalinism because their desire for more autonomy was labeled "bourgeois nationalism"; their reaction "took the form of a revival of Slovak nationalism and protest against the vestiges of Stalinism still alive in Czechoslovakia."[7] The challenge continued at the May 22 meeting of the Czechoslovak Writers' Union, at which time the delegates in a sense picked up where they had left off in 1956. The Slovak poet, Laco Novomeský, who had been denounced along with Gustav Husák as a nationalist in 1950, spoke at both the Bratislava and Prague conferences. In Prague he gave a speech in which he said that the "tragedy of the whole situation [was] . . . that we misled and confused a whole generation. . . . To this generation we must return confidence, trust, and truth; however, we must find them in ourselves first."[8] On May 27 and 28 the Congress of the Slovak Journalists' Union, meeting in Bratislava, further challenged the Party on its cultural policy. The Czechoslovak Writers' Union was to play a crucial role in the reform efforts again a few years later, at its meeting in June 1967.

At the same time the increasing number of challenges were heard in the realm of culture, another important development was taking place in the sphere of economics.

From the late fifties, the increasingly disastrous state of the economy . . . which culminated in an unprecedented crisis in 1963, had given rise to decentralizing proposals. These ideas, following Soviet leads, culminated in the elaboration of the New Economic System, or Model, by a team led by Professor Ota Šik. The System was accepted officially in 1965, and introduced at the beginning of 1967. . . . What was important about the introduction of the New Economic System . . . was that it made an ideological and practical breach in the wall of Novotny's neo-Stalinist model.[9]

The efforts to bring about change in Czechoslovakia were successful, though only for a brief period, because the crises in the economic and cultural spheres converged with a political crisis within the Party. What happened in 1968 was new only in the way in which it brought together ideas that had already been developed in the preceding years. Still, the process of rethinking was very gradual and was accomplished only in stages through the period after 1956.

The Philosophical Critique

During these years, as more and more people became involved in the process of rethinking, it became clear that philosophy had a major role to play in providing a coherent expression for the often inchoate strivings in all areas of society, especially in the artistic and cultural sphere. The task of giving theoretical expression to this revival of creativity in art and culture was aided by the emergence of a new understanding within Marxist philosophy of man and his creative role in the world—an understanding that was exceptionally well represented by the philosophers Kosík and Sviták. Kosík's and Sviták's tasks were different, but they complemented one another. Kosík began with a study of the Czech Radical Democrats of the nineteenth century and attempted to find in them a clue to understanding something of the nature of Czech culture. He then went on to draw on virtually all modern currents of philosophy in an attempt to create a synthesis and a new understanding based on this synthesis.[10] This work came out in 1963, entitled *Dialektika konkrétního* (*The Dialectics of the Concrete*), drawing on several papers Kosík had presented at various philosophical conferences through the preceding years. This work was of great significance, drawing as it did on the different currents of philosophical thought but transforming them into something genuinely new— something that was authentically Marxist as well.

In *Dialectics of the Concrete,* Kosík followed the pattern set by all serious West European Marxist scholars as well as by those in East Europe who were committed to a serious study of Marx, as opposed to mere apologetics. This thinking drew on the main currents of European thought, such as existentialism and phenomenology. In addition, Kosík, like any of the above type of thinker, could not have failed to take into account the writings of György Lukács as part of the intellectual heritage of twentieth-century Marxism; he most certainly would have been familiar with the work of those of his contemporaries in the field worthy of note—whether from Eastern Europe or the West. This stance is in particular contrast to the approach taken by Soviet Marxist scholars and those connected with the more orthodox view in East Europe. These scholars were characterized by their refusal to come to terms with other philosophical currents in any serious or open fashion.

Existentialism and phenomenology were of particular significance to Kosík because of the way they center on man and his activity.[11] Kosík was important in systematically providing a theoretical foundation for this new understanding of man, whereas Sviták's contribution lay in building on this foundation with his interest in a philosophy of aesthetics and culture. His major book in this regard was *Lidský smysl kultury* (*The human meaning of culture*), a series of essays written over the years from the early 1950s to 1968 dealing with the problematics of philosophy and art.[12]

Ivan Sviták is of particular importance in the revival of culture and the arts in Czechoslovakia after 1956 because of the way in which he, as a philosopher of culture, applied the new understanding of man and his creative activity, which was then appearing in East European Marxist thought, in his essays on art and aesthetics. By dealing with art and culture directly in his writing, he helped to formulate a new theory of the role of art as well, based on the concept of man's creative activity in the world, or *praxis*. Sviták's particular genius lay in the way he managed to interpret the new philosophical concepts for the realm of culture, but this was not his activity, per se. He is a philosopher of culture, and as such deals with culture and art, looking at works of art for their significance and meaning in terms of their portrayal and understanding of man and his world and of man in the world.

Sviták's essays were quite controversial, and his own career reflects this reaction. He was a member of the Institute of Philosophy in Prague, where his lectures and

writings were banned as early as 1955. Almost all of his
subsequent writings were originally lectures that either
were not allowed into print or were confiscated as soon as
they appeared in print. The years 1955 through 1964 saw
him suspended from and then reappointed to the Institute
three times. He still managed to contribute to a wide variety of conferences, including one in Dubrovnik, Yugoslavia, in 1963 on "Man Today." In fact, 1963 was a
particularly good year for Sviták in this regard, as—in addition to the above—he participated in the Conference on
the Theory of Literature at Liblice and another held there
devoted to the works of Franz Kafka (which was an event
having far-reaching repercussions on Czechoslovak cultural life).[13]

In 1964 Sviták was expelled from the Institute and
from the Party—though the Institute's Party organization itself refused to fire him, as did the next higher level
in the Party hierarchy. Nevertheless, in 1966 he was able
to lecture at Charles University in Prague as part of a series of lectures on "Philosophical Anthropology," though
the course was banned by the dean of the Philosophic Fac-
ulty before its end. It was during 1968, however, that
Sviták came into his own again. His essays and lectures
were published in book form, and he took an active part
in public discussions in various newspapers over the
course of that year. He had prepared another book, entitled *Hlavou proti zdi* (Head against the wall), when the
invasion prevented its publication.[14] This was a collection
of some of his newspaper articles and essays, including
one, "The Genius and the Apparatus," which appeared in
his book, *Man and His World—A Marxian View.*

Both Kosík and Sviták took an active part in public
debate. In the case of Kosík, he entered this debate at the
time of the Fourth Congress of the Union of Czechoslovak Writers in 1967; by 1968, both were active. The significance of all this philosophical activity was that it put
into words and gave a theoretical base to the new direction in art and culture. Artists had been straining against

the leash that the concept of socialist realism had become for them. Although the artists' activities cannot be viewed as dependent on or even as springing from the new philosophical understanding of man, this philosophy came at the right moment for them. In a certain sense, art and philosophy were developing in a parallel fashion but with a difference: in addition to straining in its own area against the same limits that art encountered in its field, philosophy was by its very nature given the additional task of formulating and expressing the problem theoretically. Kosík himself alludes to this fact when discussing the nature and role of philosophy in the world.

The new Marxist philosophy of man was a philosophical reaction against the Stalinist-inspired orthodoxy and, at the same time, the theoretical expression and foundation for the struggle. Without it, the same struggle going on in the arts would have been less self-conscious and would have reacted against the confining strictures of socialist realism without, in fact, having a clearly formulated idea of why or in whose name it was carrying on this struggle. In the last instance, both the struggle in philosophy and that in the arts were against the narrow conception that their role was to be socially edifying and, by extension, against a certain understanding of the nature of reality held by the proponents of orthodoxy. In both philosophy and the arts, a new vision of reality was emerging—one diametrically opposed to that which had been prevalent up to that time. It fell to philosophy to give voice to this vision.

The orthodoxy, Marxism-Leninism, stressed that man was conditioned—indeed, determined—by the social and historical forces arising from the mode of production and the production-relations. "Man is an ensemble of social relations" was the famous saying by Marx.[15] In this view, only the working class, because of its historical position in the declining capitalist system, had the possibility of being the agent of real change. But even this possibility was as much a result of the "objective forces" at work as it was of any conscious effort. Hence Lenin's view that it was up to the vanguard of the working class to act in the name of the workers in order to effect change—but this too sprang from a perception of necessity, of an understanding of the historical and social forces at work.[16] The vanguard of the working class, the Communist Party, thus became the interpreter of historical necessity for the working class and for society at large. Under Stalin this became fixed and reduced to a set of formulas, with a rigid set of historical conditions determining the nature of society and social relations, and the Party acting only as the agent of this process in interpreting it to the people. In the end, the whole conception was reduced to a legitimation of the Party's activities—whatever they were—and in this sense served merely as a legitimizing ideology for power. The individual had no part to play in all this, for the individual was seen as an outcome of "objective" social relations over which he or she had no control.

In epistemology this had its corollary in Lenin's concept of "reflection" (otrazhenie), where there is an "objective reality" and man's task is to mirror it in his understanding as closely as possible and to act on this basis.[17] The practical outcome of this philosophy was that the Party had the central position in the society and had all the power in its hands. If it was seen as the only true interpreter of historical necessity and it most clearly reflected the "objective" world in its views, then its position in society followed logically from these assumptions. Just as logically followed the concept that all other facets of society should work together toward facilitating the Party's position and task. This was especially important for the arts and for philosophy because the role they played in influencing attitudes and forming the consciousness of the masses was more direct than that of other facets of society, though the task of raising consciousness to the perception of historical necessity was shared by all.

It was from this way of conceiving reality, and, by inference, the Party's role in society, that the whole concept of the socially edifying role of the arts and philosophy arose. Against this perception of reality, philosophy and the arts were waging their struggle.

Kosík wrote in an essay on Hegel that philosophy is no longer philosophy if it refuses to investigate reality in its full breadth, in all its internal interconnections; gives up its revolutionary, critical nature in favor of apologetics—thinking that it is thereby defending socialism and serving the Party; or views development from the perspective of the given moment and a given need only, instead of examining it dialectically in terms of overall development and the contradictions inherent in any given historical situation.[18] According to Kosík, philosophy during the time of the "Personality Cult" was predicated on "revealed truth"; instead of basing itself on arguments to be verified, it based itself on "revealed truth" to be believed. Philosophy must investigate reality not as a mere collection of atoms that have nothing to do with one another but as an "internally-differentiated, developing whole." "Why did we view socialism before in a one-sided, dried-out way, and only now are coming to conceive of it as a contradictory but rich, concrete, specific reality which grows out of our activity, our work and our creation?"[19]

"The Art of Philosophy," in the book *Man and His World*, by Sviták reflects the concerns of the philosophical and artistic communities to define the nature of their activity and its place. It constituted an attempt to clear the air for an understanding of what philosophy actually was and to dispel some illusions as to what its role should be. This effort was common to many people in both philosophy and the arts; at this stage, they wanted to obtain some measure of "breathing room," to gain greater flexibility for their endeavors. To accomplish this task, they had to win ground away from the Party's "guidance," or interference in philosophical and artistic matters. This, however, entailed first and foremost a theoretical clarification—if only for their own sake—of what the role of philosophy or art actually is—that is to say, what it should be.

The question of role—in this case, social role—presupposes, however, the more basic question of philosophy or of art. Therefore, Sviták asks the question "What is philosophy?" He started out by asking whether philosophy in fact existed in the Czechoslovak setting of that time because—according to him—to ask that question was in keeping with philosophy's task of asking the most fundamental question, the question of existence. By beginning his essay with this question, Sviták implied several things from the outset. He implied a certain conception of philosophy. Further, he implied that philosophy, according to this conception, was nonexistent in the Czechoslovak social setting. Philosophy—defined here for the sake of simplicity as "love of wisdom"—had become "an aversion to thinking . . . ,a system of dogmas based on an emotional bias in favor of socialism."[20]

At the same time, these pages contain both a mockery and a challenge in the statement that most people had tended to forget that social consciousness was determined by social relationships in the present time as well. What caused the appearance of such a situation in philosophy? This question is answered indirectly in Sviták's discussion of the leading role of the Party, wherein he suggests that the nonexistence of philosophy in the true sense of the word was an outcome of Party interference in matters pertaining to science and art. This situation, however, was brought about—in Sviták's view—by a misconception as to what this "leading" role entailed. "It was thought," Sviták writes, "that party spirit meant serving the interests of the Party. . . . We are now abandoning this practice forever and beginning to make room for real theoretical work, laying emphasis on the significance of theory as creative work, as the discovery of the new."[21]

With this statement, the battle lines were clearly drawn. Sviták was saying that the Party had no right to demand of philosophy something that would mean the negation of philosophy. To be sure, the Party could ask that philosophers disseminate and popularize the basic tenets of Marxist-Leninist philosophy. But it erred in making this philosophy's sole function—meanwhile subordinating the theoretical aspects of philosophy to the rulings of the Party, based on Party needs. Theory is responsible only to reality, to facts, Sviták claimed, and not to the Party. The battle was joined after this, as Sviták attacked some of the most fundamental assumptions of Marxism-Leninism (as it was then understood) and, by extension, its very nature. The stress on the creative character of philosophy meant that the Party was no longer the final authority. This interpretation went against the Party practice of attempting to "direct" art and philosophy in the same way it attempted to run the economy by directives.

In stressing the creative role of philosophy, Sviták was consistent with the main thrust of the new understanding of Marxism that was beginning to emerge; at the same time, he was attacking the Leninist views of the role of the Party as the final arbiter and authority. The Party claimed to be in possession of the highest level of consciousness, for which reason it reserved the right to interpret reality. By emphasizing "facts" and reality, Sviták was in effect undermining that claim—as well as referring to the tendency exhibited by the Party under Stalin of distorting facts to suit its own purposes. "Philosophy," he stressed,

> fulfills its social role only if it lights the way when empiricism is left helpless, if it raises basic questions and answers them, if it turns problems into self-evident truths and if it is capable of looking at self-evident truths as if they were problems—to put it simply if it thinks, and only if it thinks, never otherwise.[22]

PRAXIS

The concept of "praxis," whether explicitly a part of any given work or not, is the key to understanding the whole of Marxist humanism. It is certainly the crucial idea for the struggle that was going on between orthodox Marxism-Leninism and the Communist Party on the one side and the proponents of the new Marxist philosophy of man and the artists on the other. It is the new way of understanding praxis as man's creative mode of living in the world, as the recognition that reality is a *human* reality with man as the *subject* as well as the *object* of it, that is so fundamentally different from the Marxist-Leninist view of the world. In this new view, each person takes on significance and can take part in creating his reality, in this case social reality. This belief radically undermines both the Party's claim to be the sole agent for interpreting historical necessity and the view that art is to assist by helping to educate the "new socialist man."

Art is part of the creative activity of man in creating his world, and philosophy as "critical thinking" can never be made into apologetics. Therefore, the very *concept* of "revolutionary human *praxis*" is a revolutionary one—not because of the word *revolutionary* but because of the realization that man makes his social reality and can therefore change it. Dialectics is the means of explaining social phenomena on the basis of the practical objective activity of historical man. For Kosík, the "concrete," or "concrete totality," is the key concept of this entire thinking because it is not a statement about how reality can be *known* but a statement about the nature of reality itself. Reality conceived of as "concrete totality" is reality in the form of a structured, developing, and self-creating whole—a whole that makes it possible for any arbitrary or chance fact to be comprehended *as part of this whole.*[23] This is not a given, however. True reality is not evident for all to see but must be uncovered, sought out. This is the significance of the dialectics; it is dialectically that the distinction between appearances and actual facts is made. Appearances, the world of everyday phenomena that has been taken by most as the "real" world, have to be transcended if the true nature of reality is to be comprehended.

This world of appearances is what Kosík calls "pseudo-concreteness," and it is the pseudo-concreteness that can be overcome dialectically. Reality does not reveal itself to man directly through things—the nature of reality is at once revealed and hidden by phenomena— "pseudo-concreteness" arises when one assumes that the phenomena in and by themselves reveal the nature of reality. Dialectics is the method whereby the phenomenon is separated from the essence. It is critical thinking, whereby a "thing in itself" is arrived at by getting beyond appearances to the reality within.[24] This process in thinking, in knowing, means, however, that for man to know a "thing in itself" he must transform it into a "thing for *himself*".[25] This goes back to a prior question, "How is reality created?" and shows immediately the fundamental difference from Lenin's epistemology. Kosík goes further, however, and carries this idea beyond the epistemological category by stating that this is also the nature of reality.[26]

It is through praxis that we arrive at reality because this means that we perceive reality as our product. This is not an idealist conception; the world or reality is not created by the mind; rather, it is necessary to realize that man's products and social relations were all created by man. Nature can be changed and transformed, but social reality can be changed in a revolutionary way because it is a product of man.[27] In neither case is anything meaningful for man unless he makes it a "thing for himself." It is in this context that the destruction of pseudo-concreteness means revolutionary human praxis, which is the same thing as the "humanization" of man, critical dialectical thought that goes beyond appearances to the "thing in itself." This entails the "realization of truth and the creation of reality, as *every* individual has a part in the creation of his truth, as a socio-historical being."[28]

Kosík takes issue with the existentialist stance, criticizing it for its lack of a social dimension. This is important for an understanding of praxis. Though praxis is *also* the individual's creative activity, it is not *only* the individual that is concerned. Man, and thus also each individual, creates his world by creating the forms and social relations of which he is a part; each individual alone "does not change the world, but only his stance toward the world. Existential modification is not the revolutionary transformation of the world, but the individual drama of the individual in the world."[29] There is a subtle but crucial difference between the individual acting in the social context through praxis to change his world and the existentialist position toward the world of which he is a part.

Kosík is careful to differentiate between fetishized, false praxis and the authentic meaning of this concept. He speaks of fetishized praxis as an outcome of the desacralization of nature, and of the desacralization of man, where nature is conceived of as an "object for exploitation" and a "conglomerate of mechanical forces," and man in turn becomes a being that can be "shaped and formed," or, in other words, manipulated.[30] Machiavelli was the theoretician for the modern era, according to Kosík, because he recognized this trend and described it. Authentic praxis, in contrast, is the answer to the questions, "Who is man?" "What is human social reality?" and "How is that reality produced?" "*Praxis is the sphere of human being.*" As such, praxis is in opposition to the Aristotelian tradition, and thus implicitly in opposition to Leninism.[31] Kosík adds a further dimension when he says:

> Praxis has one further dimension: in its events, in which a specifically human reality is produced, a reality which exists independently of man is simultaneously taking place in a certain way. Man's openness to nature altogether is pro-

duced in praxis. In the "onto-creative" process of human praxis ontological possibilities are found, that is, possibilities of understanding of being itself. The creation of (human social) reality is a prerequisite for an openness to and understanding of reality altogether. Praxis as the production of human reality is simultaneously a process in which the universe, and reality in its own existence, are discovered.[32]

Kosík stresses that, although man creates *his* world, this is not all there is to reality:

> Reality is not (authentic) reality without man, in the same way that it is not (only) man's reality. It is the reality of nature as an absolute totality, which is independent not only of man's consciousness but also of his very existence, and it is the reality of man, which—in nature and as an integral part of nature—makes human social reality. This reality goes beyond nature, and defines for itself in history its own position in the universe. Man does not live in two spheres, nor does he inhabit history with part of his being and nature with another. *As man he is always at one and the same time* in both nature and in history.[33]

Sviták uses the concepts "critical thinking" and "laws of development" or "laws of evolution" of society, where the former means an understanding of the latter and harmony with them. At first glance, this usage might appear to negate the possibility of any real transformation of society and to undermine the entire concept of praxis as man's creative activity in changing his world. This seeming contradiction, however, can be explained: although Sviták uses some of the old terminology, borrowed from the deterministic approach to social reality, in actuality something quite different is concealed behind the idea of "law of development." Critical thinking, dialectics, does not mean recognizing and conforming to necessity as in the deterministic outlook; rather, it means the perception of the nature of reality in the concrete totality of man and his world.

Sviták in turn is concerned with showing in an essay on Camus that socialist humanism represents a more complete understanding of man than does existential-ism.[34] His treatment of Camus seems lacking in depth—some of the points he criticizes seem to be dealt with too facilely at times. This lack of depth may be traceable to the date of writing. Alternatively, it may also stem from a characteristic of Sviták's thought; his insight—though very penetrating at times—sometimes tends to view all other modes of thinking exclusively in terms of the compatibility with or similarity to socialist humanism.

The problem of pseudo-concreteness and the world of appearances is analyzed by Kosík in another way, through the concept of "care" (starost, Sorge). Although the concept was originally Heidegger's, Kosík adapted it to his own use. For Kosík, "care" means the way in which the individual is woven into a network of relations that, in relation to him, appear in the form of the practical-utilitarian world.[35]

Care refers to the world of "given" with which the individual has to deal, with the world of social relations which is the natural world to the individual. It is not recognized as being a "fetishized" world, where in the popular mind (which Kosík equates with philosophical ideology) the network of social relations seems to be a world of finished, ready-made apparati, arrangements, relations, etc. These Kosík calls "procuring," and they are fetishized because the individual does not realize that they have been *created* by him, by man, and are not something fixed in relation to him. He moves about in the world, conscious of himself as subject—not as subject in the true sense, man as the creator of his social relations, but only as a subject who is "involved" in this network of social relations and activity without being aware of the true nature of these ties.[36]

Another aspect of this outlook is man's relation to nature, because this mode of living in the social sphere implies a specific approach to nature as well. Nature is viewed as a laboratory and as a source of raw materials, and man's relation to it is one of a conqueror and creator (in one sense) of the material for production. The consequence of viewing nature in this way is that man's life is made much poorer. This attitude toward nature cuts off the aesthetic side of man's existence at its roots. Even more important, with the loss of the view of nature as something that was *not* created by man or by anyone else, man loses the awareness that he himself is part of a great whole, by comparison with which he becomes aware of his own smallness and his own greatness.[37]

Furthermore, in the world of care, man loses sight of his own true temporality; he is constantly thinking only in terms of the future and thus devalues the present. He does not evaluate the present in terms both of his future goals, plans, etc. *and* of his past. He does not *live* in the present but, rather, is constantly in transition through the present, with eyes only for the future.[38]

It is significant that, although Kosík later writes about this topic explicitly in terms of capitalism, here he is writing in general terms only; at *no* point does he even suggest that the world of care is *only* a capitalist phenomenon. Although he does not apply this world directly to socialism either, it is clear that he considers it a problem of the modern age, regardless of the kind of economic system operative. This is why his analysis could be applied to the specific Czechoslovak situation. Furthermore, the reference to "philosophical ideology" could be understood to pertain to that context as well, particularly when one understands "ideology" in the Marxian sense of fetishized views of the world, ways of explaining one's own activities apologetically and then taking this explanation to be the truth—forgetting its origins.

IDEOLOGY

Traditionally in Soviet Marxism "ideology" had been used exclusively with reference to the bourgeoisie— meaning, in essence, "bourgeois ideology." Gradually the meaning of the term changed in Soviet usage and it took on a more general connotation. At this point "class ideology" became a popular concept—the idea that ideology was bad only when it lacked the proper class base, i.e., anywhere except under socialism.[39]

By linking the fetishization in everyday consciousness ("procuring") with philosophical ideology, Kosík was cutting through this subterfuge and restoring something of the original Marxian content to the understanding of the term *ideology*. In so doing, he also drew the distinction between true philosophy and ideology; he used the term *philosophical ideology* rather than just *ideology*. This distinction played a very important role in Czechoslovakia at that time, because it clarified the struggle then going on within philosophy between those adhering to the "new" way of thinking and those continuing to defend the orthodox Marxist-Leninist position.[40]

Kosík differentiates between ideology and theory, defining ideology as the way of thinking that views "categories, ideas, conceptions as something independent, self-sufficient and absolute," in contrast to the view that sees them as a "theoretical expression of reality, as they express the 'forms of being, the conditions of existence' of reality itself."[41] Kosík sees three distinct and historically separate definitions of ideology at work yet notes that there is a tendency for them to become confused. Marx (in the beginning) and Engels (throughout his life) used the term to mean "false consciousness," in the sense of an "upside-down, illusory conception of reality." Lenin used it to indicate that ideology was a "reflection of class conditions in the minds of people," and Stalin, in his *Short Course*, "talked about the ideological and theoretical principles of the Party as if he were talking about two separate matters."[42]

The distinctions Kosík points out in the meaning of ideology are very important for an understanding of the way the term was used in Czechoslovakia during the period in question. Kosík himself favors the first definition—false consciousness—at least by usage. He speaks of Marxism as the philosophical expression of the ideas of the working class, but he never refers to this as ideology and always carefully indicates that, although Marxism may encompass this element, it is not *only* the reflection of working-class ideas of conditions. In fact, although one could assume from Kosík's presentation in *Dialectics of the Concrete* that "fetishized" praxis is merely an outcome of class conditions—which is in a sense true—Kosík goes much deeper in his analysis. He goes beyond classes per se to what lies beyond the class struggle or the existence of classes. Because of his interest in going beyond them as phenomena, he really even treats the whole matter of classes and the class struggle rather matter-of-factly. Here again he implicitly departs from Lenin. Kosík's understanding and mention of ideology as false consciousness was prophetic, however. He himself differentiates between philosophers who stay on the surface of matters and deal only in subjectivism and those who attempt to go deeper by way of dialectics to an understanding of problems.

Another facet of the discussion of theory and ideology that Kosík brings out is the subject of reason. He examines the nature of reason and criticizes the common assumption that views reason only as the "independent reason of the Cartesian man." This reason is criticized because it in fact is not independent but depends on the "reason" of society, which is greater than the reason of Cartesian man. In this view then, the "transcendental" reason of the society takes the form of transcendental "regularities," which man fails to see as springing from the social activity of human beings. "Reason" and science thus concern themselves only with learning to know these "regularities" and, in the name of freedom as "recognition of necessity," submitting themselves to them.[43]

Although Kosík here again is writing of modern capitalist society, certain aspects of his description would seem to apply also to the situation pertaining in the socialist societies. It seems particularly applicable to societies in which Stalin's legacy was still fairly strong—as in Czechoslovakia—but in some ways it would apply to any

Marxist-Leninist society. Reason is not, according to Kosík, the "recognition of necessity"—historical, social, or otherwise. It was in the name of historical necessity that the Communist Party claimed its legitimacy and role as leader, vanguard of the working class—and, by extension, of all of society. In contrast, Kosík goes on to elaborate on what reason is or should be.

> Reason is the reason of an individual, but the reasonableness of his reason is not that it is without presuppositions, but that it *includes reasonable premises as the premises of its own reasonableness.* Therefore, there is no direct evidence of Cartesian reason; reason is communicated by rationally apportioned and rationally created (social) reality.[44]

The central theme of the new understanding of philosophy is once again revealed in this passage; "reasonableness" as such rests ultimately on the rational ("reasonable") creation of reality, which is the task Kosík ascribes to dialectical reason, i.e., praxis. This goes back also to an earlier discussion of epistemology and to the claim that dialectical reason—or "critical thinking," as it was called there—is not merely an epistemological method. It is also an ontological method, a statement not only about *knowing* reality but also about the *nature* of reality. As such, it is also the answer—or part of the answer—to the question "How is reality created?"

"Rationalist reason," examined in more detail, is seen to give birth to irrationality because it creates realities that it can neither understand nor control, neither rationally explain and comprehend nor rationally order—because it starts from the wrong premises. It takes itself for granted, and it cannot therefore encompass—either practically or theoretically—the world as a whole.[45] Kosík here draws a distinction between "rational" and what he terms "efficient," where "efficient" denotes utilitarian behavior. "Rational" would then refer to the true state of reasonableness, whereas "efficient" is seen only in the aberration of this reason. Reason is then merely technique, in this understanding, and encompasses the technical side of life, or that which can be reached technically. Human values and meanings are left to the domain of the irrational, as a logical outcome of this understanding of reason. "Dialectical reason," on the other hand, is characterized by the fact that it "does not exist outside of reality and does not leave reality out either. It exists only by virtue of the fact that it realized [actualized] its own reasonableness, i.e., it creates itself in the form of dialectical reason only insofar as in the historical process it creates a reasonable reality."[46]

Kosík applied his analysis of reason to the concrete social situation in a speech he gave at the Fourth Congress of Czechoslovak Writers in June 1967. It was a short speech, entitled "Reason and Conscience," and took its inspiration from Jan Hus. It is noteworthy from the point of view of Kosík's philosophy in that it implicitly repeats his idea of the "reasonableness of reason," continuing the distinction between "false reason" and "true reason" and applying that distinction explicitly to the Czechoslovak situation.

Sviták also dealt with the question of ideology in a manner similar to Kosík's. The issue was an extension of the basic struggle with the Party and the struggle to arrive at a workable definition of philosophy and art. For Sviták it was a question of "direct contact with the deepest needs of our life, or the death of thought—that is the alternative facing creation in science and art."[47] Ideology is a consequence of ignoring dialectics, in Sviták's view. Thinking dialectically means to be aware of contradictions—specifically, in this context, the internal contradictions within society. Several features are characteristic of ideology.

First, ignoring dialectics means that ideas become fixed and concepts become absolute because an unchanging "truth" is at issue, not an ongoing process. The second result of ignoring dialectical thinking is that conflicts within society are also ignored; only a bright

picture is painted by the official view. This picture, more-
over, is one that then *becomes* reality for those within
this framework. How does one know whether it is reality—or only one's perception of reality—that is at issue?
Whereas Kosík formulates the issue philosophically, theoretically, Sviták makes of it a direct confrontation:

> Theoretician, artist, do you intend to [e]mbellish the exist-
> ing conditions with the ornament of your abstractions, and
> give theory or art an appearance of depth at variance with
> the truth, or do you intend to make your thinking an instru-
> ment for the reshaping of these conditions?[48]

"EVERYDAYNESS"

Kosík uses yet another concept with which to characterize the world of appearances—that of "everydayness." Everydayness is similar to pseudo-concreteness and to the
fetishized world. It is the instinctive, subconscious and
unconscious, unreflective mechanism of acting and living: things, people, movements, tasks, the surroundings
are not perceived in their originality and authenticity.
They are not examined and do not appear. They merely
are and they are seen as an inventory, an integral part of
the *familiar* world.[49]

Everydayness is the phenomenological world, a world
in which reality both reveals itself and hides itself at the
same time and in a specific way. The individual creates
relations on the basis of *his own* experience, possibilities,
and activity, and he therefore regards this reality as his
very own world. This view is disturbed only when in
some way the everydayness is shaken, at which time the
everydayness becomes problematical to him.[50]

This introduces the subject of "everydayness and
history."[51] Why are these examined in juxtaposition like
this? What is their connection? "Everydayness" to the average person means the natural atmosphere or familiar

reality. "History," on the other hand, is viewed as the transcendental reality going on behind his back and interjecting itself into his everydayness in the form of catastrophes. For the individual, history becomes synonymous with fate when everydayness and history are separated, when it is not recognized that they interpenetrate each other and interact. Everydayness separated from history is emptied to an absurd unchangeability, whereas history torn from everydayness changes into an absurdly powerless colossus that interrupts everydayness like a catastrophe but cannot change it—that is, it cannot separate out its banality and fill it with some content. When this happens, everydayness turns into a "religion of everyday" and loses its historical dimension. It becomes banal and anonymous, and it dictates to every individual his behavior, actions, tastes, and even his protest against banality. The "religion" or everyday awareness of daily life regards human existence as something manipulable, and it behaves with it and explains it on this basis.[52]

Kosík asks further why people look for meaning in history. Even though people make history, why does it seem to them that they are mere instruments, carrying out some higher purpose? Kosík disputes the idea that some external factor gives meaning to history—history *is* the struggle for meaning, for "reasonableness," against unreason. "Man actualizes himself, humanizes himself, in history."[53] Kosík goes on to argue that certain qualities, such as tragedy, absurdity, etc., may exist *within* history, but history in itself is none of these. He also talks about history as *continuity*, as that which enables man to learn from his past. Then, in a short, cogent passage, he describes the relation of the individual to history:

> The connection of the objectified and materialized *praxis* of mankind—called "substance," "the objective spirit," "culture," or "civilization" and deciphered in materialist theory as the historical unity of the forces of production and the conditions of production—produces a historically attainable

"reason" for society. This "reason" is independent of all specific individuals and therefore beyond individuality, but in
actuality has its existence *only through* the activity and reason of individuals. The objective social substance, in the
form of materialized forces of production, of language, and
forms of thinking is *independent* of the will and consciousness of individuals, but *exists* only through their activity,
thinking and speech.[54]

Kosík ties in everydayness by implication to the socialist "reality" of which he is a part. He says that the
materialist thesis which holds that man is an ensemble of
social conditions, but does not add that he is the *subject*
of these conditions, makes of the "interpretation" of
something only a choice of whether to put the *real* subject into the empty space or to put a mystified subject
there—a mystified "ideology" or a mystified "we," for
whom the authentic individual is transformed into an instrument or a mask.[55] This is a scarcely veiled attack on
what Kosík refers to as "vulgar materialism," meaning
the Stalinist legacy in orthodox Marxism-Leninism.
Those still operating in terms of this legacy were indeed
guilty in their approach of precisely the error that Kosík
so roundly condemned, and this must have been immediately apparent to his contemporaries—at least to those
who had begun to think on their own about what was
transpiring in Czechoslovakia.

Whereas man as "care" represented pure subjective
activity and involvement in the world, man as "homo
oeconomicus" represents the opposite extreme, according
to Kosík—the world conceived of only "objectively"
where man, too, becomes an object among objects. "The
subject abstracts from his subjectivity and becomes an
object and an element of the system. Man is a unit which
is determined by its function in the system of regularities
(regular laws)."[56] This way of viewing man is a result of
the rise of science—in this case, specifically political
economy. This new science wants to transform man into
something that can be counted and analyzed, just as any

other object of investigation, for the *real* for modern science is that which can be expressed mathematically. Political economics sees economy as a *system of regularities* that man comes to know; only then does it ask what the relation is of man to this system. " 'Homo oeconomicus' is man as an integral part of the system, and as such must be equipped with those basic characteristics which are unavoidable for the movement of the system."[57]

Although Kosík here for the first time explicitly mentions capitalism and is critical of it, he is talking of it both in terms of the present and in terms of its place in the rise of the modern world. He asks the question of what kind of man, with what kind of psychic properties, the system must make in order to function; this question can be asked of any system, not only of capitalism. Man is changed into a part of the system, into an object. "Man's world becomes a physical world, and the science of man becomes the science of man-object, i.e., a social physics."[58] Man is not seen as being in a specific era, and reality is taken as a once-and-for-all given, rather than the then-state of affairs being recognized as belonging to a specific historical time and place. The alternative is to see that "man always exists within a system, and as an integral part of this system is reduced to certain facets (functions) or forms (one-sided and objectivized) of his being. At the same time, he is always greater than the system and *as a person* cannot be reduced to the system." "The existence of concrete man extends in a span between nonreducibility to the system and the possibility of going beyond the system to the actual placement and practical functioning within the system (of historical conditions and relations)."[59] So, the two extremes of nonauthenticity in the modern age can be characterized by the terms *care* and *homo oeconomicus*. In neither of them does man realize that *he* is behind social relations and social products, regardless of the kind of society he is in.

THE CRITICAL FUNCTION OF ART

To be able to discern the truth about alienated everydayness and to transcend nonauthenticity, man must put a
certain distance between it and himself, rid it of all famil-
iarity, and apply a certain "force" to it.[60] Here Kosík is
setting the stage for the first real mention of the role art
has to play in the world, and what he says is again a dia-
metrical opposition to the prevailing concept of art as
"socialist realism."

> Into what kind of "forced" metaphor and likenesses must
> man and his world be transformed for people to see their
> own real face and recognize their own real world? It seems to
> us that one of the main principles of modern art, poetry and
> theater, graphic arts and film is the "violence" on everyday
> reality, the destruction of pseudo-concreteness.[61]

By coming out with this statement in his philosophy,
Kosík was at the same time implicitly making a very
strong political statement in the context of his environment. The issues alive at that time find their expression
in Kosík's philosophy—even though his writing is by no
means polemical and the nature of both his work and the
task he set for himself are purely philosophical. Kosík
would have it understood, though—not as a "dead" discipline, divorced from reality, but as a living enquiry into
the nature of reality and man's place in it.

Reality has the characteristic of being both expressed
in and hidden by the phenomena of our everyday lives, so
in what way do we penetrate to the essence of a thing behind or in its external manifestations? Man can know reality, can penetrate to the essence of things, in two ways:
through philosophy and through art. "It is for this reason
that art and philosophy have such a specific meaning for
man and such a special mission. Art and philosophy are
in their functions vitally important, irreplaceable, and
nothing can be substituted for them. Rousseau would
have said that they are inalienable."[62]

This understanding of art and philosophy is in marked contrast to what is termed here "sociologism," which is the tendency to replace the idea of "social being" with "conditions," where the conditions change and the "human subject" merely reacts to these changes—as if the subject were merely a collection of mental capabilities. In this view, "conditions change and unwind, and the human subject goes along parallel with them and photographs them. Man becomes a photograph of conditions."[63] He renders them artistically or scientifically, learning to recognize and represent them. Kosík's emphasis is in marked contrast to Lenin's theory of "reflection" and, although the difference had been implicit from the very beginning, it was made more or less explicit with this attack on "sociologism."[64] Man perceives the world and makes it his own through this sensual activity, but he "discovers the meaning [sense] of things by *creating* a human meaning [making human sense] for them."[65] Otherwise they are indeed "senseless."

Art, like praxis, makes an indelible mark on all human activity. "Every work of art has a twofold character, in an indivisible unity: it is an expression of reality, but simultaneously produces reality—that reality which does not exist outside of the work of art or before it but precisely only in the work of art."[66]

Kosík argued that reality could not be conceived of only in terms of "economic factors," which led him to once again stress man's creative role and activity in producing his world. This creative activity in the form of praxis was then compared with the role of art, and the nature of a work of art was the subject of enquiry. In fact, art could not be separated from praxis, as if it were a separate category, any more than philosophy can be separated. They are both a part of praxis, as man's creative mode of being in the world, and as such cannot be considered apart from this context. To attempt to do so renders the discussion meaningless—as Kosík shows when he argues against reducing Shakespeare's plays to "nothing more than an artistic reflection of the class struggle in the era of primary accumulation."[67] Why must *art* convert a thing into something other than itself, merely reflect it in an "artistic" way? That art did, in fact, do just this was the prevailing attitude in terms of the Marxist-Leninist orthodoxy of the day, and Kosík was showing that this attitude expected from art something completely irrelevant. If a work of art has this twofold character in relation to reality, what does this say about reality? What is expected of art? Must the "reality" that art at once reflects and makes be that which men *assume* to be reality? "How does man know," Kosík asks, "whether this reality that man assumes he knows is not in fact only his *idea* of reality?"[68] If this were true, and man's *idea* of reality were indeed the same as reality itself, the artist's function *would* be merely to represent and illustrate it. But this is not the case. "A work of art is not a representation of *ideas* about reality. As a work of art and as art it represents *reality*, and, simultaneously *produces* reality, the reality of beauty and art."[69]

An "economic factor" is any particular facet of the whole of society which is given undue emphasis and is not seen as a part of the whole. It is viewed as if it were independent of the rest of the whole and of man and his activity. In the modern age, this takes on in particular the form of the economy as an independently understood, autonomous phenomenon but, in fact, this autonomy is only an apparent one. Instead of being understood as "economic structure," economy is taken to be the one special factor that determines all other factors in the society. The concept of the economy as the "privileged factor" that determines all other facets of the society does not take into account the origin of the society but simply tries to explain society as something "given." In contrast, the true materialist view holds that the "social whole (socio-economic formation) is created and constituted by the economic structure. The economic structure creates the unit and interdependence of all spheres of social life."[70] In this statement, the economic structure is conceived to be "the ensemble of social relations which people occupy in production and in relation to the means of production."[71]

This analysis, and the differentiation between the concepts "economic factor" and "economic structure," are particularly important for any discussion of the role of art from the materialist perspective. Some who claimed to be materialists were also caught in the tendency to explain everything in terms of the economic factor as only one of many aspects of society, yet the one that plays the dominant role. The effect of Kosík's analysis is to refute this view and to widen the approach. This had implications for his own time as well. Because Stalinism had simplified Marxism to just such an understanding of the role of the economy as Kosík described under the term *economic factor*, everything in society, including art, tended to be explained in terms of this one factor. Making the distinction between the two approaches opened the way to a new understanding of art and a new perspective in philosophy.

The concept of class struggle is bound up closely with the understanding of the economic structure but, just as "structure" became "factor" in the common approach, the whole idea of class struggle was also drastically simplified and began to lose its original meaning. Instead of basing a concept of class struggle on the above understanding of the economic structure as the ensemble of social relations occupied in production and in relation to the means of production (and therefore going deeper into the matter), the commonly held approach assumed that the class struggle was the basic reality from which to operate. From this approach came such ideas as the "class character" of a work, whether of philosophy or of art. The whole concept of class character played a large role in the orthodox conception of art, and the shift from thinking in terms of economic factors to the understanding of

economic structure undermined at the same time the
simplistic view of the class-struggle and the class character of any activity then prevalent in the socialist societies
of Eastern Europe. This action was necessary in order to
clear the way for any new understanding of culture and
artistic activity.

After reiterating the statement that one cannot begin
one's analysis with the economy as if it were something
that was already the most basic reality, beyond which no
enquiry could possibly go, Kosík maintains that to work
on this assumption is to make a fetish, a thing, out of the
economy. Any enquiry must penetrate more deeply, to
man, who makes social reality. "The primary nature of
economy is not a result of some higher degree of reality
for specific human products, but comes from the central
meaning of praxis and work in making a human
reality."[72]

In the Renaissance, work was perceived as creation, as
truly creative activity whose products said something
about the character of the artist as well. This ceased to be
the case after the rise of capitalism and the advent of the
peculiarly capitalistic division of labor, because work
then ceased to be a creative activity that said something
about its creator and instead became devaluing toward
man himself. "The authentic world is an objective world
of things and objectified human relations, in comparison
with which man is the source of errors, subjectivity, uncertainty, and chance—therefore imperfect reality."[73]
The economy, in the sense of economic factor, becomes
the highest reality for man. This is in contrast to the true
understanding of economy as economic structure, the
"basic structure of human objectivization, as the ground
plan and outline of human relations, as an elementary
level of human objectivization, as the economic base
which determines the superstructure."[74]

Kosík then turns to an examination of work as an integral part of being, in which man is changed and becomes
objective and the objects of his work are transformed

from their original, natural state and in some way thereby "humanized." It is through this activity that man makes the human world, *his* world.

Work is that sphere of man's activity that is carried out under "the pressure of outside necessity, the fulfillment of which makes possible the existence of the individual."[75] The activity that is not done out of necessity—whether natural or social—is not work, but "free creation," whatever area it is in. However, there can be no separation of work and freedom, as Kosík stresses, because work creates the basis for human freedom and free creative activity. The economy, then, is "that sphere of human reality in which the unity of necessity and freedom, animality and humanity is historically produced. The economy is the sphere of necessity (objective work efforts) in which the historical prerequisites for human freedom are produced."[76] A note of caution should be sounded here, however, with regard to one point. Work is conceived of in the *philosophic* sense, not in the *economic* one, for whereas work in the former sense is where the human social reality is produced, it is in the latter sense only the production of a specific historical form of social wealth.[77] In drawing this distinction, Kosík is, by his own admission, following Marx's observations in his *Grundrisse*.[78]

Although the tension between the opposing points of view might not be immediately perceived by the uninformed or casual reader, anyone who was aware of what was going on and who had more knowledge of Marxist philosophy would need no explanation. It is as if the whole preceding section had been leading up to one remark:

> Marxism is not a mechanical materialism which would reduce social knowledge, philosophy and art to "economic conditions," and whose analytical activity would then depend on discovering the earthly core of spiritual formations. On the contrary, materialist dialectics shows how the historical subject concretely promises relevant ideas and a

complete set of forms of knowledge. Knowledge is not reduced to conditions, but the process by which *the concrete
subject produces and reproduces social reality, and in it is
simultaneously produced and reproduced*, is brought to the
center of attention.[79]

Kosík takes care to differentiate between "conditions"
and "being" and, again, through this stresses the fact that
man has a central place, that he is *not* determined only by
events external to him.

Kosík continues his discussion of the relation between philosophy and economics in Marx's thought, and
in so doing he examines the relation between the young
Marx and the Marx of *Capital*. He begins his discussion
of *Capital* by asking what it meant for Marx to have begun this work with an analysis of commodities and to
have ended it with an examination of classes; he proceeds
to show the dialectical nature of Marx's thought—the
way of getting behind appearances to the essence of phenomena. *Capital* is also treated as a literary work and, as
such, is compared to Hegel's *Phenomenology of the
Mind*. Both are characteristic of a specific literary genre,
that of odyssey. Hegel's *Phenomenology of the Mind* is an
odyssey of the mind, whereas *Capital* is an odyssey of
concrete historical praxis.[80] In this discussion, as in the
earlier ones, the organic unity of Marx's thought, from
the *Economic and Philosophic Manuscripts of 1844*
through *Capital*, becomes apparent.

As a work of art itself, though in the sphere of philosophy, *Dialectics of the Concrete* exhibits precisely the
twofold nature Kosík ascribes to an art work: it reflects
reality while at the same time producing a reality found
only within this work. It has an internal consistency that
reflects the cogency of the analysis for the world it describes and out of which it springs. Because of these two
features, Kosík had a profound influence on the struggle
going on between the orthodoxy and those trying to
break out of old forms in both philosophy and art. "Art,
in the proper sense of the word, is simultaneously de-

mystifying and revolutionary, for it leads man out of his ideas and prejudices about reality to reality itself and its truth."[81]

Kosík also asks why a work of art not only serves as a witness to its own time but also manages to transcend it. His answer is that, *in addition* to serving as a witness of a particular era, the work *also* becomes an essential element of human existence, and of a class or nation's existence. It becomes a part of human social reality and becomes meaningful from this interaction between the particular era and the universal human aspects represented in the work of art. This process takes place in every era, as each time must understand for itself the characteristics of being human. This fact is portrayed in the following words:

> The historical stages in the development of humanity are not empty forms from which life has evaporated *because* humanity has reached higher forms of development, but rather, through man's creative activity—praxis—are constantly being integrated into the present. The part concentrated in the present (in the dialectical sense, "superseded") creates human nature, that "substance" which includes both objectivity and subjectivity, both material relations and objectivized forces and the ability to "see" the world and explain it through various modes of subjectivity, that is, scientifically, artistically, philosophically, politically, etc.[82]

Sviták was also concerned with the meaning of art, particularly in modern culture. Modern culture, the modern spirit, is increasingly rationalistic and caught up with science and technology; consequently, there is a tendency to ignore the spiritual and emotional sides of man, to have as an ideal the complete control over feelings and emotions. This would lead to a dull sort of man, a functionary without any vision.

Sviták, while painting this unflattering picture of modern society, also stresses that "at the very core of human life there lies another source of spiritual activity—the power of the imagination, of creative fantasy—the eternal source of art."[83] Here is the key to understanding the nature and meaning of art. Art, says Sviták, is therefore intimately connected with the meaning of man. It involves a conception of the world, and therefore of man and his activity in the world, which is man's creativity. "Art invariably calls for an explanation of the meaning of man, it is an appeal to a dimension unknown in nature."[84]

By referring to "a dimension unknown in nature," Sviták is once again referring to the specific character of man, as opposed to other animals—man's culture. Man is formed not only by nature but by culture, by society, and therein lies a clue to his meaning. Man is to a large degree what his culture makes of him, but he is also the creator of culture. Culture involves man's self-perception, and it is partly through his self-perception that man defines his meaning. This self-perception changes historically, but common to it at all times is man's attempt to understand himself. Art is one form of this attempt.

Sviták goes on to speak of transformation in culture as a transformation in social consciousness and, thus, as a transformation of man's perception of himself. In this, of course, are transformations in man's objective reality as well, for man's self-perception is not something that exists independently of his objective being in the world. According to Sviták, transformations in social consciousness include five basic features:

1. The transformation of the content of a given culture, that is, the dialectical process which changes culture in its very essence and reflects the contradictions of the age;
2. The transformation of the structure of social consciousness, especially changes in the particular forms of social consciousness and in the relations between these forms;
3. The transformation of the social characteristics of those who produce culture and of those who consume it, that is, the transformation of the whole cultural aspect of the various social strata and classes;
4. The transformation of the type of man as determined by the combination of all his social relationships, both

those which remain stable and those which change, that is, the overall transformation of the historically transient human type;

5. The transformation of the forms of life in society, of modern man's way of life.[85]

The above discussion of the transformation in social consciousness is important background to an understanding of the nature of art. Art is not something that takes place independently of culture and its transformations; it is intimately involved in these transformations. Art both reflects these changes and helps to create them, but art cannot be understood except in relation to culture and its transformation. In a certain sense, art is therefore a form of social consciousness. This feature is one that Sviták is concerned to stress because he believes it is unrealistic to attempt to view art as a phenomenon that exists suspended in a vacuum, independent of its social context. To stress this feature of art is therefore a necessity, but it does *not* mean that art is *only* a social process. This is the other side of the coin, and Sviták is equally concerned that it be understood. "Art participates in the revolutionary transformation of culture as art, through art, and in no other way."[86]

In another context, Sviták further develops the theme that through art man sees the different forms of social consciousness, his different perceptions of himself historically, that the meaning of art is precisely to show the meaning of man.

The riddle of Hamlet and the riddle of the Theban sphinx are one and the same, and their solution is man, not only figuratively and abstractly, but also concretely—man as a living existence. . . . Man is a living riddle, not only to others but also to himself, precisely because he is capable of changing his own meaning. He knows that life has no external meaning apart from life itself. Modern man is a riddle to himself, and also the solution to the riddle, as Hamlet is, because he, too, knows that either he creates and guarantees his own meaning or he is absurd.[87]

It is the unique contribution of the modern age that human life is viewed in terms of praxis.

Art is a part of the transformation of social consciousness, but as art it also has its own character and undergoes its own transformations independent of those taking place around it. This is to say that art does not merely reflect the changes going on around it but undergoes change in and of itself. Although these internal changes relate to those in the social context, the relationship is much more subtle and complex than if changes in art were only a reflection in some sense of general social changes. Hence, both sides of art must be understood if there is to be any understanding of the meaning of art. Art is influenced by its social context, but at the same time is engaged in creating new forms of social consciousness, in transforming culture. That is why art is revolutionary. The artist "is always shaping the world according to his imagination, he is creating. . . . [He] does not imitate the world, does not reflect it passively, but forms it and reshapes it, reshapes reality, stylizes it and deforms it."[88] In doing this, the artist is "giving shape to man's hopes," he is "a symbol of the struggle to give his age a human face."[89] Thus, for Sviták, art must be viewed as a way man expresses his perception of himself, and man's perception of himself is also the perception of his activity in the world.

These conceptions of the meaning of art and the social role of art are fundamentally different from those expressed in the official, Marxist-Leninist view of art then in force. Art is not a reflection of social processes, as that view would have it. Neither can art be regulated or told that it should serve to illustrate the view of man officially held at any given moment. For this reason, art *is* revolutionary because it cannot be subjected to the demands of the social system. Man must constantly redefine his own meaning, and this redefinition is open-ended. Therefore a work of art, though a reflection of its age, is more than that. It is not "the simple representation of our human condition; it is rather a stimulus to man's insight into himself, it is an incentive to a deeper understanding of man as man."[90]

In an essay entitled "Man and Poetry," in his work *Man and His World*, Sviták developed the theme that art—and thus also poetry—is a statement about man and his meaning, and that this statement changes along with changes in man's social consciousness historically. "The meaning of poetry is the cultivation of human sensibility, perceptiveness and understanding of the world."[91] This understanding of the meaning of poetry prepares the ground for a new conception of the social role of poetry, of art, where art is not expected to serve a specific social or educational function but is involved in the most basic task of humanizing man, of changing his perceptions of himself and his world. "Poetry stimulates man's contact with his personality, it adds to his most precious consciousness of himself, it makes him aware that he is a unique, ephemeral being, perceiving a unique, ephemeral world, that he is an existence open to the world."[92]

"Man and Poetry" is a lyrical essay in its own right. Sviták speaks of poetry as a "vision of the world," and in so doing shows the way in which poetry is at once an agent of man's ability to perceive reality and to create his reality.[93]

> The poem integrates us into the universe, into the absurdity of being, into the chaos of existence, not through the operations of reason and logic, but immediately and directly by evoking the world of values and deeper levels of meaning; the poem returns us to our place among mankind, in an ordered world, in the universe; it gives us back our humanity.[94]

Both here and later, where he speaks of poetry as helping to penetrate to the essence of phenomena through its insight, Sviták is expressing the perception of art as one of the ways in which man orders the primal chaos into a structured whole and penetrates to reality, to essences, to the "thing-in-itself." Also, Sviták again expresses here the insight that in poetry, in art, man is "torn out of the context of abstractions and portrayed in the actual constellation of the living moment."[95] In both Kosík and Sviták there is the perception that art is violent in a certain way—it does violence to some conceptions of reality and "forces" man to penetrate beyond appearances. Poetry by its very nature is radical; writing poetry is a revolutionary act.

In viewing poetry as a human act and looking at its role over the ages, Sviták goes beyond even the humanist content usually found in his philosophy, and he touches on the mystery of being. Poetry, he says, "cannot surrender its original meaning, which is to make up poetic, graphic fables about man, to create myth. . . . Poetry reveals to man the secret aspect of human existence itself, and that has been its function in all the myths of the past."[96] This statement, coming from a Marxist philosopher who had been engaging in polemics against religion, illustrates the extent to which the new conception of man in Marxism constituted a radical departure from the conception by Stalinism—even from that of orthodox Marxism-Leninism. The statement provides a view of the radical character of this new philosophy of man and the creative possibilities for an understanding of culture based on this philosophy, on this conception of man, as it indeed enables man to be open to his creative possibilities.

The Prague Spring

In 1968, both Kosík and Sviták were increasingly caught up in the tempo of political change; both tried, through their writing and other activity, to influence the course of events.

In the series of articles entitled "Our Present Crisis," which appeared in *Literární listy* in the spring of 1968, Kosík was extremely outspoken.[97] It is evident that his thinking had changed considerably over the twelve-year period in question; though his basic themes remained remarkably similar during this time, the practical consequences he drew from his thought became progressively more radical. In speaking of the crisis in Czechoslovak society that spring, Kosík demonstrated this radicalization well. In 1958, he had been quite bold for his time by writing so critically on the subject of classes, but at that time he was still calling for a return to the Leninist norms of "democratic centralism."

Even in his 1958 call for "democratic centralism," however, Kosík stressed that a "return to Lenin" could not mean a return to the pre-Stalinist days in actuality but that Lenin must be viewed in light of the requirements of the modern age. He saw Marxism as a "philosophy of everyday life and the everyday relations of people"—in addition to being a "theory of historical growth or a strategy for class struggles.[98] Therefore, if socialism did not give meaning to the everyday lives of people and enable them to realize their longings for a full life of feeling, something was wrong.

In "Our Present Crisis" in 1968 Kosík begins by saying that what is at question is a search for meaning in the life of the society, the nation. This is the essence of the "Czech Question." He writes elsewhere that in Palacky's time the Czech nation was threatened by a worldwide process of centralization but that now it is threatened instead by a system of universal manipulation. Indeed, the characteristic feature of politics in the modern world, according to Kosík, is mass manipulation. "Politics as mass manipulation is possible only in a system of universal manipulation."[99] In Czechoslovakia there is a growing danger that the political nation will be

> transformed into an indifferent mass, i.e., a mass of residents who have lost the ability and desire to differentiate between truth and falsehood, good and evil, better from worse in their actions, thinking and in their lives as a whole.[100]

In this search the opportunity exists for transforming society and replacing old forms with new, but the danger exists also of not effecting *this* transformation and of merely changing one set of circumstances for another, equally bad set.[101] Implicit in this statement is Kosík's central idea, praxis, whereby man as both subject and object of his social conditions has the capacity to change those conditions in a radical and revolutionary way. Seen in this context, the article becomes a call to action and the practical side of the philosophical concept of praxis. In his philosophy Kosík has said that man is capable of transforming his society through revolutionary praxis— in his article he was calling on people to actually put this theory into "practice."

Kosík again attacked "the leading role of the Party" as practiced and understood at that time. "Politicians talk of the 'leading role of the party'," Kosík wrote, "by which they mean . . . the ruling position of a power group."[102]

These remarks signify a radical departure from Lenin's conception of the "leading role of the Party." Although the argument could be made that, in fact, Kosík was calling only for a return to "democratic centralism," his article leads one to question that assumption. He talks about both the "Party-masses" and the "non-Party masses" being manipulated by the "power group," and he proposes that "instead of the old obsolete alliance of Party and non-Party members, a new political alliance of communists, socialists, democrats, and other citizens might be created. Socialist democracy is either an all-inclusive democracy, or it is not democracy at all."[103] This proposition is something far more than "democratic centralism," even if the Party had been viewed as having a "guiding" function, as some had suggested.[104] Lenin had definite ideas about the role of the Party as the "vanguard of the proletariat," a role that furthermore was necessitated by the political situation under the Czar, where an elite party of revolutionaries was absolutely essential to the success of the revolution, and a mass party was an impossibility.

Also inherent in the call for a new alliance, a new "socialist democracy," was the basic theme of man's creative activity as a subject of his social conditions as well as their object, and therefore of the necessity for social conditions that would allow man to be creative—hence, an end to Party interference in philosophy and art and an end to the theory that their function was to serve the Party in its role as edifier of the masses. "Edification" became here "mystification," the creation of a false consciousness. But according to the philosophy formulated by Kosík, it was precisely the *nature* of art and philosophy to *de*mystify, to cut through appearances to the essence of phenomena. This held true for any society, not only the Czechoslovak one, but it grew out of the specific conditions pertaining in that society at that time, and—while transcending this role—constituted an attempt to explain the developments in that society philosophically.

In an interview he had with Antonin Liehm, Kosík himself summed up much of the discussion about the importance of the new philosophy. Many themes that found expression in Kosík's writings were mentioned in the course of the interview. In talking about Czechoslovak culture during the period from 1956 to 1968, Kosík had the following to say:

> There is another question which intrigues me; namely, why our culture proved so effective, so vital. There was a definite cross-fertilization between literature, art, and philosophy, so that we can truly speak of culture in the broadest sense of the word. . . . There was a particular cultural "common denominator" which emerged during the last few years and which manifested itself especially clearly in our cinema. . . . The fundamental reality of Czech culture hinged on the question; "What is man?" That is the political, critical, revolutionary essence. . . . The real fundamental polemic of our culture lay in the fact that against the official—one might say "reigning"—concept of Man, it put forth an entirely different concept of its own.[105]

Kosík goes on to explain what he means by "official" concept of man. Rather than some explicit doctrine, it is a concept of Man implicit in the regime's political, economic, and moral functioning, one which was, at the same time, mass-produced by the regime because it required precisely this sort of human being. . . . In dealing with the question, "What is Man?", culture naturally formulated its answer quite differently. While the official view saw human characteristics in terms of Man's limits, emptiness, simplicity and lack of dynamism, Czech culture emphasized Man as a complex creature, continually alive, elastic, striving to overcome conflicts, a being irreducible to a single dimension.[106]

Further on, Kosík gave his assessment of Stalinism and put forward the contention that it was not, in fact, some *distortion* of socialism but a "full realization of an entirely different conception of socialism."[107] This conception rested on a fundamentally different view of man. Stalinism is characterized as follows:

> The conception of history as necessity unfolding with the inevitability of natural, scientific law; the self-justification of socialism as both necessary and inevitable; the conception of man as *homo oeconomicus* or a manipulable unit; the reduction of dialectics to a few elementary features; the perception of truth as a utilitarian tool—the sum of these ideological presuppositions shows us the source from which the well-known Stalinist period originated.[108]

Kosík saw philosophy as needing to clarify some of its more fundamental questions, and he saw the significance of the "Prague Spring" and the whole era leading up to it as challenging those involved to a thoroughgoing reexamination of some of its underlying assumptions, both philosophical and in terms of the "social, political, and economic functioning of socialism; that is, of the socialist working model."[109]

This was the task Kosík set himself, and one he fulfilled to an extraordinary degree in *Dialectics of the Concrete*. In his interview, Kosík was calling for exactly that—a systematic reformulation of the most fundamental philosophical assumptions of socialism, based on a radically new view of man and his world. Kosík's other work is important in helping him to clarify his ideas and as a means of making them widespread in the society—a task he also viewed as essential and without which he considered philosophy useless. This view is in character with the call for a "socialist democracy" and, both through his philosophy and his attempts to disseminate this new understanding, Kosík was actively engaged in attempting to create a new society as well. It is out of these attempts that his far-reaching influence on the rebirth of culture after Stalinism comes, as well as his fundamental significance as the philosopher of this rebirth. If the Phoenix was rising from its ashes, this was due at least in part to Karel Kosík.

Sviták was instrumental in interpreting the new philosophy of man for the cultural context, and, in a sense, he served as a bridge between the systematic thinking of Kosík and the realm of art and culture. It was not the case, however, that Sviták was solely an interpreter for Kosík. In fact, as has been stressed, the thought of both men sprang from a common source, the new conception of man that was then emerging in East European Marxist philosophy.

CONCLUSION

The Yugoslav Praxis Group in the East European Context

The Common Task

THE PRECEDING SECTIONS HAVE PRESENTED A picture of the activity of critical thinkers in Eastern Europe who used Marx as the basis for a humanist critique of society and ideology. Although their activity sprang out of conditions specific to postwar Eastern Europe, it was analogous to an earlier critical movement that took place within Marxism in Western Europe, represented by such thinkers as Rosa Luxemburg, Antonio Gramsci, György Lukács, and Karl Korsch.

What these figures in both Eastern and Western Europe shared—aside from any specific points of agreement—was an attempt to reevaluate critically certain "givens" in Marxist theory in light of changing circumstances. Although all of them were aware of and to some degree sympathetic to the Russian experience, none was inclined to accept it uncritically. Their theoretical activity had the effect of an immanent critique that caused a ferment within Marxism, continually challenging tendencies toward dogmatization.

They were following in the footsteps of Bernstein's revisionism in that they did not approach Marxism as a faith to which they had to give their uncritical allegiance.

174

They, like Bernstein, were interested in an analysis of their reality as a means of evaluating the theoretical tenets of Marxism for themselves. They did not believe that historical laws as inevitable conditions fixed the pattern of events or prescribed their course of action.

Similarly, the activity of the East European critical Marxists was a reaction to changing circumstances in the world, as well as to the ossification of Marxist theory. These thinkers also set out to reevaluate "givens" in their world and to remain open to a variety of intellectual approaches. They also did not approach Marxism as a faith demanding belief. Although most were wholeheartedly for the development of socialism in the early stages after the war, they never divorced their support of Marxism from their critical thinking. For them, as for their intellectual predecessors, this propensity for individual thought was what most threatened the ideological unity so prized by their contemporaries. They initially may have been sympathetic in some sense to the Soviet experiment, but they were also sharply critical of its shortcomings. By virtue of their questioning, the immanent critique of Marxist theory that had begun earlier in Western Europe was now continued in an East European context. In this sense, the East Europeans studied here were the torchbearers for the critical perspective within Marxism. They were not alone in this task—they shared it with some West Europeans, most notably the "Frankfurt School"—but they were the primary figures in this undertaking. It is they who were concerned most explicitly and systematically with reviving Marx's critical outlook and further developing it in light of contemporary circumstances.

Within each of the three countries covered so far in this study—Poland, Hungary, and Czechoslovakia—it has been possible to see the fundamental unity of purpose and orientation that characterized the work of the individuals involved. This unity was based on their shared commitment to rediscovering the humanist content in

Marx, despite the fact that each thinker went about it in his or her own way. In fact, this unity is all the more striking precisely because of the individual variations on the theme.

Just as within each of the countries there existed a unity in diversity among different thinkers, so there was an underlying unity among the theorists from different countries. Marxist humanism and its critique of Stalinism developed differently in each country; the starting time and the rate of development differed from one country to another. Although the Polish, Czech, and Hungarian cases were similar in their broad historical outlines, the Yugoslavs had a radically different political history following the break with the Soviet Union. Still, a conceptual unity emerged from the activity of all of these individuals, in four different countries, a unity that at first glance might seem astonishing.

The reader will have noted the presence of similarities and the existence of some conceptual overlap among the representatives of different countries. What may not always be clear is that these points of convergence were neither accidental nor planned; they sprang from a shared conceptual framework that informed the activity of all of these thinkers. This common conceptual framework was the commitment to a critical reappraisal of Marxism that sought to rediscover and emphasize the radically humanist context in Marx's work. The impetus for this reconstruction of Marxist theory was the reaction to Stalinism—both the political system and its legitimizing ideology.

Given that critical intellectuals in Poland, Hungary, and Czechoslovakia shared a broadly similar background and context, it is not too surprising that they should evince many conceptual similarities. Nevertheless, each country's experience differed enough from the others that this theoretical overlap should not be viewed as being a matter of course. What is more difficult to account for is the degree to which the Yugoslavs share in this conceptual unity, as on the surface their experience was quite different from that of the rest of Eastern Europe.

Although superficially quite different, the Yugoslavs in fact shared a great deal in common with their counterparts in the rest of Eastern Europe. The apparent differences spring from the obvious: Yugoslavia was not part of the Soviet bloc. Even prior to the break in 1948, the Yugoslav communists had their own power base as a result of the Partisan war against the Germans. They were neither beholden to nor dependent on the Soviet Union or the Red Army for their position; instead, they enjoyed broad legitimacy with the population. In fact, the major cause of the eventual split was the Yugoslav assertion of their equality with the Soviet Union, both in doctrinal matters and in domestic political life.

The split between Stalin and Tito in 1948 only confirmed Yugoslavia's separateness, even though the Yugoslavs themselves were for a time convinced that only a tragic misunderstanding was taking place. This conviction on the part of the Yugoslavs provides a key for understanding some of the underlying similarity between the Yugoslav experience and that of the rest of Eastern Europe. The reason the Yugoslavs were so convinced that some terrible misunderstanding was at the root of the split was because they were not trying to be different. If anything, they were trying to be more Stalinist than Stalin, which was their real sin. Still, at the time of the break, Yugoslavia had very much a Stalinist system, which the Yugoslavs only later tried to change when they began to search for a counterclaim to ideological legitimacy against the Soviets.

At the time of the break, some of the Yugoslav thinkers who later were to be identified with the Marxist humanist orientation centered in the journal *Praxis* were completing their studies in philosophy, but they had come to have doubts about Stalinist ideology even before that time.[1] It was to them that the major work of providing ideological justification for the Yugoslav position was to fall:

> What was needed in the realm of theory was not simply a superficial critique of the more grotesque aspects of the Soviet experience, but a clear and complete alternative to the Stalinist philosophical system. . . . This was a task for which the new regime's ideologists . . . were not prepared. Thus it fell to a small but dynamic group of young university philosophers to return to the Marxist classics in search of a new theoretical framework, to which they found the key in the only recently discovered writings of the young Marx. But in so doing they laid the foundations for a conflict between politics and philosophy that would erupt into the open only a decade later.[2]

In Yugoslavia these young philosopers found themselves engaged in a two-pronged critique of Stalinism very similar to that carried out by critical thinkers elsewhere in Eastern Europe. The first part involved a critique of the Stalinist political system, which was characterized as a system of bureaucracy. This critique began earlier in Yugoslavia than in other parts of Eastern Europe; in Yugoslavia it started to take shape by the end of 1949, whereas it came into being in the other parts of Eastern Europe only after the Twentieth Soviet Party Congress and Khrushchev's speech in 1956.

The second part of the critique was in the realm of philosophy; in Yugoslavia, as elsewhere, the prevailing Marxist approach came under attack. Although this approach was sometimes referred to as Marxism-Leninism, its central features could be subsumed under the headings "dialectical materialism" and "historical materialism." In Yugoslavia the critique of the Stalinist political system was encouraged, whereas in much of the rest of Eastern Europe it was more tolerated than encouraged. The critique of dialectical and historical materialism was encouraged in Yugoslavia only to the extent that the thrust of the criticism was directed against the Soviets; the irony of the situation was that this philosophy continued to dominate at the same time it was being criticized in the Soviets. In the rest of Eastern Europe, any philosophical critique of Stalinism that developed had to fight a long battle, whereas the Yugoslav critics of Stalinist philosophy scored a dramatic breakthrough as early as 1960.[3]

Another parallel between the Yugoslav experience and that of the other East European countries also contributed to the similarities in the humanist critique of Stalinism. This parallel was the consequence of yet another irony of the Yugoslav situation. The Yugoslavs developed a critique of the Stalinist political system and instituted far-reaching reforms designed to transform the Yugoslav political reality away from the Soviet model. These reforms were, first, the institution of workers' self-management in 1950 and, second, the restructuring of the Communist Party into the League of Communists in 1952.[4] The irony lay in the fact that, in both cases, the reforms were imposed from above, and vestiges of the old, Stalinist way of doing things still remained. This tension has remained with Yugoslavia to the present in some respects. The parallel was that the Yugoslav critical thinkers set about trying to eliminate the vestiges of Stalinism from their society just as their counterparts were doing elsewhere in Eastern Europe.

The critique of the Stalinist political system and its ideology was common to the critical thinkers from all four countries. Beyond that, however, lay the fundamental source of their unity, the "return to the Marxist classics in search of a new theoretical framework." It is not only *that* they criticized Stalinism which was significant; what was most important was the *nature* of their critique and its theoretical foundations. These thinkers represented an approach that came to be known as "Marxist humanism" or "socialist humanism." It was this common approach that assured the conceptual unity that emerged from the separate activity of philosophers and sociologists in four countries over a period of many years.

The central feature of the Marxist humanist critique of Stalinism was the concept of *praxis*. Praxis referred to human creative activity as constituting human reality, in contrast with Stalinism's stress on human reality as determined by "objective laws" external to human activity. The concept of praxis was present, explicitly or implicitly, in the work of all of the thinkers who represented the Marxist humanist orientation; indeed, this was the defining characteristic for this orientation. This is not to say that every individual representing this approach used the concept identically, but the basic outlines were the same in all cases.

The use of the term *praxis* most often brings to mind the group of Yugoslav theorists who gathered around the journal of that name from 1964 onwards, and it was their activity that probably brought the most outside recognition to Eastern European Marxist humanism. Several of their theorists expressed the sense of the term well, and it would be instructive to see how their use of the concept compares with that of some other figures from other countries.

The best single statement from the *Praxis* group on the nature of praxis comes from Predrag Vranicki:

> We see man as *par excellence*, a being of practice, a being who freely and consciously transforms his own life. . . . Man exists and develops only by transforming his natural and social reality and . . . in this way he transforms himself also.[5]

Gajo Petrović develops the concept more fully in his essay, "Marx's Concept of Man." In trying to come to grips with how Marx defined what it is to be human, Petrović writes: "Therefore, what makes a man man is . . . his whole way of Being, the general structure of his relationship toward the world and toward himself. This way of Being, which is peculiar to man, Marx designates by the word *praxis*." He goes on to further define the term as "universal-creative self-creative activity, activity by which man transforms and creates his world and

himself."⁶ This activity is what defines what it is to be
human; in it, man realizes what Marx called his "species being."

Several other characteristics follow from this understanding of praxis, according to Petrović. First, he says
that to define praxis as universal-creative, self-creative
activity means to define it as free, conscious activity.
This in turn is to understand man as a social history, for
"if man is a creative self-creative being that constantly
creates and changes himself and his world, he is necessarily not always the same." Therefore, only man has a
history. "Furthermore, if this activity is what makes man
human, then it can never be stopped if he is to continue
to be human."⁷ Man is man if he realizes his historically
created human possibilities, according to this view, but
what if he does not realize these possibilities? This is
where Marx's concept of alienation ties in with his concept of praxis; alienation is what prevents, or interferes
with this self-realization.

The concept of praxis was also developed explicitly by
Kosík in his *Dialectics of the Concrete*. He writes about
praxis in a way very close to that of Petrović:

> *praxis* is the sphere of human being . . . [It is] the exposure of
> the mystery of man as an onto-formative being, as a being
> that *forms* the (socio-human) reality and *therefore* also
> grasps and interprets it (i.e., reality both human and extra-
> human, reality, in its totality) . . . *praxis* is active and self-
> producing in history . . . since the socio-human reality is
> *formed* by *praxis*, history becomes a practical happening
> in which what is human is distinguished from what is
> inhuman.⁸

Praxis is for Kosík also the central category, as was
seen in the earlier analysis of Marxist humanism in
Czechoslovakia.

These are some examples of how praxis was developed
as a key concept in Marxist humanism. Of the Hungarians, Márkus developed it most in his discussion of human essence and history, but it is also present in Heller's

treatment of value and need. The concept also figures throughout the writings of the Polish thinkers, especially Baczko, Kołakowski and Bauman.

As was seen in Petrović and Kosík, praxis as human self-creative activity is closely linked to a normative understanding of "human essence," or "human nature." This means that praxis "refers to good or ideal human activity and presupposes that this activity is good or best precisely because it realizes in action one's best latent and actual dispositions."[9] Implicit in this is the claim that certain human dispositions are optimal. From this also comes the basis for social theory. "A good society is . . . a *praxis* society; a society whose basic structure and institutions (a) maximally exemplify social principles derived from the norm of *praxis*, and (b) maximally promote lived *praxis*."[10] This link was developed most fully by Márkus in his work *Marxism and Anthropology: The Concept of "Human Essence" in the Philosophy of Marx*, but it is present to one extent or another in the writings of all of the theorists.[11] Heller discusses it at length in her works on value and need.

The concepts of praxis and human essence together form the core of the humanist Marxism that grew up in Eastern Europe. It is on these two concepts (or this dual concept) that the entire humanist approach rests. Other categories developed in this orientation are linked conceptually to the above and, taken together, they constitute a well-rounded and well-developed vision of human reality. Based on this normative understanding of what human reality is in its essence, it becomes possible to hold up to scrutiny any given social reality. The critique of Stalinism was only the beginning of this endeavor; when that was accomplished, the critique expanded to include both the Stalinist legacy in Eastern Europe and the capitalist system of the West.

Two other concepts featured prominently in the works of the Marxist humanist theorists: "need," in the sense of "authentic" or "human" needs; and "alienation." The concept of authentic human needs was developed most fully by Ágnes Heller. She termed them "radical needs" and devoted an entire book to examining Marx's use of the concept. The concept of need was also used extensively by Baczko. He saw clearly the way in which this concept was integrally linked to that of praxis. As he put it succinctly:

> In [Marx's] understanding of the "plenitude of human need" and the "wealth of needs," the idea of the universality of man is joined in Marx with the *Faustian idea of man* as a being never content, a being for whom self-realization is an unending process, a being who constantly transcends himself and continuously creates his own new and as yet unfulfilled possibilities.[12]

The concept of "alienation" was a two-edged sword. It carried within it both the understanding of how a given social reality prevented the full realization of human possibilities, and the vision of what "de-alienation" would look like. Once an awareness had been developed as to what in a given setting was alienating—based on an analysis of the concrete structures of a society—it became possible to formulate specific steps by which the situation could be overcome. This analysis led many of the Marxist humanists to progress from a philosophical critique of orthodox ideology to addressing social and political issues in their own societies. In Poland, this progression was particularly evident in the works of Hochfeld and Bauman (although not limited to them, as Baczko used his study of Rousseau to examine the concept thoroughly). The theoretical "discovery" of the possibility of alienation in socialist societies played an important role in the ferment in Czechoslovakia in the 1960s, but it was in Yugoslavia that "alienation" was used most extensively.

Taken together, need and alienation led to another theme that was very important to all of these thinkers—that of "community." Humans have a need for other humans, for human relationships, and one characteristic of modern societies is that people are alienated from each other (and from themselves). Hence it becomes very important for some sense of authentic community to be restored. The problems of the nature of authentic community and of possible ways in which to (re)establish such a community figured prominently in the work of Baczko (particularly in his study of Rousseau), Heller, and various members of the *Praxis* group.[13]

The discussion of the problem of community was linked closely in the writings of the *Praxis* group to the critique of political alienation. Their examination of this topic led them to the most far-reaching political analysis of any of the Eastern Europeans.[14] This circumstance is traceable due largely to the specific conditions present in Yugoslavia. Several philosophers who were later to form the nucleus of the *Praxis* group were very active in redefining Yugoslav socialism following the Cominform break, and the central feature of this new definition was socialist self-management. In Yugoslav political life, the reality of self-management never equaled even its official theoretical dimensions, but these dimensions themselves were not accepted as final by the *Praxis* theorists. They continued to grapple with the idea of self-management long after its incorporation into the official political lexicon, and the more they developed the theme conceptually, the more acute became their critique of the Yugoslav reality. This critique finally led to the eruption of conflict between them and the authorities. Ironically, Yugoslavia attracted world attention to its experiment in "self-managing socialism" largely because of the theoretical activity of the *Praxis* group in exploring self-management, but it is these same theorists who were so much a thorn in the side of the political establishment.

Several other themes were linked to each other and to the central themes of praxis and human essence. These themes, which were explored by various theorists, were history, totality, and rationality. *History* was very important, as was seen in the discussion of the concept of praxis earlier. History is the context for praxis—there could be no praxis without the historical continuum of past to future. *Totality* refers to the comprehensive approach to the study of reality, in which individual facts are understood as part of a context, a larger whole. It is a holistic approach to reality and is closely tied to the use of the dialectic to show the development of a reality over time through its own internal dynamic. Kosík devoted the most space to an exposition of the themes of history and totality, but others also looked at them, particularly some of the *Praxis* group.[15]

The concept of *rationality* was one to which considerable attention was given by Kosík especially, but it also featured in the work of Mihailo Marković, for example. The main focus was on the contrast between technical or "instrumental" reason and a more comprehensive understanding of rationality as a dimension of human activity.[16] The discussion of rationality was linked especially to that of totality, but it constituted a part of the critique of alienated political reality as well.

It can be seen from the above discussion that the core themes of Marxist humanism were held in common by all of the Eastern Europe thinkers examined in this study. Different thinkers focused more intensely on certain concepts, but all relied on the shared framework. They all returned to a reexamination of Marx's works, particularly to the newly discovered works of the "young Marx." They shared the conviction, however, that it was impossible to somehow draw a distinction between the "young Marx" and the "mature Marx," as was done by those of a more orthodox persuasion.

Given the emphasis on the humanist nature of Marx's thought, it could be expected that the thinking of these individuals should develop along similar lines and use the same conceptual framework. Any inquiry into the humanist categories in Marx would discover that Marx stressed certain key concepts that, when followed through, would yield similar results in analysis. Still, it is important to stress yet again that the thinkers from the four Eastern European countries represented here arrived at similar conclusions on the basis of an independent reappraisal of Marx's thought. Not only was the activity of each group or grouping of thinkers carried on largely independently of one another, in many cases the same held true of individuals within a given country. Taken together, their work forms a mosaic, a comprehensive pattern composed of variations on an overall theme of Marxist humanism. This work was not simply an explication of Marx's thought but rather a further development of it in light of the specific circumstances faced in each country.

So far, the activity of the Eastern European Marxist humanists has been characterized primarily in terms of their theoretical undertakings. This picture, while necessary, is somewhat one-sided if it conveys the impression that they were involved *only* in thinking or that their thought was somehow separated from the reality surrounding them. Nothing could be further from the truth. Their theoretical activity was labeled revisionism and was very much a political event in and of itself. Their activity was political in another sense also. Aside from the fact that *any* activity that did not support the Party's position at any given moment was suspect, every facet of life was politicized in Eastern European societies. This situation also contributed to the underlying similarity among the different areas.

In addition, all of the Marxist humanists were actively engaged in efforts to reform and change their society. They initially were involved in the attempt to create more leeway for philosophical endeavors free of Party control and the necessity of engaging in apologetics for Party policy. This fight for the autonomy of thought in "professional" philosophy expanded to include demands for the autonomy of *all* cultural life. This battle raged for many years, sometimes more intensively than at other times, with varying results. Although the most visible achievements in this struggle were found in Czechoslovakia in the 1960s, culminating in the "Prague Spring" of 1968, the efforts of these intellectuals had an impact elsewhere as well.

It has been stressed here that the Marxist-humanist intellectuals arrived at their positions independently of one another. This holds true for all of them to one degree or another, but the assertion should be qualified to give a more rounded picture. First, none of them worked in a vacuum—each lived in a specific historical context. This meant that as they went about their work they had certain objectives in mind and were aware of those involved in similar undertakings.

In some cases, as mentioned earlier, there were distinct groups, which had regular contact and dialog. In the case of Hungary, those associated with the Budapest School met often to exchange ideas and were also involved in dialog with Lukács. This latter dialog was important to them, both for shaping their ideas and for presenting them with the opportunity to define their position in relation to his.

In the case of the Yugoslavs, many of the critical intellectuals had been working together since the early 1950s and the experience of founding the journal *Pogledi*.[17] Although this experiment was short-lived, it taught them a great deal and, more important, it cemented the bonds among them. As a result, after their 1960 defeat of the orthodox Marxist position in philosophy, they were ready for a new undertaking. The founding of a new journal, *Praxis*, was very important for giving them an outlet, and even more important for bringing them together to discuss issues.

In this latter regard the Yugoslavs were singularly fortunate in being able to institutionalize their encounters in the Korčula Summer School, which met yearly from 1963 through 1973. Here they were able not only to get together among themselves but also to create an international institution, in which intellectuals from other parts of Eastern Europe and from Western Europe were able to participate. Korčula became a symbol for the creative interchange of ideas among the different participants. In 1968, those present signed documents critical of the Soviet invasion of Czechoslovakia, and they addressed telegrams to Tito and Kádar (the latter from the Hungarian group, led by Ágnes Heller).[18]

Although the Korčula Summer School was very significant for the chance it gave Eastern and Western European critical Marxist thinkers to interact with one another, by the time this possibility occurred their basic positions had already been established. For this reason it is possible to assert that the East Europeans developed their positions independently of one another and of the Western Europeans, even though in later years interaction among the different areas became more common.

The End of Philosophical Revisionism in Eastern Europe

Philosophical revisionism in Eastern Europe was in one sense a transitory phenomenon. By the end of 1968 it had for all practical purposes come to an end in Poland and Czechoslovakia, with many of its leading figures from these countries leaving for exile at about this time. In Hungary, because of different circumstances due in part to Kádar's policies, it lasted until 1977, when most of its adherents there also went into exile. Only the case of Yugoslavia diverges from this pattern, and even there it could be argued that the divergence was only apparent.

The journal *Praxis* was closed in February 1975, and eight of the Belgrade members of the group were suspended from their teaching posts at Belgrade University in January 1975. From then until December 1980 they were engaged in attempts to get reinstated. In December 1980 they were dismissed formally, but in 1981 they were employed in research positions in the newly created Center for Philosophy and Social Theory within the Institute of Social Sciences at the University of Belgrade. The *Praxis* group—or at least some members of it—were involved in the publication of a new international edition of *Praxis* in 1981, in the tradition of the earlier International edition. The question raised by the events, however, is whether the activities after 1975 should be viewed in the same light as those prior to that time. Although the Zagreb contingent did not suffer the repressive measures undergone by the "Belgrade Eight," it can be argued that the closing of *Praxis* signified the end of an era. With the loss of their journal, the *Praxis* group lost the only major outlet left to them for expressing their ideas publicly, but even more, it had a dramatic impact on their identity. The observation was made in reference to them that "the specific form which dissident thinking assumes in a given historical instance may have a profound impact on its ability to persuade others and sustain itself."[19] In the case of the *Praxis* group, the loss of the journal does seem to have influenced the ongoing activity of the group and their impact on the Yugoslav scene.

Another aspect of the transitory nature of philosophical revisionism is separate from the question of repression and exile, and it is this second dimension that also has some bearing on the case of the *Praxis* group. This second dimension of the fate of philosophical revisionism relates to the death of Marxism as a serious medium for discourse in most of Eastern Europe. Prior to 1989, it might have seemed paradoxical to make an assertion about the demise of Marxism in Eastern Europe when one could hear Marxist terminology used in official pronouncements on a regular basis. This fact only reinforces the point, however. It was only in official ideological language that Marxist terms were employed, and not even those uttering the sounds took their content seriously any more. Kołakowski writes in his history of Marxist thought that:

revisionism could be effective only as long as the party took the traditional ideology seriously and the apparatus was in some degree sensitive to ideological questions. But revisionism itself was a major cause of the fact that the Party lost its respect for official doctrine and that ideology increasingly became a sterile though indispensable ritual.[20]

After the changes of 1989, Marxist terminology ceased to be heard even in official pronouncements. Marxism had been so discredited in the popular mind that any kind of Marxist discourse had become suspect. Consequently, no government official would now dream of employing these categories, even though many of the former dissidents now in positions of governmental authority had originally been influenced to one degree or another by critical Marxist thinking. That revisionism was a "major cause" of the breakdown of the official ideology is open to dispute. It certainly played a role, but it seems more likely that, in light of the everyday reality that the Eastern European populace experienced, the ideological pronouncements came to sound increasingly hollow. Philosophical revisionism was, however—as Kołakowski himself pointed out—a victim of the phenomenon as well, whether or not it alone undercut its position by virtue of its critique. Even among the "revisionists" themselves a wide variety of responses to Marxism has emerged: some, like Kołakowski, reject Marxism altogether; others, like Stojanović, speak in terms of some kind of "post-Marxism." Kosík, on the other hand, remains much closer to the critical Marxist thought that he formulated in the 1960s.

Philosophical revisionism no longer exists in Eastern Europe. As a historical phenomenon in this region it played a dramatic role, and it was very influential on the course of events there. Like all historical phenomena, it had a dual nature. On the one hand, it had its day and then receded into the category of things past, partly because of official repression. On the other, it left its legacy on subsequent events there, and on the intellectual hori-

zons of contemporary life in general.[21] One example of
this legacy was the relationship of events in Poland associated with the Solidarity movement in 1980–81 to the
themes of work-place democratization explored by Hochfeld, Bauman, and Hirszowicz. Their discussion of this issue was related in turn to the first, tentative attempts at
founding workers' councils in Poland in 1956. Another
example can be found in Czechoslovakia. The Charter 77
movement there carried on the attempts to create a more
human and rational social order which had been so much
a part of the 1960s and the Prague Spring.

Perhaps the best example of the legacy of revisionism,
however, was found in Yugoslavia. This legacy was the
entire concept of self-management for which Yugoslavia
became famous. The *Praxis* thinkers played a large role in
the initial formulation of this concept, and their critique
of its application in the Yugoslav context served to further develop the concept and influence the reality. Their
defense of a critique of Yugoslav society independent of
the party line certainly left its mark. It won for them as
individuals partial reinstatement to academic posts in
1981 (in the case of the Belgrade professors), but, more important, it seemed to have an effect on the willingness of
the political leadership to tolerate such criticism. The
most important impact of the *Praxis* group cannot as yet
be measured. It combines the legacy of past activities
with the ongoing efforts of the group members. From the
perspective of 1992, however, it seems clear that, although individual members of the group still retain some
of this former influence and still play an active part in
Yugoslav life, there is no such thing as a *Praxis* group any
more, per se; the former members of the group have all
gone their own way.

In writing on the "timelessness" of a work of art,
Kosík observed that "the work's life is not a result of its
autonomous existence, but of the mutual interaction of
the work and mankind."[22] In the same way, it can be said
of the Marxist humanists in Eastern Europe that their

work lives on because of this mutual interaction. The questions they raised and the themes they worked through have had a tremendous impact on the development of Marxist thought; they were indeed among the principle torchbearers of the critical tradition in Marxism. Especially as more of their work becomes accessible in other languages, their impact will continue to be felt.

One of the historical ironies of Eastern Europe is that the adherents of the official ideology, after fighting revisionism for so long, tried to co-opt the movement by adapting its language to fit their use. This attempt met with more success among foreign onlookers than it did at home.[23] That the attempt was made is testimony to the extent of the influence that philosophical revisionism had on intellectual life in postwar Eastern Europe. The varieties of Marxist humanism that grew up there left their mark, and the depth of the imprint has yet to be finally determined.

Notes

Bibliography

Index

NOTES

Introduction: The East European Context

A combination of the Introduction and Conclusion to this study appeared previously as an article entitled "East-European Marxist Humanism," in *Praxis International* (Oxford) 3, no. 3 (October 1983).

1. Gerson Sher, *Praxis: Marxist Criticism and Dissent in Socialist Yugoslavia* (Bloomington: Indiana University Press, 1977) pp. 10, 20–21.

2. The only possible exception here would be the case of East Germany, where the work of Rudolf Bahro, *Die Alternative: zur kritik des realexistierenden Sozialismus,* Frankfurt: Europäische Verlagsanstalt, 1977 (English version, *The Alternative in Eastern Europe,* London: NLB Press, 1978) and others has been quite critical of the political reality. This German critique does not fall within the purview of the present study, however, because it was not developed from the perspective of Marxist humanism.

3. The label was applied to Bernstein following the publication in 1899 of his book, *Evolutionary Socialism* [German title: Die Voraussetzungen des Sozialismus und die Aufgaben der Sozialdemokratie] (New York: Schocken Books, 1901). The book was meant to clarify some thoughts that he had first put forward from 1886 in a series of articles entitled "Problems of Socialism" in a periodical of the German Social Democratic Party,

Die Neue Zeit. The book had a powerful impact on the socialist movement of the day—particularly within the German Social Democratic party—because Bernstein called into question several fundamental tenets of Marxist doctrine as it had been understood up until that time. First, and most important, he disputed Marx's contention that the working class was becoming ever more impoverished, which was to lead the working class to a spontaneous revolution when the situation became unbearable. Bernstein emphasized the democratic character of socialism and attacked the concept of dictatorship by a revolutionary, avant-garde party. He also attacked the idea that the whole aim of the socialist movement was to achieve some final goal—without regard to how it reached that goal. He stressed, rather, that gradual reform of socioeconomic and political conditions was the task of the socialist movement, leading to greater democracy and a more equitable society. Even though much of what Bernstein had to say was only an expression of the reality of the German Social-Democratic party, which preached revolution and practiced reform, for Bernstein to give voice to this was equivalent to pointing out the fiction of the emperor's new clothes. It stirred up a hornet's nest of debate, the echoes of which can still be heard.

4. Sher, p. xiii.

5. See: J. M. Bochenski, "The Great Split," *Studies in Soviet Thought* 8 (March 1968): pp. 1–15.

6. Although a comprehensive treatment of the phenomenon of Marxist humanism in Eastern Europe calls for the inclusion of Yugoslavia and the *Praxis* group, they will not be given a comprehensive section of their own here because they have been the subject of two very good studies that, between them, cover the ground thoroughly. The first is Sher's work noted above; the other is David Crocker's *Praxis and Democratic Socialism: The Critical Social Theory of Marković and Stojanović* (Sussex: Harvester Press, 1983). A portion of this work forms the basis for an essay by Crocker in John Burke, et al., *Marxism and the Good Society* (London: Cambridge University Press, 1981). The decision not to devote a separate section solely to the *Praxis* group does not mean, however, that they are not included. They are examined in the concluding chapter as part of the comparative analysis of all four varieties of Marxist humanism.

Chapter 1: Polish Revisionism: Critical Thinking in
Poland from 1953 to 1968

1. Z. Brzezinski, *The Soviet Bloc* (Cambridge, Mass.: Harvard University Press, 1967), p. 243. See also Witold Jedlicki, *Klub krzywego koła* (Paris: Instytut Literacki, 1963); *Tygodnik powszechny*, Oct. 13, 1957, has an account of the "Club of the Flaming Tomato" in Kraków.

2. Brzezinski, p. 244.

3. R. M. Fernandes, "Antinomies of Freedom: On the Warsaw Circle of Intellectual History," Ph.D. dissertation from Columbia University, 1976, pp. 144–45. See also p. 209, notes 8 and 12. Fernandes has very good notes, which cover many facets of the discussion going on in Poland around 1956 and later, and a comprehensive bibliography.

4. Leszek Kołakowski, *Światopogląd i życie codzienne* (Warsaw: PIW, 1957), p. 5.

5. Zbigniew Jordan, "Rewizjonizm Polski (dok.)," *Kultura* (Paris) 1, 171 (Jan.–Feb. 1962), p. 40. A German version of this article is: "Der philosophische Hintergrund des Revisionismus in Polen," in *Hinter dem eisernen Vorhang* 8, 1962, nr. 7/8, nr. 9.

6. Ibid.

7. Several of these are: Fernandes, "Antinomies of Freedom"; Gesine Schwann, *Leszek Kołakowski: Eine marxistische Philosophie der Freiheit* (Stuttgart: Verlag W. Kohlammer, 1971), originally a Ph.D dissertation at Freie Universität in Berlin; "A Leszek Kołakowski Reader," *Triquarterly* 22 (Fall 1971). Schwann has a good chronological bibliography that is helpful for tracing the development of Kołakowski's thought.

8. "Zwolnieni ze stanowisk na Uniwersytecie Warszawskim," *Trybuna ludu*, March 26, 1968, pp. 1, 4.

9. Fernandes, p. 3; Kroński's major piece of writing is *Rozważania wokół Hegla* (Warsaw: PWN, 1960), published posthumously as a collection of his essays. For a comprehensive review of Kroński's life and work, see the chapter on him in Fernandes's dissertation.

10. In his preface to *Zarys marksistowskiej teorii społeczeństwa* (Warsaw: PWN, 1964), Bauman states, "My theoretical views were formed under the influence of Prof. Julian Hochfeld, to whose inspiration and criticism, broad intellectual horizons, and eternal creative unrest in large measure I owe

198   *Notes to Pages 19–23*

their present form." In addition, Bauman draws heavily on Hochfeld throughout the book, quoting from him extensively. As to the way in which Hochfeld oriented Bauman (and Hirszowicz) to the practical study of society, Bauman stated, in a letter to this author, that: "it was Hochfeld who suggested to us that the humanist potential of Marxism can be developed by the study of the socio-political structure rather than by philosophical anthropology—the suggestion we followed." Hochfeld wrote an article on the *Sejm:* "Z zagadnien parlamentaryzmu," *Nowe drogi* 4 (April), 1957. For an account of this activity, see Maurice D. Simon and Roger E. Kanet, eds., *Background to Crisis: Policy and Politics in Gierek's Poland* (Boulder, Colo.: Westview Press, 1981), p. 29.

11. See Fernandes, p. 210 (note 15), for an account of this attempt. See also Hochfeld's article, "Rewizje i tradicje," in *Przegląd kulturalny* 11, no. 17 (April 1957).

12. Cf. Zygmunt Bauman, "Traktat o biurokracji," *Twórczość* 9 (1957). Cf. also Sher, *Praxis: Marxist Criticism and Dissent in Socialist Yugoslavia,* p. 136ff. The critique played a large role in Czechoslovakia in the 1960s.

13. Bauman, "Traktat o biurokracji." Cf. Bronisław Baczko on this in "O stylu filozofowania," *Myśl filozoficzna* 4 (24), 1956, note 12.

14. Bauman, "Traktat o biurokracji," p. 103.

15. Ibid., p. 117.

16. See Fernandes, p. 209, note 12, for a list of those taking part in the debate and the specific articles where it was aired.

17. Baczko, "O stylu filozofowania," p. 13.

18. Ibid., p. 8.

19. Bauman, "O przezwyciężenie dezintegracji filozofii marksistowskiej," *Myśl filozoficzna* 6 (26), 1956. Cf. Baczko, "O stylu filozofowania," and Kołakowski, "Światopogląd i krytyka," "Światopogląd i edukacja." See Fernandes, p. 209, note 12, for a list of the contributors.

20. Ibid., p. 134.

21. Jerzy K. Wiatr and Zygmunt Bauman, "Marksizm i socjologia współczesna," *Myśl filozoficzna* 1, 1957.

22. Ibid., p. 3, footnote 1.

23. Ibid., p. 6. When Wiatr and Bauman speak of the ideal, where the "ideology" of the proletariat becomes "science," they depart from their definition of ideology as a "deformed reflec-

tion" of reality; even though they qualify the term in the new context, they seem to be shifting definitions. The "ideology" of the proletariat is conceived of here in two mutually conflicting senses.
24. Ibid.
25. Ibid., pp. 7–8. "Doublethinking" appears in English in the Polish text.
26. Ibid., p. 10. Cf. Zbigniew A. Jordan, *Philosophy and Ideology* (Dordrecht: Reidel, 1963), pp. 246–49 for a brief discussion of sociology in Poland during those years.
27. Ibid., p. 19. Later, on the same page, Kołakowski is quoted approvingly with his now famous lines from "Intellectuals and the Communist Movement" that the party needs intellectuals to ensure that its decisions are wise, not to marvel at the wiseness of its decisions. (*Towards a Marxist Humanism* [New York: Grove Press, 1968] p. 171; Polish original in *Nowe drogi* 9 [87], 1956, p. 31).
28. L. Kołakowski, "Permanent vs. Transitory Aspects of Marxism," in *Towards a Marxist Humanism*; Polish original is "Aktualne i nieaktualne pojęcie marksizmu," *Nowa kultura* 4, 1957. This is taken up in the Wiatr/Bauman essay on page 17; also, later, Bauman comes back to this issue in "Modern Times, Modern Marxism," *Social Research* 3, 34 (Autumn 1967), p. 409ff.
29. E. V. Kas'ianova, "Marksizm li eto," *Voprosy filosofii* 4, 1957. See *Polytika* 33, 1957, for Wiatr's rebuttal. Cf. here Ivan Sviták, "The Art of Philosophy," in *Man and His World: A Marxian View.*
30. Maria Hirszowicz, "Ideologia i nauka," *Myśl filozoficzna* 6, 1956, p. 23. Cf. here her article "Problemy interpretacji Marksa," *Studia filozoficzne* 3 (1959): 3–28.
31. Hirszowicz, *Konfrontacje socjologiczne: Marksizm i socjologia współczesna* (Warsaw: Książka i Wiedza, 1964), p. 77.
32. Ibid., p. 120. Cf. Kosík's discussion of the "economic factor" and "care" in *Dialectics of the Concrete*. Translated by Karel Kovanda with James Schmidt. Boston Studies in the Philosophy of Science, vol. 52; Synthese Library, vol. 106. Dordrecht/Boston: D. Reidel, 1976.
33. Cf. Kołakowski's essay in *Triquarterly* 22 on "The Epistemological Significance of the Aetiology of Knowledge."
34. Hirszowicz, *Konfrontacje socjologiczne*, p. 361.

35. Ibid., pp. 361–62. (See note 22).

36. Cf. Ágnes Heller's "Towards a Marxist Theory of Value."

37. Leszek Kołakowski, "Światopogląd i krytyka," in Światopogląd i życie codzienne (Warsaw: Panstwowy Instytut Wydawniczy, 1957), p. 65. Originally published in Nowa kultura 3, 1955.

38. Ibid., 68.

39. Kołakowski, "Wizjonerstwo i dogmatyzm." Originally published in Przegląd kulturalny 43, 1955.

40. Kołakowski, "Światopogląd i edukacja," in Światopogląd i życie codzienne, p. 30. Originally published in Przegląd kulturalny 11, 1956.

41. Ibid., p. 48.

42. B. Baczko, "Hegel, Marks, i problemy alienacji," Studia filozoficzne 1, 1957, p. 56.

43. B. Baczko, "Kryptoproblemy i historyzm," Studia filozoficzne 3 (6), 1958, p. 76.

44. Ibid., p. 78.

45. Ibid., p. 85.

46. Ibid., p. 92.

47. Ibid.

48. Hirszowicz, Konfrontacje socjologiczne, p. 77.

49. The book Wizje ludzkiego świata was devoted to an analysis of many of the modern currents of sociology through an examination of representative figures.

50. Bauman, Zarys marksistowskiej teorii społezceństwa, p. 494.

51. Z. Bauman, "O potrzebie socjologii partii," Myśl filozoficzna 2 (28), 1957.

52. Ibid., p. 6.

53. Ibid., p. 22. Cf. Julian Hochfeld, "Marksizm i sociologia stosunków polityczynch," Studia sociologiczne-polityczne 1, 1958.

54. Bauman, "Vilfredo Pareto i teoria elit," Myśl filozoficzna 3, 1957. That Bauman should have been aware of and used Pareto in the Poland of 1957 is significant in itself.

55. Ibid., p. 32.

56. Ibid., p. 33.

57. Fernandes, pp. 227–28. See also his note 3, p. 295, where he says that one of the first examples of this "double edge" was found in the essay, "Catholicism and Humanism," Po Prostu 3, 1956, reprinted in Światopogląd i życie codzienne, (Warsaw: PWN, 1957).

58. Fernandes, p. 230.

59. Ibid.

60. In Polish, *Świadomość religijna i więź kościelna*, (Warsaw: PWN, 1965); translated into French as *Chrétiens sans eglise*, (Paris: Gallimard, 1969).

61. Fernandes, p. 253.

62. Kołakowski, *Świadomość religijna i więż kościelna*, p. 52.

63. Ibid., p. 51.

64. Ibid., p. 100.

65. Ibid., p. 237.

66. Ibid., p. 100.

67. Fernandes, p. 245.

68. Kołakowski, "Istota i istnenie w pojęciu wolności," in *Światopogląd i życie codzienne*. Also in German as "Marxismus und personalistischer Freiheitsbegriff," in *Das Problem der Freiheit im Lichte des Wissenschaftlichen Sozialismus*, Konferenz der Sektion Philosophie der Deutschen Akademie der Wissenschaft zu Berlin, 1–10 März, 1956. Protokoll. (East Berlin, 1956).

69. Kołakowski, "Istota i istnenie w pojęciu wolności," p. 106 (p. 155 in the German).

70. Ibid., pp. 110–11 (p. 158 in the German).

71. Ibid., p. 114 (p. 160 in the German). Cf. here Mihály Vajda, "Law, Ethics, Interest," *Telos* 34 (Winter 1977/78).

72. Ibid., p. 122. (p. 165 in the German).

73. Ibid., p. 124ff. (p. 166ff in the German). Cf. Ágnes Heller's *Theory of Need in Marx*.

74. Kołakowski "Światopogląd i życie codzienne," in the book of the same title. Originally found in *Przegląd kulturalny* 37/38, 1956.

75. Ibid., p. 198.

76. Kołakowski, "Responsibility and History," part 3: "Conscience and Social Progress," in *Towards a Marxist Humanism*, p. 140. Polish original, "Odpowiedzialność i historia," published in *Nowa kultura* 35/37/38, 1957.

77. Kołakowski, *Świadomość religijna i więż kościelna*, p. 282.

78. Kołakowski, "Responsibility and History," part 1: "The Escapist Conspiracy," pp. 96–97.

79. Ibid., p. 108. Cf. Heller, "Towards a Marxist Theory of Value."

80. Kołakowski, "Responsibility and History," part 2: "The Opiate of the Demiurge," p. 122.

81. Kołakowski, "Responsibility and History," part 4: "History and Hope," pp. 143–144. Cf. here Heller on "valid values," in "Towards a Marxist Theory of Value."

82. Ibid., p. 155.

83. Kołakowski, "The Escapist Conspiracy," p. 99 (Emphasis in the original).

84. Kołakowski, "The Concept of the Left," in *Towards a Marxist Humanism.* Polish original in *Po prostu,* 8, 1957.

85. Fernandes, p. 243.

86. Kołakowski, "The Concept of the Left," p. 82.

87. Ibid., p. 243. See also his article "The Escapist Conspiracy," p. 96. Cf. here Vladimir Kusin's discussion on the importance of defining "models" of socialism to the Prague Spring in his chapter on philosophy in *Intellectual Origins of the Prague Spring* (Cambridge: University Press, 1971).

88. Baczko, "O stylu filozofowania," *Myśl filozoficzna* 4 (24), 1956, p. 13.

89. Ibid.

90. B. Baczko, "Hegel, Marks, i problemy alienacji," *Studia filozoficzne* 1, 1957, p. 56.

91. Ibid., p. 44.

92. Ibid., p. 52.

93. Ibid., p. 53, citing Jean Hyppolite, *Études sur Marx et Hegel* (Paris: 1956), p. 160.

94. Karl Marx, *Economic and Philosophic Manuscripts of 1844* (Moscow: Foreign Language Publishing House, 1959), p. 75, cited in B. Baczko, "Marx and the Idea of the Universality of Man," p. 188.

95. Baczko, "Marx and the Idea of the Universality of Man," p. 190. In Erich Fromm, ed., *Socialist Humanism: An International Symposium.* (Garden City, N.Y.: Doubleday and Company, 1965; Anchor Books edition, 1966).

96. Ibid., p. 189.

97. Ibid. Cf. also here Ágnes Heller, *The Theory of Need in Marx* and "Towards a Marxist Theory of Value," for a comparable analysis taken much further.

98. Ibid.

99. Baczko, *Rousseau—samotność i wspólnota,* p. 49, citing Rousseau, *Emil,* vol. 1, pp. 50–51 and vol. 2, p. 42–43 of Pol-

ish edition, published in Wrocław in 1955; and, *Rozprawa o nierówności* [Discourse on inequality], in *Trzy rozprawy z filozofii społecznej*, Warsaw, 1956, pp. 196–197, 199–202.

100. Baczko, "Marx and the Idea of the Universality of Man," p. 190, citing Marx, *Economic and Philosophical Manuscripts*, as found in Erich Fromm, *Marx's Concept of Man* (New York: Frederick Ungar Publishing Co., 1962), p. 137. (Emphasis is Baczko's.)

101. Baczko, "Marx and the Idea of the Universality of Man," p. 192.

102. Ibid., p. 193. Compare the analysis on p. 194 of the effect of alienation on individuality with that in Kosík's *Dialectics of the Concrete* under the heading of "care."

103. Baczko, *Rousseau—samotność i wspólnota*, p. 27. Compare this with Kosík's formulation of the "pseudoconcrete." Cf. also G. Márkus, *Marxism and Anthropology.*

104. Ibid., pp. 55, 56. Cf. Bauman, *Socialism: The Active Utopia*, especially chapter 1.

105. Ibid., p. 38.

106. Ibid., p. 30. Compare with Kosík's use of the concept "care."

107. Ibid., p. 31, 46, 56. Cf. Jürgen Habermas' work on the subject. A good outline can be found in chapter 4 of Thomas McCarthy's *The Critical Theory of Jürgen Habermas* (Cambridge: MIT Press, 1978), entitled "Foundations: A Theory of Communication."

108. Baczko, *Rousseau—samotność i wspólnota*, p. 127. Cf. Kosík on the role of philosophy and art in providing this "distance"; this theme is also touched on by Baczko at the end of his section on the "Antinomies of Solitude," p. 494. There is also a parallel between Kosík and Baczko on the question of the relation of a work of art to its creator and others.

109. Ibid., p. 165.

110. Ibid., p. 349.

111. Ibid., pp. 148–49

112. Ibid., p. 296. "Everyday life" is a category taken up by such Marxist thinkers as Henri LeFevre, Karel Kosík, and Ágnes Heller especially.

113. Kołakowski, "Cogito, materializm historyczny, ekspresyjna interpretacja osobowości" in *Kultura i fetysze*; originally published in *Studia socjologiczne* 3, 6 (1962): 132.

114. Ibid., p. 128. Cf. Habermas in this regard (note 54).

115. Bauman, *Socialism: The Active Utopia*, p. 43. See note 63 for reference to Baczko and Heller.

116. Baczko, *Rousseau—samotność i wspólnota*, p. 368. Cf. Heller's distinction between "Einzelwesen" and "Individuum" in her article "The Marxist Theory of Revolution and the Revolution of Everyday Life."

117. Ibid., p. 58.

118. Ibid., p. 62. Cf. Ágnes Heller on community in *The Theory of Need in Marx* and in her article on "Individual and Community," in *Social Praxis* 1, 1 (1973).

119. Ibid., p. 290. The word in Polish used here is *Ład*, which translates only as *order* into English but is a term that signifies more than *Porządek*, which is the other, more commonly used word for *order*.

120. Ibid., p. 312.

121. Kołakowski, "Historical Understanding and the Intelligibility of History," in *Triquarterly* 22. Polish version in *Kultura i fetysze*, French version in *Praxis* (int. ed.) 1/2, 1966, p. 14.

122. Ibid., p. 117.

123. Bauman, *Zarys marksistowskiej teorii społeczeństwa* (Warsaw: PWN, 1964), p. 11 (Emphasis in original).

124. Bauman, "Marksa wizja ludzkiego świata," *Argumenty* 17 (255), April 28, 1963, p. 11. Cf. Kołakowski's critique of positivism in his book *The Alienation of Reason* (New York: Doubleday, 1968); published originally as *Filozofia pozytywistyczna* (Warsaw: PWN, 1966).

125. Ibid. Cf. Kosík in *Dialectics of the Concrete* on "Concrete Totality."

126. The question of alienation is taken up by Bauman in the sequel to the article on "Marx's Vision of the Human World," entitled "The Anti-Alienation Perspective" (Perspektywa antyalienacjna), in *Argumenty* 19 (257), May 12, 1963.

127. Bauman, *Zarys marksistowskiej teorii społeczeństwa*, p. 482.

128. Ibid., p. 495.

129. Ibid., p. 549. For more discussion of this theme, see the chapter on Gramsci in *Wizje ludzkiego świata*.

130. Kołakowski, "Karl Marx and the Classical Definition of Truth," in *Towards a Marxist Humanism*. Polish original in *Studia filozoficzne* 2, 1959; also reprinted in Kołakowski, *Kultura i fetysze* (Warsaw: PWN, 1967). Cf. here also Bochenski,

"The Great Split," in *Studies in Soviet Thought* 8, 1 (March 1968): 1–15.

131. Ibid., p. 39.

132. Ibid., p. 54.

133. Ibid., p. 56.

134. Ibid., p. 59.

135. Ibid., pp. 63–64. The "world of things" is "that world upon which man has already imposed 'substantial forms'" (p. 57); it would be interesting to explore further how what Kołakowski says here fits into the theme of reification/fetishization. These concepts generally refer to what is the "second" world of Kołakowski, the world of values, the human world. His later discussion of how the natural sciences and the humanities/social sciences compare in their approach to value judgments (pp. 64–65) sets the stage, but does not people it. Cf. Kosík's discussion of "pseudo-concreteness" in *Dialectics of the Concrete.*

136. Ibid., p. 66. Cf. "Cogito, materializm historiczny, ekspresyjna interpretacja osobowości" in *Kultura i fetysze* (German version in *Traktat über die Sterblichkeit der Vernunft* (Munich: Piper, 1967); also "The Epistemological Significance of the Aetiology of Knowledge," in *Triquarterly* 22 (Fall, 1971). See Ágnes Heller, "Towards a Marxist Theory of Value" on the question of values.

137. Kołakowski, "Cogito, materializm historiczny, ekspresyjna interpretacja osobowości," in *Kultura i fetysze;* originally published in *Studia socjologiczne* 3 (6), 1962, p. 132.

138. Ibid., p. 117. Cf. Kołakowski, *Świadomość religijna i więź kościelna,* p. 74, for a similar discussion.

139. Ibid., pp. 112–113.

140. Baczko, "Marx and the Idea of the Universality of Man," pp. 195–196. (Emphasis is Baczko's)

141. Hirszowicz, *Konfrontacje socjologiczne: Marksizm i socjologia współczesna* (Warsaw: Książka i Wiedza, 1964), p. 55.

142. Hochfeld, "Dwa modele humanizacji pracy," *Studia o marksowskiej teorii społeczeństwa,* p. 237. Published originally in *Kultura i społeczeństwo* 3, 1961.

143. Ibid., p. 239. See here the discussion in "Poland and Britain."

144. Ibid., p. 242. Cf. Bauman on culture as the human artificial environment at the beginning of his *Zarys . . . .*

145. Ibid., p. 244.

146. Ibid., p. 246ff.

147. Ibid., p. 249, 254.

148. Ibid., p. 255. Hochfeld draws in this discussion on David Riesman's *The Lonely Crowd*; Rosenberg and White, eds., *Mass Culture*; and W. Kornhauser, *The Politics of Mass Society*.

149. Ibid., p. 256. Cf. Baczko's discussion of this in *Rousseau: samotność i wspólnota*.

150. Ibid., p. 263.

151. Ibid., p. 264.

152. Hochfeld, "Poland and Britain: Two Concepts of Socialism," *International Affairs* 33 (1957) 4. Published by the Royal Institute of International Affairs, London (originally an address given at Chatham House on October 16, 1956), p. 4.

153. Ibid., p. 6.

154. Ibid., p. 8.

155. Ibid., p. 9.

156. Hirszowicz, *Konfrontacje socjologiczne*, p. 187.

157. Ibid. Cf. Gerson Sher, *Praxis*, p. 151ff, on self-management.

158. Kołakowski, "Intellectuals Against Intellect," *Daedelus* (Summer 1972). Cf. "Intellectuals and the Communist Movement," *Towards a Marxist Humanism*. Polish original in *Nowe drogi* 9, 1956.

159. Ibid., p. 15.

160. Hirszowicz, *Komunisticzny lewiatan* (Paris: Instytut Literacki, 1973; Biblioteka kultury, vol. 234).

161. Ibid., p. 122.

162. Baczko, "Rousseau and Social Marginality," *Daedelus* (Summer 1978); see Fernandes's notes for further discussion of Baczko on Rousseau.

163. See note 4, this chapter. For this theme in his later works, see "Intellectuals Against Intellect"; "The Myth of Human Self-Identity" in L. Kołakowski and S. Hampshire, eds., *The Socialist Idea* (London; Weidenfeld and Nicolson, 1974); also, see Kołakowski, *Main Currents of Marxism*, vols. 1–3 (Oxford: Clarendon Press, 1978). Translated by P. S. Falla. See also this author's review essay on *Main Currents of Marxism* in *Philosophy and Social Criticism* 8, 1 (Spring 1981).

164. George L. Kline, "Beyond Revisionism: Leszek Kolakowski's Recent Philosophical Development," *Triquarterly* 22,

p. 14. Cf. also here G. Kline, "Leszek Kolakowski and the Revision of Marxism," in G. Gomori, C. Newman, eds., *New Writing in Eastern Europe* (Chicago: Quadrangle, 1968). The same essay appeared originally in G. Kline, ed., *European Philosophy Today* (Chicago: Quadrangle, 1965).

165. Bauman, *Socialism: The Active Utopia*, p. 108.

166. Bochenski, "The Great Split," *Studies in Soviet Thought* 8, 1 (March 1968).

Chapter 2: The Budapest School

1. Zbigniew Brzezinski, *The Soviet Bloc* (Cambridge: Harvard University Press, 1960; Rev. and enl. ed., 1967, p. 158 (in 1967 ed.).

2. Ibid., p. 210.

3. Ibid., p. 162.

4. François Fejtö, *A History of the Peoples' Democracies*, translated by Daniel Weissbort (New York: Praeger Publishers, 1971); originally published as *Histoire des démocraties populaires: Après Stalin* [Paris: Editions du Seuil, 1969]), p. 24.

5. Ibid., p. 25.

6. Brzezinski, p. 218.

7. Fejtö, p. 60–61.

8. Brzezinski, p. 219–220.

9. Fejtö, pp. 113–15, citing article in *Pravda* (Moscow), Dec. 26, 1961.

10. Hans-Georg Heinrich, *Hungary: Politics, Economics and Society* (Boulder, Colo.: Lynne Reinner Publishers, 1986), p. 41.

11. Although both terms are accurate, *Budapest School* will be used in the present context because it expresses the relationship of the group as a whole to Lukács better than does the expression *Lukács School*. The latter term implies that those in the group were all disciples of Lukács, but this in fact was not the case. To the extent that they are followers of Lukács, this means only that they share many of his concerns, and that these concerns serve as the basis for their work. Even those who were closest to him, however, and derived the most inspiration from him differ from Lukács in the way they address these common

concerns. It can be said that their work was along the lines Lukács summarized in an interview late in life, when he said that a revival of Marxism "requires two processes: methodologically, back to Marx; for the understanding of reality, a forward move toward a Marxist interpretation of contemporary phenomena." Interview with Lukács on "Some Questions of Peaceful Coexistence" in *Kortars* (Budapest: May 1968); cited in Serge Frankel and Daniel Martin, "The Budapest School," *Telos* 17 (Fall 1973), p. 124.

In addition to the influence Lukács exerted on the group, the works of Antonio Gramsci and Karl Korsch had considerable influence on members of the group, as they acknowledged on various occasions.

12. Kenneth A. Megill, "Philosophy in Hungary," *International Philosophical Quarterly* 9 (June 1969): 277.

13. Ivan Völgyes, "Limited Liberalization in Hungary," *Current History* 70, no. 414 (1976): 107, citing, in footnote 2, expulsion notice in *Szociologica* 1 (1973): 44–45.

14. See Note 11.

15. See Heller's comments on this in her interview in "Marxist Ethics and the Future of Eastern Europe," *Telos* 38 (Winter 1978–79), pp. 166–68. This interview provides an excellent overview of Heller's own intellectual development, as well as that of the Budapest School as a whole.

16. Ibid., p. 155.

17. The proceedings of the conference were published as *Das Problem der Freiheit im Sozialismus,* Konferenz der Sektion Philosophie der Deutschen Akademie der Wissenschaft zu Berlin, 1–10 März, 1956. Protokoll. [East] Berlin, 1956]. Both Kołakowski and Kroński delivered papers at the conference; see note 68 in chapter 1 of this study for details on Kołakowski's paper, and the Bibliography for Kroński's.

18. Heller, "Marxist Ethics and the Future of Eastern Europe," pp. 156–57. Heller here describes the influence Kołakowski had on her intellectual development, as well as differences in their later directions.

19. Ibid., p. 159

20. György Márkus, *Marxism and Anthropology: The Concept of "Human Essence" in the Philosophy of Marx.* Translated by E. de Laczay and G. Márkus. (Assen, The Netherlands: Van Gorcum, 1978]. Translation of *Marxizmus es antropologia,* 2d ed. (Budapest: Akademiai Kiado, 1971.]

21. Andrew Arato, "Introduction: Issues in the Marxian Theory of History," *International Journal of Sociology* 4 (Spring 1974): 8. This essay has a brief recapitulation of the first two chapters of *Marxism and Anthropology* in it.

22. Márkus, "Human Essence and History," *International Journal of Sociology* 4 (Spring 1974): 88.

23. Ibid., p. 84.

24. Ibid., p. 95.

25. Ibid., p. 92. (Emphasis in original). See Márkus's extended discussion of this theme in his footnote 26. Some other themes discussed by Márkus are as follows: for a discussion of the individual, see p. 99 of "Human Essence and History"; "revolutionary *praxis*" appears on p. 101, and in footnote no. 12. The problem of community comes out in his "Marxist Humanism," *Science and Society* (Summer 1966): 283; that of everyday life and knowledge appears in "The Marxian Concept of Consciousness," *Cultural Hermeneutics* 3 (1975): 25, similarly as in Heller's "Towards a Sociology of Knowledge of Everyday Life," *Cultural Hermeneutics* 3 (1975).

26. Márkus, "The Marxian Concept of Consciousness," p. 27; citing Marx, *Grundrisse der Kritik der politischen Oekonomie*, (Dietz Verlag, 1953), pp. 113–14. (Emphasis added by Márkus).

27. Márkus, "Human Essence and History," p. 103. See his footnote 48 for more on this. Contrast this approach to Heller's discussion in *The Theory of Need in Marx* (New York: St Martin's Press, 1974). See also p. 109 in Márkus.

28. Ibid., p. 101. See also Mihály Vajda, "Law, Ethics and Interest" in *Telos* 34 (Winter 1977–78): 173–80.

29. Ágnes Heller, *The Theory of Need in Marx*.

30. Jean Cohen, review of *The Theory of Need in Marx*, by Ágnes Heller, in *Telos* 33 (Fall 1977): 170, 171. Márkus and Gorz were others who dealt with Marx's theory of need.

31. Heller, *The Theory of Need in Marx*, p. 38.

32. Ibid., p. 46.

33. Heller, "Towards a Marxist Theory of Value," *Kinesis* 5 (Fall 1972): 7.

34. Ibid., pp. 9–14. Quote citing Weber found on p. 12.

35. Ibid., p. 13, citing Max Weber, "The Meaning of 'Ethical Neutrality' in Sociology and Economics", in Max Weber, *Max Weber on the Methodology of the Social Sciences* (New York: Free Press, 1949), p. 19.

36. Heller, "Towards a Marxist Theory of Value," p. 61.
37. Ibid., p. 14.
38. Ibid., p. 15.
39. Ibid., p. 16.
40. Ibid.
41. Ibid., p. 18.
42. Ibid., p. 19; in her discussion of the "essential powers of the species," Heller draws on themes elucidated in György Márkus' *Marxism and Anthropology* (Marxizmus es antropologia).
43. Ibid., p. 20.
44. Karl Marx, *Theories of Surplus Value*, vol. 2. (London: Lawrence and Wishart, 1972), p. 118; quoted in Ágnes Heller, *The Theory of Need in Marx*, p. 84.
45. Heller, "Towards a Marxist Theory of Value," p. 20; quoting Marx, *Grundrisse der Kritik der politischen Oekonomie*, p. 312.
46. Heller, "Towards a Marxist Theory of Value," p. 20.
47. Heller, *The Theory of Need in Marx*, p. 76.
48. Ibid., p. 42.
49. Heller, "Towards a Marxist Theory of Value," pp. 24 - 26.
50. Ibid., p. 28.
51. Heller, *The Theory of Need in Marx*, p. 41.
52. Ibid., p. 48.
53. Ibid.
54. Ibid., p. 50.
55. Marx, *Grundrisse*, p. 224; quoted in *Theory of Need in Marx*, p. 54.
56. Heller, *Theory of Need in Marx*, p. 55.
57. Marx, *Economic and Philosophic Manuscripts of 1844* (London: Lawrence and Wishhart, 1970), p. 169; quoted in *Theory of Need in Marx*, p. 56. (Translation modified by Heller.)
58. Marx, *EPP*, p. 150; in *Theory of Need in Marx*, p. 57.
59. Heller, "Towards a Marxist Theory of Value," p. 28.
60. Heller, *The Theory of Need in Marx*, p. 64.
61. See Ágnes Heller and Ferenc Fehér, "Forms of Equality," *Telos* 32 (Summer 1977); also, see Ferenc Fehér, "The Dictatorship Over Needs," *Telos* 35 (Spring 1978). Reference will be made to both of these articles at a later point in this paper.
62. Mihály Vajda, "Law, Ethics and Interest," pp. 173–79.
63. Ibid., p. 177.
64. Ibid., p. 179.

65. Ibid. Quoted by Vajda from Lukács, "The Role of Morality in Communist Production," in *Political Writings, 1919–1929*, ed. Rodney Livingston (London: NLB, 1972), p. 51.

66. Heller, *The Theory of Need in Marx*, p. 68. (See note 34 above.)

67. Ibid., p. 71 (For her discussion of social needs, see pp. 67–73).

68. Ibid., p. 74. Emphasis is Heller's.

69. Ibid., p. 76.

70. Ibid., p. 78.

71. Ibid., p. 80.

72. Ibid.

73. Ibid., p. 81ff.

74. Ibid., p. 84.

75. Ibid.

76. Ibid., p. 86.

77. Ibid., p. 90.

78. Ibid., p. 95.

79. Karl Marx, *Critique of Hegel's Philosophy of Right* (Cambridge: Cambridge University Press, 1970), pp. 137, 138; quoted in Heller, *The Theory of Need in Marx*, p. 88, 89. (Translation modified by Heller.)

80. Heller, *The Theory of Need in Marx*, p. 86.

81. Ibid., p. 88.

82. Heller, "Towards a Marxist Theory of Value," p. 70.

83. Heller, *The Theory of Need in Marx*, p. 96.

84. Ibid., p. 125.

85. Ibid., p. 17.

86. Maria Márkus and Andras Hegedüs, "Free Time and the Division of Labour," in Hegedüs et al., *The Humanization of Socialism* (London: Allison and Burky, 1976). *Kozgazdasagi szemle*, no. 10, 1971.

87. Heller, *The Theory of Need in Marx*, p. 130.

88. Heller, "Towards a Marxist Theory of Value," p. 27. Heller refers in this discussion to Georg Lukács, *Die Eigenart des Aesthetischen* (Neuweid, 1963). Cf. Kosík, *Dialectics of the Concrete*, pp. 66–86.

89. Ibid., pp. 53, 54. Here Heller refers to Lukács's "Heidelburg Aesthetic Fragments" (manuscript), and to "Subject-Object Beziehungen in der Aesthetik," *Logos* 7 (1917): 1–39. Cf. Kosík here also.

90. Ibid., p. 55.
91. Ferenc Fehér, "Is the Novel Problematic? A Contribution to the Theory of the Novel," *Telos* 15 (Spring 1973): 47–74. This version is translated from the French but is a chapter from *Az antinomiak Koltoje (Doestojevszkij es az individuum valsaga)* (Budapest: Magveta Kiado, 1972).
92. Georg Lukács, *Die Theorie des Romans* (Berlin: Luchterland, 1965); in English, *The Theory of the Novel* (Boston: MIT Press, 1971).
93. Fehér, p. 47, citing Lukács: *Theorie*, pp. 23, 26, 35, 53; *Theory*, pp. 30, 33, 40–41, 56.
94. Ibid., p. 49. See discussion of György Márkus's development of the concept of human essence.
95. Ibid., p. 50.
96. Ibid., p. 58. See discussion of this theme as regards Heller.
97. Ibid., p. 67. This theme appears throughout Fehér's writings. Cf. Kosík, p. 66–86.
98. Ibid., p. 71.
99. Ibid., p. 74.
100. Ibid., p. 51.
101. Ibid., pp. 51, 61, 67.
102. Ibid., p. 74.
103. Heller, "Towards a Marxist Theory of Value," p. 56. Cf. David Crocker, *Praxis and Democratic Socialism: The Critical Social Theory of Marković and Stojanović* (Sussex: Harvester Press, 1983) for a similar discussion.
104. Ibid., p. 57.
105. It is perhaps better to say here "social theory" rather than "social sciences," although she herself uses that term, because of the connotations the latter term carries with it today. Cf. Richard Bernstein, *The Restructuring of Social and Political Theory* (Philadelphia: University of Pennsylvania Press, 1978) for an excellent discussion of this problematic. The use of "social theory" for "philosophy" also raises possibilities for discussion along the lines of Marcuse's *Reason and Revolution: Hegel and the Rise of Social Theory* (Boston: Beacon Press, 1960), and the overcoming of philosophy and its change into social theory. Cf. also Karel Kosík on this in his *Dialectics of the Concrete*, pp. 99–106. (*Dialektika konkrétního*, pp. 113–21.)
106. Heller, "Towards a Marxist Theory of Value," p. 59.

107. Maria Márkus and Andras Hegedüs, "Tendencies in Marxist Sociology in the Socialist Countries," in Hegedüs et al., *The Humanization of Socialism: Writings of the Budapest School* (London: Allison and Busby, 1976), p. 131. Hungarian version in *Kortars*, no. 12, 1968.

108. Maria Márkus and Andras Hegedüs, "The Role of Values in the Long-Range Planning of Distribution and Consumption," in *The Humanization of Socialism*, p. 143. Hungarian original in *Kozgazdasagi szemle*, no. 9, 1969.

109. Ibid., p. 146, 147.

110. Ibid., p. 160.

111. Ibid. Cf. discussion in Gerson Sher, *Praxis: Marxist Criticism and Dissent in Socialist Yugoslavia* (Bloomington: Indiana University Press, 1977), on the way in which the *Praxis* group dealt with the question of self-management.

112. Ferenc Fehér, "The Dictatorship Over Needs." Cf. Fehér and Heller, "Forms of Equality."

113. Ibid., p. 32. Emphasis Fehér's.

114. Ibid. Emphasis Fehér's.

115. Ibid., p. 34.

116. Ibid., pp. 34, 35. Cf. Kosík's discussion of rationality on p. 56ff. of his *Dialectics of the Concrete*. (*Dialektika konkrétního*, pp. 68ff.)

117. Ibid., pp. 41, 42.

118. Ibid., p. 40.

119. Ibid., p. 42.

120. Heller, "Marxist Ethics and the Future of Eastern Europe," p. 158.

121. Ibid. Since elsewhere in the same interview Heller stresses that she identifies with Western Europe and looks at the implications for her outlook on Eastern Europe, and remarks that Kołakowski by contrast opted for Eastern Europe, it would be interesting to speculate on the extent to which this characterization applies in his case. Heller clearly implies it, whether intentionally or not.

122. In this regard see Heller, *Alltag and Geschichte* (Berlin: Luchterhand, 1970); one chapter is available in English as "Individual and Community," *Social Praxis* 1, 1 (1973): 11 - 22. Also see "Marxist Ethics and the Future of Eastern Europe" in *Telos* 38 (Winter 1978–79): 153–74.

123. Heller, "Individual and Community," p. 15.

124. Ibid., p. 19.

125. Ibid., p. 21, 22.

126. Heller, "Theory and Practice: Their Relation to Human Needs," *Social Praxis* 1, 4 (1974): 373.

127. Heller, "The Marxist Theory of Revolution and the Revolution of Everyday Life," *Telos* 6 (Winter 1971): 213. Cf. Kosík, p. 42ff.

128. Ibid.

129. Ibid., p. 214. Cf. Kosík on "care" in *Dialectics of the Concrete*.

130. Ibid., p. 215.

131. Ibid., p. 216.

132. Ibid., p. 218.

133. Heller, "Theory and Practice," 373.

134. Heller, "The Marxist Theory of Revolution," 222.

135. Maria Márkus and Andras Hegedüs, "Community and Individuality," in *Humanization of Socialism*, p. 98. Hungarian original in *Kortars*, no. 12, 1970.

136. Ibid., p. 93.

137. Ibid., p. 91.

138. Heller, "Marxist Ethics and the Future of Eastern Europe," p. 161.

139. Heller, *Renaissance Man* (London: Routledge and Kegan Paul, 1978), p. 90. Translation of *A reneszánsz ember* (Budapest: Akademiai Kiado, 1967).

140. Ibid., p. 100, 101.

141. Ibid., p. 114.

142. Ibid., p. 120.

143. Ibid., p. 157. Cf. also Heller, "Towards a Sociology of Knowledge of Everyday Life," 7–18; Translation of "Hit vagy bizaton" [Faith or confidence], in *Ertek es tortenelen* [Value and history], (Budapest: Magreto, 1969), pp. 76–91. Translated by John Fekete.

144. Heller, *Renaissance Man*, p. 445.

145. Serge Frankel and Daniel Martin, "The Budapest School," *Telos* 17 (Fall 1973), pp. 122–33; originally published in *Tagebuch*, June 6, 1973. Translated from the German by Ruth Heydebrand.

146. Ibid., p. 130.

147. Márkus and Hegedüs, "Tendencies in Marxist Sociology in the Socialist Countries," p. 130. Márkus and Hegedüs are

in a position similar to that in Poland of Hochfeld, Hirszowicz, and Bauman, of looking at the sociopolitical structure rather than "philosophical anthropology."

148. For these discussions see Jeff Herf's review of *The Humanization of Socialism* in *Telos* 35 (Spring 1978): 238–43, and the interview with Heller, "Marxist Ethics and the Future of Eastern Europe," p. 172.

149. "The Position Paper of the Cultural Political Work Collective Operating Next to the Central Committee of the Hungarian Socialist Worker's party on the Anti-Marxist Views of Several Social Researchers," in *Telos* 17 (Fall 1973).

150. Heller, "Marxist Ethic and the Future of Eastern Europe," p. 158.

151. It may be that some of them are following Kołakowski's path, particularly Mihály Vajda, but information for this is slight at present.

152. Heller, *The Theory of Need in Marx*, p. 130.

Chapter 3: Czechoslovakia: The Philosophical Background of the Prague Spring

A portion of this chapter appears in different form in "Marxist Critique and Czechoslovak Reform." Chapter on Czechoslovakia in *The Road to Disillusion: From Critical Marxism to Post-Communism in Eastern Europe*, Ray Taras, ed. (Armonk, N.Y.: M.E. Sharpe, 1992). A different version of part of this chapter appeared in *Denver Quarterly* 12, no. 4 (1977) as "Philosophy of Man and the Revival of Culture in Czechoslovakia, 1956–1968."

1. Tad Szulc, *Czechoslovakia Since World War II* (New York: Grosset and Dunlap; paperback edition published by arrangement with Viking Press, 1972), p. 155.

2. *Literární noviny* (Prague), April 21, Nov. 17, Dec. 1, Dec. 29 (1956); Mar. 9 and Mar. 16 (1957); Jan. 4 (1958).

3. Szulc, p. 128.

4. Vladimir V. Kusin, *The Intellectual Origins of the Prague Spring* (Cambridge: University Press, 1971), p. 29.

5. Ibid., p. 28.

6. Szulc, p. 180.

7. Ibid., p. 183.

8. Ibid., p. 184.

9. A. Oxley, et al., *Czechoslovakia: The Party and the people* (London: Allen Lane; The Penguin Press, 1973), p. xiii.

10. Kusin, p. 37.

11. J. M. Bochenski, "The Great Split," *Studies in Soviet Thought* 8, no. 1 (March 1968).

12. Ivan Sviták, *Lidský smysl kultury* (Prague: Československy spisovatel, 1968).

13. Kafka's work was extremely important to the Czech intellectuals for the way in which it raised the question of alienation, and for its use as part of what Kosík called "the artistic destruction of pseudo-concreteness," or fetishized reality. Cf. Kosík, "Hašek a Kafka neboli groteskní svět," in *Plamen* 6 (1963). Serbo-Croatian version in *Dijalektika krize* (Belgrade, 1983); English version in *Cross-Currents* (Ann Arbor, Mich., 1983, Michigan Slavic Materials no. 23, University of Michigan, Department of Slavic Languages and Literatures, pp. 127–36.), 2; reprinted in Kosík, *Crisis of Modernity* (Collection of Kosík's articles translated from the Serbo-Croatian edition, *Dijalektika krize*, and from additional Czech materials from the 1960s provided by Kosík.) Edited by James Satterwhite, in the series "Modern Social and Political Thought in East-Central Europe." Series editors: Lyman Legters, Janos Bak. Forthcoming, by Rowman and Littlefield Publishers.

14. It was subsequently published in the United States as *The Czechoslovak Experiment: 1968–1969* (New York: Columbia University Press, 1971).

15. Marx goes into this in the preface to *A Contribution to the Critique of Political Economy*, in *The Marx-Engels Reader*, ed. Robert C. Tucker (New York: W. W. Norton, 1972), p. 3.

16. V. I. Lenin, "The State and Revolution," *Collected Works*, vol. 25, 4th ed., trans. and ed. S. Spresyan and Jim Riordan. (Moscow: Progress Publishers, 1964), p. 404.

17. V. I. Lenin, *Materialism and Empirio-Criticism* (New York: International Publishers, 1927; New World Paperbacks, 1970), p. 128. "Matter is a philosophical category designating the objective reality which is given to man by his sensations, and which is copied, photographed and reflected by our sensations, while existing independently of them." See all of discussion under "Does Objective Truth Exist," pp. 120–29; also, the reader is referred to L. Kołakowski's essay, "Karl Marx and the

Classical Definition of Truth," in his book *Towards a Marxist Humanism* (New York: Grove Press, 1968).

18. Karel Kosík, "Hegel a naše doba," *Literární noviny* (Prague), Nov. 17, 1956.

19. Ibid.

20. Ivan Sviták, *Man and His World: A Marxian View* (New York: Dell, 1970; Delta Books, 1970), trans. Jarmila Veltrusky. p. 6.

21. Ibid., pp. 8, 9.

22. Ibid., p. 17.

23. Kosík, *Dialektika konkrétního: Studie o problematice člověka a světa* (Prague: ČSAV, 1966), p. 29.

24. Ibid., p. 14.

25. Ibid., p. 19.

26. Ibid., p. 28.

27. Ibid., p. 17.

28. Ibid.

29. Ibid., p. 61.

30. Ibid., p. 152.

31. Ibid., pp. 153–54. See the essay by Kołakowski again; also Bochenski, "The Great Split," p. 11. Kołakowski's interpretation of the Aristotelian position is unique and interesting, and it would tend to resemble Kosík's own understanding as it is implicit in his work.

32. Ibid., p. 156.

33. Ibid., p. 172.

34. Sviták, "Existence, absurdita a revolta," in *Lidský smysl kultury* (Prague: Československy spisovatel, 1968).

35. Kosík, *Dialektika konkrétního*, p. 47.

36. Ibid., p. 49.

37. Ibid., pp. 51, 52.

38. Ibid., p. 52.

39. J. Sedlak discusses this point briefly in his essay, "Filosofie a dnešek," *Literární noviny* (Prague), Dec. 1, 1956.

40. Kusin, p. 51.

41. Kosík, "Hegel a naše doba."

42. Kosík, "Přeludy a socialismus," *Literární noviny* (Prague), Mar. 9 and 16, 1957.

43. Ibid., p. 69.

44. Kosík, *Dialektika konkrétního*, p. 69.

45. Ibid., p. 70.

46. Ibid., p. 74. Here Kosík is concerned about much of the same thing as is J. Habermas. For a further discussion of this topic in Kosík, see his articles "Iluze a realismus" and "Rozum a svědomí" (both in *Literární listy* 1 [1968]). "Rozum a svědomí" (Kosík's speech at the Writer's Congress) appeared in English in A. Oxley, et al., *Czechoslovakia: The Party and the People*, pp. 26–29; Serbo-Croatian version in *Dijalektika krize* (Belgrade, 1983). Another English version is found in Kosík, *Crisis of Modernity*. For further discussion on the subject of dialectical reason, see "Antinomie morálky," *Plamen* 9 (1964), also in *Dijalektika krize* and *Crisis of Modernity*.

47. Sviták, *Man and His World*, p. 35.

48. Ibid., p. 25.

49. Kosík, *Dialektika konkrétního*, p. 53.

50. Ibid., pp. 54–55.

51. Ibid., p. 55.

52. Ibid., pp. 55–57.

53. Ibid., p. 164.

54. Ibid., p. 165.

55. Ibid., p. 58.

56. Ibid., p. 61. Cf. Kosík, "Hašek a Kafka neboli groteskní svět," in *Plamen* 6 (1963), especially the last two sections: "Who Is Švejk," and "Hašek and Kafka." Serbo-Croatian version in *Dijalektika krize* (Belgrade, 1983); English version in *Cross-Currents* (Ann Arbor, Mich. 1983): 2, reprinted in Kosík, *Crisis of Modernity*.

57. Ibid., p. 63. Cf. collection of articles in the journal *Filozofija* (Belgrade) 4, 1967, under the heading "Homo Oeconomicus i humanizacija društva."

58. Ibid., p. 66.

59. Ibid., p. 68.

60. Ibid., p. 60.

61. Ibid.

62. Ibid., p. 88.

63. Ibid., p. 91.

64. Lenin, *Materialism and Empirio-Criticism*, p. 128. See also Kołakowski, "Karl Marx and the Classical Definition of Truth," in *Towards a Marxist Humanism*.

65. Kosík, *Dialektika konkrétního*, p. 91.

66. Ibid., p. 87.

67. Ibid., p. 88.

68. Ibid., p. 87.
69. Ibid.
70. Ibid., p. 78.
71. Ibid., p. 79.
72. Ibid., p. 82.
73. Ibid., p. 83.
74. Ibid., p. 82.
75. Ibid., p. 143.
76. Ibid., p. 145.
77. Ibid., p. 146.
78. Ibid., p. 58.
79. Ibid., p. 84.
80. Ibid, pp. 126–27.
81. Ibid., p. 88.
82. Ibid., pp. 102–03.
83. Sviták, Man and His World, p. 58.
84. Ibid., p. 59.
85. Ibid., p. 60.
86. Ibid., p. 61.
87. Ibid., p. 97.
88. Ibid., p. 63.
89. Ibid., p. 62.
90. Ibid., p. 79.
91. Ibid., pp. 105–06.
92. Ibid., p. 108.
93. Ibid.
94. Ibid., p. 112.
95. Ibid., p. 114.
96. Ibid., pp. 120, 121.
97. As excerpted and translated in A. Oxley, et al., *Czechoslovakia: The Party and the People*, pp. 48, 110, 160. A complete translation, including sections previously unpublished, is in Kosík, *Crisis of Modernity*.
98. Kosík, "Přeludy a socialismus," *Literární noviny* (Prague), Mar. 9 and 16, 1957.
99. Kosík, "Iluze a realismus," *Literární listy* (Prague), 1 (1968).
100. Ibid.
101. Oxley, et al., p. 48.
102. Ibid., p. 112.
103. Ibid., p. 162.

104. See the debate on "The Role of the Party" in G. Golan, *The Czechoslovak Reform Movement* (Cambridge: University Press, 1971), pp. 163–76.
105. A. J. Liehm, *The Politics of Culture* (New York: Grove Press, 1967), p. 397.
106. Ibid., p. 398
107. Ibid., p. 404.
108. Ibid.
109. Ibid., p. 405.

Conclusion: The Yugoslav Praxis Group in the East European Context

1. Gerson Sher, *Praxis: Marxist Criticism and Dissent in Socialist Yugoslavia* (Bloomington: Indiana University Press, 1977), p. 16–17.
2. Ibid., p. 10.
3. Ibid., pp. 10, 32–33
4. Sher, p. 10.
5. Predrag Vranicki, "On the Problem of Practice," *Praxis* (International Edition) 1, 1 (1965), quoted in Sher, *Praxis*, p. 70. See the discussion on the varying approaches of the *Praxis* group to this concept in Sher, *Praxis*, pp. 68–87. Also see David Crocker, *Praxis and Democratic Socialism: The Critical Social Theory of Marković and Stojanović* (Sussex: Harvester Press, 1983), where he closely examines their use of this idea. Several of the *Praxis* group were introduced to Western audiences by Erich Fromm in his *Socialist Humanism: An International Symposium* (Garden City, N.Y.: Doubleday and Company, 1965; Anchor Books edition, 1966).
6. Gajo Petrović, *Marx in the Mid-Twentieth Century* (Garden City, N.Y.: Doubleday and Co., Anchor Books, 1967), p. 78. Translation of *Filozofija i marksizam* (Zagreb: 1965).
7. Ibid., p. 79.
8. Kosík's, *Dialectics of the Concrete*, trans. Karel Kovanda with James Schmidt, Boston Studies in the Philosophy of Science, vol. 52; Synthese Library, vol. 106 (Dordrecht/Boston: D. Reidel, 1976), p. 136–37. Emphasis is Kosík's.
9. Crocker, *Praxis and Democratic Socialism*, p. 47; all of chapter 3 is also devoted to this theme.

10. Crocker, "Praxis and Democratic Socialism" (original manuscript), p. 105. A slightly altered rendition of the same statement is found in the published book on p. 227. All of chapter 7 in the book is devoted to this subject.

11. Márkus, *Marxism and Anthropology: The Concept of "Human Essence" in the Philosophy of Marx*, trans. E. de Laczay and G. Márkus (Assen, The Netherlands: Van Gorcum, 1978). Translation of *Marxizmus es antropologia*.

12. Baczko, "Marx and the Idea of the Universality of Man," in Erich Fromm, ed., *Socialist Humanism*, p. 190. Emphasis is Baczko's.

13. For a discussion of how members of the *Praxis* group dealt with the problem of community, see Sher, *Praxis*, p. 117ff., and Crocker, pp. 74, 171–79.

14. Ibid., p. 105ff, p. 136ff.

15. See Sher, p. 84ff.

16. In addition to Kosík, Marković takes up this question in several places in his book *From Affluence to Praxis* (Ann Arbor: University of Michigan Press; Ann Arbor Paperbacks, 1974).

17. See Sher for an account of these events, on pp. 23–29.

18. Sher, p. 190.

19. Sher, p. xiii.

20. Leszek Kołakowski, *Main Currents of Marxism*, trans. P. S. Falla. Vol. 3: *The Breakdown* (Oxford: Clarendon Press, 1978), p. 465.

21. For an extensive discussion of this theme, see Ray Taras, ed., *The Road to Disillusion*.

22. Kosík, p. 81.

23. The best case in point is Adam Schaff, who after bitterly fighting Kołakowski turned around and wrote *Marxism and the Human Individual* (N.Y.: McGraw Hill, 1970). Originally published as *Marksizm i jednostka ludzka* (Warsaw: PWN, 1967). Another example in Poland is Marek Fritzhand, who found it not at all strange to assert that the Party's program represented the fulfillment of humanist aspirations. Also, the Soviets felt compelled to address the issue in a short book entitled *Problemy gumanizma v marksistsko-leninskoi filosofii*, ed. A. G. Myslivchenko and L. N. Suvorova (Moscow: Izdatelstvo Politicheskoi Literatury, 1975). Kołakowski himself alluded to this phenomenon in his book *Świadomość religijna i więź kościelna* (religious consciousness and ecclesiastical ties), where he dis-

cussed the ability of the Catholic Church, specifically the Jesu-
its, to incorporate ideas—such as mysticism, for instance—that
could otherwise represent a threat to it. He wrote that "the
Catholic Church displayed an exceptional genius in its relationship to mysticism; it demonstrated that it was able to make into
its own property ideas which in principle were contrary to its
own order, and to use them to increase its own glory" (p. 394).

BIBLIOGRAPHY

The list of sources consulted in the writing of this study is divided into the following sections:

I. General Works
II. Poland
III. Hungary
IV. Czechoslovakia
V. Yugoslavia

I. General Works

Bahro, Rudolf. *Die alternative: zur kritik des realexistierenden Sozialismus*. Frankfurt: Europäische Verlagsanstalt, 1977. English version, *The Alternative in Eastern Europe*. London: NLB Press, 1978.

Bernstein, Eduard. *Evolutionary Socialism*. German title: Die Voraussetzungen des Sozialismus und die Aufgaben der Sozialdemokratie. New York: Schocken Books, 1901.

Bernstein, Richard. *The Restructuring of Social and Political Theory*. Philadelphia: University of Pennsylvania Press, 1978.

Brzezinski, Zbigniew. *The Soviet Bloc*. Cambridge, Mass.: Harvard University Press, 1960. Rev. and enl. ed., 1967.

De George, Richard T. *The New Marxism*. New York: Pegasus, 1968.

Fejtö, François. *A History of the Peoples' Democracies.* Translated by Daniel Weissbort. New York: Praeger Publishers, 1971; originally published as *Histoire des démocraties populaires: Après Stalin.* Paris: Editions du Seuil, 1969.

Fetscher, Irving. "New Tendencies in Marxist Philosophy." *East Europe* (May 1967): 9–14.

Fromm, Erich, ed. *Socialist Humanism: An International Symposium.* Garden City, N.Y.: Doubleday and Company, 1965; Anchor Books, 1966.

Heinrich, Hans-Georg. *Hungary: Politics, Economics and Society.* Boulder, Colo.: Lynne Rienner Publishers, 1986.

Lebeder, A. *Esteticheskie Vzglady A. V. Lunacharskogo.* 2d ed., rev. and corr. Moscow: Iskusstvo, 1970.

Lefebvre, Henri. *Everyday Life in the Modern World.* New York: Harper and Row, 1971; Harper Torchbooks, 1971.

Lenin, Vladimir Illiich. *Collected Works,* vol.25, 4th ed. Edited and translated by Stepan Apresyan and Jim Riordan. Moscow: Progress Publishers, 1964.

———. *Materialism and Empirio-Criticism.* New York: International Publishers, 1927. New World Paperbacks, 1970.

Lobkowicz, Nicholas, ed. *Marx and the Western World.* Notre Dame/London: University of Notre Dame Press, 1967.

Lunacharski, A. V. *Sobranie sochinenii.* Edited by I. Anisimov. Vol. 8: *Estetika, literaturnaia kritika.* Moscow: Khudozhestvennaia Literatura, 1967.

Marcuse, Herbert. *Reason and Revolution: Hegel and the Rise of Social Theory.* Boston: Beacon Press, 1960.

Marx, Karl. *Critique of Hegel's Philosophy of Right.* Cambridge: Cambridge University Press, 1970.

———. *Economic and Philosophic Manuscripts of 1844.* London: Lawrence and Wishhart, 1970.

———. *Grundrisse der Kritik der politischen Oekonomie,* Dietz Verlag, 1953.

———. *Selected Works,* vol. 1. Edited by V. Adoratsky. Moscow: Co-Operative Publishing Society of Foreign Workers in the USSR, 1935.

———. *Theories of Surplus Value,* vol. 2. London: Lawrence and Wishart, 1972.

Morby, E. S., et al., eds. *University of California Publications on Modern Philology,* vol. 69. *Soviet Literary Theories: 1917–1934,* by Herman Ermolaev. Berkeley and Los Angeles: University of California Press, 1963.

Myslivchenko, A. G., and Suvorova, L. N., eds. *Problemy gumanizma v marksistko-leninskoi filosofii: istoriia i sovremennost'*. Moscow: Izdatelstvo Politicheskoi Literatury, 1975.

Tokes, Rudolf L., ed. *Opposition in Eastern Europe*. Baltimore: The John Hopkins University Press, 1979.

Trotsky, Leon. *Literature and Revolution*. Ann Arbor: University of Michigan Press, 1960; Ann Arbor Paperbacks, 1960.

Tucker, Robert C., ed. *The Marx-Engels Reader*. New York: W. W. Norton, 1972.

Vaughn, James C. *Soviet Socialist Realism: Origins and Theory*. New York: St. Martin's Press, 1973.

Weber, Max. "The Meaning of 'Ethical Neutrality' in Sociology and Economics," in Max Weber, *Max Weber on the Methodology of the Social Sciences*. New York: Free Press, 1949.

Zhdanov, A. "Sovetskaia literatura—samaia ideinaia, samaia peredovaia literatura v mire." Speech at the First All-Union Congress of Soviet Writers, Aug. 17, 1934. Reprinted by Gospolitizdat in 1953.

II. Poland

Baczko, Bronisław. "Absolut moralny i faktyczność istnienia," In *Wokól myśli Stanisława Brzozowskiego*, pp. 127–78. Edited by Andrzej Walicki and R. Zimand. Kraków: Wydawnictwo Literackie, 1974.

——.*Człowiek i światopoglądy*. Warsaw: Książka i Wiedza, 1965.

——."Demokracja i konserwatysm w utopii J. J. Rousseau," In *Filozofia i utopia*, pp. 5–51. *Archiwum historii filozofii i myśli społecznej*, no. 10 (1964). Edited by B. Baczko, Jan Garewicz, Leszek Kołakowski. Instytut Filozofii i Socjologii, PAN. Warsaw: PWN, 1964.

——. "Filozofia francuskiego oświecenia i poszukiwanie człowieka konkretnego." *Studia filozoficzne* 2–3 (1960).

——. "Hegel, Marks i problemy alienacji." *Studia filozoficzne* 1 (1957): 36–58.

——. "Horyzonty problemowe polskiego heglizmu," In *Polskie spory o Hegla, 1830–1860*. Zakład historii filozofii

nowożytnej i myśli spolecznej, Instytut Filozofii i So-
ciologii, PAN. Warsaw: PWN, 1966.

——. "Kryptoproblemy i historyzm," *Studia filozoficzne* 3, 6
(1958): 76–102.

——. "Marksizm wspólczesny i horyzonty filozofii," In *Filozofia i socjologia XX wieku*, Część 2, pp. 403–19. Seria
myśli i ludzie 2; Filozofia nowożytna i współczesna. Edited by B. Baczko. Warsaw: Wiedza Powszechna, 1965.

——. "Marx and the Idea of the Universality of Man." In
Erich Fromm, ed., *Socialist Humanism: An International
Symposium*. Garden City, N.Y.: Doubleday and Company,
1965; Anchor Books ed., 1966.

——. "O stylu filozofowania," *Myśl filozoficzna* 4, 24 (1956):
3–28.

——. "Oświeceniowe konfrontacje kultur," *Argumenty*, Pt. 1.
June 21, 1964, pp. 1, 10. Pt. 2: "Cechy oświeceniowej kon-
frontacji." June 28, 1964, p. 4.

——. "Rousseau and Social Marginality," *Daedelus* (Summer
1978): 27–40.

——. *Rousseau—samotność i wspólnota*. Warsaw: PWN,
1964.

——. "Walor rzeczowści." *Nowa kultura*, July 6, 1958, p. 4.

Bauman, Zygmunt. *Culture as Praxis*. London and Boston:
Routledge and Kegan Paul, 1973.

——. "Economic Growth, Social Structure, Elite Formation:
The Case of Poland," In *Class, Status and Power*, 2d ed.,
pp. 534–40. Edited by S. Lipset and R. Bendix. New York:
Free Press, 1966. Reprinted from *International Social Science Journal* 5, 16 (1964): 203–16.

——. *Hermeneutics and Social Science*. New York: Columbia University Press, 1978.

——. "Kilka uwag teoretycznych o zasadzie centralismu
demokratycznego." *Nowe drogi* 3 (1957): 93–101.

——. *Kultura a społeczeństwo*. Warsaw: PWN, 1966.

——. " 'Kulturologia' a dychotomiczność świata ludzkiego."
Kultura i społeczeństwo 10, no. 2 (1966).

——. "Marksa wizja ludzkiego świata." Pt. 1: *Argumenty*,
Apr. 28, 1963, pp. 1–11. Pt. 2: "Perspektywa antyalien-
acyjna." *Argumenty*, May 12, 1963, p. 3.

——. "Modern Times, Modern Marxism." *Social Research*
34 (Autumn 1967): 399–415.

———. "Osobowość—kultura—struktura społeczna." *Studia sociologiczne* 2, 17 (1965): 203–33.

———. "O potrzebie socjologii partii." *Myśl filozoficzna* 2, 28 (1957): 3–26.

———. O przezwyciężenie dezintegracji filozofii marksistowskiej." *Myśl filozoficzna* 6, 16 (1956) pp. 133–40.

———. "Parsona teoria czynności i teoria systemu społecznego." In *Filozofia i socjologia XX wieku*, Część 2, pp. 169–99. Edited by B. Baczko. Warsaw: Wiedza Powszechna, 1963.

———. "Rousseau nasz współczesny." Review of B. Baczko, *Rousseau—samotność i wspólnota*. *Argumenty*, May 16, 1965, p. 2–3.

———. "Social Dissent in the East European Political System." *Archives Europeennes de Sociologie* 12 (1971): 25–51.

———. *Socialism: The Active Utopia*. New York: Holmes and Meier Publishers, 1976.

———. *Towards a Critical Sociology*. London and Boston: Routledge and Kegan Paul; Routledge Direct Editions, 1976.

———. "Traktat o biurokracji," *Twórczość* 9 (1957): 103–18.

———. "Vilfredo Pareto i teoria elit," *Myśl filozoficzna* 3 (1957): 3–33.

———. *Wizje ludzkiego świata*. Warsaw: Książka i Wiedza, 1964.

———. *Zarys marksistowskiej teorii społeczeństwa*. Warsaw: PWN, 1964.

Cieplak, Tadeusz, ed. *Poland Since 1956*. New York: Twayne Publishers, 1972.

Czerniawski, Adam. "Prawdy względne Leszka Kołakowskiego." *Kultura* (Paris) 1, 256 (Jan.–Feb., 1969): 201–04.

Czerwinski, Edward J. "Kołakowski and the Jester-Priest Metaphor." *The Polish Review* 13 (Summer 1968): 62–70.

Duvall, George. "The Politics and Philosophy of Adam Schaff: A Study of Revisionism and Humanism in Polish Marxism." M.A. thesis, University of Washington, 1973.

Fernandes, Rubem Cesar. "The Antinomies of Freedom: On the Warsaw Circle of Intellectual History." Ph.D. diss., Columbia University, 1976.

Flechtheim, Osip K. *Von Marx bis Kolakowski*. Studien zur Gesellschaftstheorie. Köln: Europaesche Verlagsanstalt Heft, 1978.

Hirszowicz, Maria. "Ideologia i nauka." *Myśl filozoficzna* 6 (1956): 3–30.

———. *Komunistyczny lewiatan.* Biblioteka kultury, no. 234. Paris: Instytut Literacki, 1973.

———. *Konfrontacje socjologiczne.* Warsaw: Książka i Wiedza, 1964.

———. "Problemy interpretacji Marksa." *Studia filozoficzne* 3 (1959): 3–28.

Hochfeld, Julian. "Marksizm i socjologia stosunków politycznych," *Studia socjologiczno-polityczne* 1 (1958): 3–24.

———. "Poland and Britain: Two Concepts of Socialism," *International Affairs* 33 (Jan. 1957): 2–11. Address at Chatham House, Oct. 16, 1956.

———. "Rewizje i tradicje," in *Przegląd kulturalny* 11, no. 17 (Apr. 1957).

———. "Z zagadnien parlamentaryzmu," *Nowe drogi* 4 (Apr.) 1957.

———. *Studia o marksowskiej teorii społeczeństwa.* Warsaw: PWN, 1963.

Jedlicki, Witold. *Klub kryzwego koła.* Biblioteka kultury, no. 89. Paris: Instytut Literacki, 1963.

Johnson, A. Ross, "Warsaw: Politics and the Intellectuals." *East Europe* (July 1967): 12–16.

Jordan, Zbigniew A. "Der philosophische Hintergrund des Revisionismus in Polen," in *Hinter dem eisernen Vorhang* 8, nos. 7/8, 9 (1962).

———. "Konflikt ideologii marksistowskiej i filozofii," *Kultura* (Paris) 3, 258 (Mar. 1969): 11–24. Text of lecture delivered at York University, Autumn 1968, as part of a cycle of lectures devoted to "European Philosophical Thought After World War II."

———. *Philosophy and Ideology.* Sovietica Series. Dordrecht: D. Reidel, 1963.

———. "Rewizjonizm w Polsce," (1) *Kultura* (Paris) 12, 170 (Dec. 1961): 15–29.

———. "Rewizjonizm Polski," (Dok.) *Kultura* (Paris) 1, 171 (Jan.–Feb. 1962): 21–44.

Kasianova, E.V. "Marksizm li eto." *Voprosy filosofii* 4 (1957): 227–29.

Kline, George L., "Leszek Kolakowski and the Revision of Marxism," In *New Writing of Eastern Europe,* pp. 82–101. Edited by G. Gomori and C. Newman. Chicago: Quadrangle, 1968. Originally published in G. Kline, ed., *European Philosophy Today*. Chicago, Quadrangle, 1965.

Kołakowski, Leszek. *The Alienation of Reason: A History of Positivist Thought*. Translated by Norbut Guterman. New York: Doubleday, 1968.

————. "Dwoje oczu Spinozy," In *Antynomie wolności: Z dziejów filozofii wolności*, pp. 219–29. Edited by Marian Druzkowski and Krystyna Sokol. Warsaw: Książka i Wiedza, 1966.

————. "The Fate of Marxism in Eastern Europe." *Slavic Review* 29 (June 1970): pp. 1–7.

————. *Główne nurty marksizmu*. Vol. 1 *Powstanie;* Vol. 2, *Rozwój;* Vol. 3, *Rozkład*. Paris: Instytut Literacki, 1976–78. English translation is *Main Currents of Marxism*. Vol. 1, *The Founders;* Vol. 2, *The Golden Age;* Vol. 3, *The Breakdown*. Translated by P. S. Falla. Oxford: Clarendon Press, 1978.

————. "Husserl—filozofia doświadczenia rozumiejącego." In *Filozofia i socjologia XX wieku*, Część 1. Warsaw: Wiedza Powszechna, 1962.

————. "Informacja i utopia." Review of Stanisław Lem, *Summa technologiae*. Kraków: Wydawnictwo Literackie, 1964. *Twórczość* 11 (1964): 115–23.

————. "Intellectuals Against Intellect." *Daedalus* (Summer 1972): 1–15.

————. *Jednostka i nieskonczoność*. Warsaw: PWN, 1958.

————. *Kultura i fetysze*. Warsaw: PWN, 1967.

————. "Marxismus und personalistischer Freiheitsbegriff," Deutsche Akademie der wissenschaften zu Berlin. *Das Problem der Freiheit im Lichte wissenschaftlichen Sozialismus*. Konferenz der Sektion Philosophie der Deutschen Akademie der Wissenschaft zu Berlin, 1–10 März, 1956. Protokoll. Berlin: Akademie Verlag, 1956.

————. "Materialismus als negative Mystik." Part 1: *Forum* 12, 138–39 (June–July 1965): 283–86. Part 2: "Uber die Unentbehrlichkeit der Metaphysik." *Forum* 12, 140–41 (Aug.–Sept. 1965): 365–68.

————. "Miejsce filozofowania Stanisława Brzozowskiego." *Twórczość* 6 (1966): 39–54.

————. "The Myth of Human Self Identity," In *The Socialist Idea*. Edited by L. Kołakowski and Stuart Hampshire. London: Wiedenfeld and Nicolson, 1974.

——. *Obecność mitu*. Biblioteka kultury, no. 224. Paris: Instytut Literacki, 1972.

——. "Pascal i epistomologia historyczna Goldmanna." *Studia filozoficzne* 3 (1957): 182–95.

——. "A Pleading for Revolution." *Archives Europeennes de sociologie* 12 (1971): 52–60.

——. "Reply." *Slavic Review* 29 (June 1970): 201–02.

——. *Świadomość religijna i więź kościelna*. Warsaw: PWN, 1965; translated into French as *Chrétiens sans eglise*, Paris: Gallimard, 1969.

——. *Światopogląd i życie codzienne*. Warsaw: PIW, 1957.

——. "Światopogląd XVII stulecia," in *Filozofia XVII stulecia*. Edited by L. Kołakowski. Warsaw: PWN, 1959.

——. "Tezy o nadziei i beznadziejności." *Kultura* (Paris) 6 (1971): 3–21.

——. *Towards a Marxist Humanism*. New York: Grove Press, 1968.

——. "What Is Socialism," In *Bitter Harvest*. Edited by Edmund Stillman. Praeger Publications in Russian History and World Communism, no. 78. New York: Frederick A. Praeger, 1959.

——. "Wokół Pascala," *Studia filozoficzne* 1 (1965): 180–84.

——. "A Leszek Kołakowski Reader." *Triquarterly* 22 (Fall 1971): Entire issue.

Kroński, Tadeusz, "Filozofia na ostrym zakręcie." *Po prostu*, May 5, 1957, pp. 1–5.

——. "Hegel i problemy filozofii historii." *Studia filozoficzne* 3 (1958): 42–75.

——. "Henri Lefebvre i renesans lewicy francuskiej." *Kuźnica*, Feb. 22, 1948, p. 5.

——. *Rozważania wokół Hegla*. Warsaw: PWN, 1960. Contains a complete bibliography of Kronski's works.

——. "Zu den Fragen der individualistischen und totalitaren Freiheitsaufassugnen." Deutsche Akademie der Wissenschaften zu Berlin. *Das Problem der Freiheit im Lichte wissenschaftlichen Sozialismus*. Konferenz der Sektion Philosophie, DAW. zu Berlin, 1–10 März, 1956. Protokoll. Berlin: Akademie Verlag, 1956.

Ladosz, Jarosław. "Marksizm a filozoficzne poglądy Kołakowskiego." *Trybuna ludu*, Apr. 13, 14, 15, 1968, pp. 5–9.

Michnik, Adam. *Kosciól, lewica, dialog.* Biblioteka kultury, no. 277. Paris: Instytut Literacki, 1977.

Pešić-Golubović, Zaga. Review of Zygmunt Bauman's *Zarys marksistowskiej teorii spoleczeństwa. Sociologija* (Belgrade) 1 (1967): 101–04.

Raina, P. K., "Der Fall Kołakowski." *Neues Forum* 14, 159 (March 1967): 209–19.

Schaff, Adam. *Marxism and the Human Individual.* N.Y.: McGraw Hill, 1970. Originally published as *Marksizm i jednostka ludzka.* Warsaw: PWN, 1967.

Schwann: Gesine, *Leszek Kołakowski: Eine marxistische Philosophie der Freiheit.* Stuttgart: Verlag W. Kohlhammer, 1971.

Simon, Maurice D. and Roger E. Kanet, eds. *Background to Crisis: Policy and Politics in Gierek's Poland.* Boulder, Colo.: Westview Press, 1981.

Szacki, Jerzy. "Historia zamiast doktryny." *Studia filozoficzne,* 4, 47 (1966): 155–62.

Tygodnik powszechny, Oct. 13, 1957.

Weiss, Andreas V. "Leszek Kołakowski und die Entfremdung." *Österreichische Ost-Hefte.* 2 (1962): 102–10.

Wiatr, Jerry, and Zygmunt Bauman. "Marksizm i sociologia współczesna." *Myśl filozoficzna* 1 (1957): 3–23.

"Zwolnieni ze stanowisk na Uniwersytecie Warszawskim." *Trybuna ludu.* Mar. 26, 1968, pp. 1, 4.

III. Hungary

Arato, Andrew. "Introduction: Issues in the Marxian Theory of History." *International Journal of Sociology* 4 (Spring 1974): 3–14.

Boella, Laura. "Radicalism and Needs in Heller." *Telos* 37 (Fall 1978): 112–19.

Cohen, Jean. Review of *The Theory of Need in Marx,* by Agnes Heller, *Telos* 33 (Fall 1977): 170–84.

Fehér, Ferenc. "The Dictatorship Over Needs." *Telos* 35 (Spring 1978): 31–42.

———. "Is the Novel Problematic? A Contribution to the Theory of the Novel." *Telos* 15 (Spring 1973): 47–74.

———. "The Last Phase of Romantic Anti-Capitalism: Lukacs' Response to the War." *New German Critique* 10 (Winter 1977): 139–54.

———. "Negative Philosophy of Music—Positive Results." *New German Critique* 4 (Winter 1975): 99–111.

———. "There Is a Verdict." Review of *No Verdict,* by Tibor Dery. *New Hungarian Quarterly* 36 (Autumn 1969): 126–36.

Fehér, Ferenc, and Agnes Heller. "Forms of Equality." *Telos* 32 (Summer 1977): 6–26.

Feenberg, Andrew. "Aesthetics as Social Theory: Introduction to Féher's 'Is the Novel Problematic?'" *Telos* 15 (Spring 1973): 41–46.

Frankel, Serge, and Daniel Martin. "The Budapest School." *Telos* 17 (Fall 1973): 122–33.

Hegedüs, Andras. "Hungary." In *The State of Sociology in Eastern Europe Today,* pp. 79–95. Edited by Jerzy J. Wiatr. Perspectives in Sociology. Carbondale: Southern Illinois University Press, 1971.

———. *The Structure of Socialist Society.* Translated by Rudolf Fisher; revised by Peter Szente. London: Constable and Company, 1977.

Hegedüs, Andras, Ágnes Heller, Maria Márkus, and Mihály Vajda. *The Humanization of Socialism: Writings of the Budapest School.* London: Allison and Busby, 1976.

Hegedüs, Andras, and Maria Márkus. "Hierarchy and the Performance Principle." *International Review of Sociology* 3 (1974).

Hegedüs, Andras, and Maria Márkus. "Modernization and the Alternatives of Social Progress." Paper prepared for the International Sociological Conference on Modernization at the Polish Academy of Sciences, Warsaw, June 11–18, 1972. *Telos* 17 (Fall 1973): 145–56. Reprinted in Hegedüs, et al., *The Humanization of Socialism* in revised form.

Heller, Ágnes. *Alltag und Geschichte.* Berlin: Luchterhand, 1970.

———. *A Theory of Feelings.* Assen, The Netherlands: Van Gorcum, 1979. Dialectics and Society, 7.

———. "Individual and Community." *Social Praxis* 1 (1973): 11–22.

———. "Lukacs' Aesthetics." *New Hungarian Quarterly* 7 (Winter 1966): 84–94.

————. "Marxist Ethics and the Future of Eastern Europe." Interview in *Telos* 38 (Winter 1978–79): 153–74.

————. "The Marxist Theory of Revolution and the Revolution of Everyday Life." *Telos* 6 (Winter 1971): 212–23.

————. "The Moral Mission of the Philosopher." *New Hungarian Quarterly* 13, 47 (Autumn 1972): 156–67.

————. *On Instincts*. Translated by Mario Fengo. Assen, The Netherlands: Van Gorcum, 1979. Dialetics and Society, 6.

————. "On the New Adventures of the Dialectic." *Telos* 31 (Spring 1977): 134–42.

————. *Renaissance Man*. London: Routledge and Kegan Paul, 1978. Translation of *A reneszánsz ember*. Budapest, Akademiai Kiado, 1967.

————. Review of *Passages from Antiquity* and *Lineages of the Absolute State* by Perry Anderson. *Telos* 33 (Fall 1977): 170–84.

————. *Svakodnevni život*. Belgrade: Nolit, 1978. Translation of German version. Hungarian original was *A mindennapi élet*, Budapest: Akademiai Kiado, 1970.

————. "Theory and Practice: Their Relation to Human Needs." *Social Praxis* 1, 4 (1974): 359–73.

————. *The Theory of Need in Marx*. New York: St. Martin's Press, 1974.

————. "Towards a Marxist Theory of Value." Translated by Andrew Arato. *Kinesis* 5 (Fall 1972): (entire issue).

————. "Towards a Sociology of Knowledge of Everyday Life." Translated by John Fekete. *Cultural Hermeneutics* 3 (1975) 7–18.

————. "The Two Myths of Technology." *New Hungarian Quarterly* 9 (Summer 1968): 135–42.

————. "The Challenge of the Counter-Culture and the New Left." *New Hungarian Quarterly* 15, 55 (Autumn 1974): 119–34.

Herf, Jeff. Review of *Humanization of Socialism*. *Telos* 35 (Spring 1978): 238–43.

Lukács, György. *Die Eigenart des Aesthetischen*. Neuweid, 1963.

————. *History and Class Consciousness*. Cambridge, Mass.: MIT Press, 1971. The German original was entitled *Geschichte und Klassenbewusstsein* and was published in Berlin and Vienna in 1923. It was republished in 1968 by Hermann Luchterhand Verlag, Berlin and Neuweid.

————. "The Role of Morality in Communist Production." In *Political Writings, 1919–1929*, Edited by Rodney Livingston. London: NLB, 1972.

————. *Die Theorie des Romans*. Berlin: Luchterhand, 1965; in English, *The Theory of the Novel*. Boston: MIT Press, 1971.

Márkus, György. "Human Essence and History." *International Journal of Sociology* 4 (Spring 1974): 82–125.

————. "The Marxian Concept of Consciousness." *Cultural Hermeneutics* 3 (1975): 19–28.

————. *Marxism and Anthropology: The Concept of "Human Essence" in the Philosophy of Marx*. Translated by E. de Laczay and G. Márkus. Assen, The Netherlands: Van Gorcum, 1978; Translation of *Marxizmus es antropologia*, 2d. ed. Budapest: Akademiai Kiado, 1971.

————. "Marxist Humanism." *Science and Society* (Summer 1966): 275–287.

————. "The Young Lukács and the Problem of Culture." *Telos* 32 (Summer 1977): 95–116.

Megill, Kenneth A. "Philosophy in Hungary." *International Philosophical Quarterly* 9 (June 1969): 267–77.

"The Position Paper of the Cultural Political Work Collective Operating Next to the Central Committee of the Hungarian Socialist Workers' Party on the Anti-Marxist Views of Several Social Researchers." *Telos* 17 (Fall 1973): 134–44.

Vajda, Mihály. *Fascism as a Mass Movement*. New York: St. Martin's Press, 1976.

————. "Karl Korsch's *Marxism and Philosophy*." In *The Unknown Dimension: European Marxism Since Lenin*, pp. 131–46. Edited by Dick Howard and Karl E. Klare. London: Basic Books, 1972.

————. "Law, Ethics and Interest." *Telos* 34 (Winter 1977–78): 173–80.

————. "Marxism, Existentialism, Phenomenology: A Dialogue." *Telos* 7 (Spring 1971): 3–29.

————. "Power and Rule in the Fascist System." *Social Praxis* 1: 159–71.

————. Review of *Prison Notebooks*, by Antonio Gramsci. *Telos* 15 (Spring 1973): 148–56. Translated by John Fekete.

————. "Truth or Truths." *Cultural Hermeneutics* 3 (1975): 29–39.

Völgyes, Ivan. "Limited Liberalization in Hungary." *Current History* 70, 414 (Mar. 1976): 107–10.

IV. Czechoslovakia

Bochenski, J. M. "The Great Split." *Studies in Soviet Thought* 8, no. 1 (Mar. 1968): 1–15.

"Další rozvoj filosofické prace." *Nová mysl* 6 (June 1959): 571–79.

Fiala, Miloš. "The Party's Leading Role in the Sphere of Art." *Rudé Pravo* (Prague), July 17, 1966. Translated in part in Radio Free Europe Research. Czechoslovak Press Survey 1826 (165, 166): 6–9.

Golan, Galia. *The Czechoslovak Reform Movement.* Cambridge: University Press, 1971.

Hajek, Jiří. "Democratization or Liberalization." *Rudé Pravo* (Prague) Apr. 1, 1966. Translated in RFE Research. Czechoslovak Press Survey 1782 (79, 87): 1–6.

Hamšík, Dušan. *Writers Against Rulers.* New York: Random House, 1971; Vintage Books, 1971.

Hawyard, Max. "The Decline of Socialist Realism." *Survey* 18 (Winter 1972): 73–97.

Hendrych, J. Speech of the Third Congress of the Union of Czechoslovak Stage and Film Artists (delivered in Prague on Nov. 29, 1965). *Rudé Pravo* (Prague), Dec. 1, 1965. Translated in part in RFE Research. Czechoslovak Press Survey 1730 (351): 2–10.

Kalivoda, Robert. "Vztah straničkosti a vědeckosti, ideologie a vedy v marxistické filosofii a teorii." *Literární noviny* (Prague), Dec. 15, 1956.

Kosík, Karel. "Antinomie morálky." *Plamen* 9 (1964). This article was reprinted in a more complete version in Italian in the journal *Critica Marxista* 3 (Jan.-Feb. 1964), taken from Kosík's talk at an international conference in Rome. Serbo-Croatian version, "Dijalektika morala i moral dijalektike," in Kosík, *Dijalektika krize* (Belgrade: NIP Mladost, 1983); English version, "The Dialectics of Morality and the Morality of Dialectics," based on Kosík's original manuscript, in Kosík, *Crisis of Modernity* (Collection of Kosík's articles translated from the Serbo-Croatian edition, *Dijalektika krize,* and from additional Czech materials from the 1960s provided by Kosík.) Edited by James Satterwhite, in the series "Modern Social and Political Thought in East-Central Europe." Series editors: Lyman Legters, Janos Bak. Forthcoming by Rowman and Littlefield Publishers. Another English version of the article is "The Dialectic of Morality and the Morality of the Dialectic," in *Telos* 33 (Fall 1977): 85–92.

———. "Česká otázka a Evropa (stručné teze)." mimeographed version obtained from Kosík.

———. "Česká otázka a Evropa." 2d. vers. Photocopy of manuscript obtained from Kosík.

———. *Česká radikální demokracie. Příspěvek k dejinám nazorovych sporů v české společnosti 19. stoleti.* Praha: Státní Nakladatelství Politické Literatury, 1958.

———, ed. *Čeští radikální demokraté. (Výbor politickych statí).* With a foreword by Karel Kosík. Prague: Státní Nakladatelství Politické Literatury, 1953.

———. *Dějiny filosofie jako filosofie: Filosofie v dějinách českého národa.* Prague, 1958

———. *Dialektika konkrétního: Studie o problematice člověka a světa.* Prague: ČSAV, 1966. The English translation of *Dialektika konkrétního* is *Dialectics of the Concrete.* Translated by Karel Kovanda, with James Schmidt. Boston Studies in the Philosophy of Science, vol. 52; Synthese Library, vol. 106. Dordrecht/Boston: D. Reidel, 1976.

———. *Dijalektika krize.* Translated and with an afterword by Aleksander Ilič. Belgrade: NIP Mladost, 1983. This is a collection of articles written by Kosík between 1961 and 1969.

———. "Dopis z 10. prosince 1513." Manuscript, 1967.

———. "Evropská levice." *Plamen* (Apr. 1969). English version, "The European Left," in Kosík, *Crisis of Modernity.*

———. "Filosofie a dějiny literatury." *Plamen* 4 (1961).

———. "Hašek a Kafka neboli groteskní svět." *Plamen* 6 (1963) pp. 95–102. Serbo-Croatian version, in *Dijalektika krize* (Belgrade, 1983); translated as "Hašek and Kafka, or, the World of the Grotesque," in the journal *Cross-Currents* (Ann Arbor, Mich. 1983) 2, reprinted in *Dialectics of Crisis.* Another English version is "Hašek and Kafka," in *Telos* 23 (Spring 1975).

———. "Hegel a naše doba." *Literární noviny* (Prague), Nov. 17, 1956.

———. "Ideologické zdání a politická imaginace." Manuscript, 1969.

———. "Iluze a realismus." *Literární listy* (Prague) 1 (1968): 1. Serbo-Croatian version, "Iluze i realizam," in *Dijalektika krize;* English version, "Illusions and Realism," in Kosík, *Crisis of Modernity.*

———. "Individuum a dějiny." *Plamen* (Oct. 1966); English version, "The Individual and History," given as a speech at the University of Notre Dame (USA). Published in *Marx and the Western World,* edited by N. Lobkowicz. Notre Dame/London: University of Notre Dame Press, 1967. Reprinted in Kosík, *Crisis of Modernity.*

———. "Intelektuál a dělník." *Orientace* 5 (1968); English version, "The Intellectual and the Worker," in Kosík, *Crisis of Modernity.*

———. "Jediná záchrana—spojenectví s lidem." Speech given at a session of the Central Committee of the Czech Communist Party in November 1968. Manuscript. English version, "The Only Chance—An Alliance With the People," in Kosík, *Crisis of Modernity.*

———. "Jinoch a smrt." Manuscript written in Jan. 1969.

———. "Krize moderního člověka a socialismus." *Plamen* 9 (1968): 22–27. Speech given in Zürich and Frankfurt am Main in June 1968. Serbo-Croatian version, "Kriza modernog čoveka i socijalizam," in *Dijalektika krize.* English version, "The Crisis of Modern Man and Socialism" in Kosík, *Crisis of Modernity.*

———. "Kultura proti nihilismu." *Literární noviny* (1964); English version, "Culture Against Nihilism," in Kosík, *Crisis of Modernity.*

———. "Machiavelli a machiavellismus." *Plamen* 2, 3 (1968). Roundtable discussion with the editors of *Plamen,* in which the following people participated: Lubomír Sohor, Jozef Macek, Petr Pithart, and František Šamalík. Serbo-Croatian version, "Tri zapažanja o Makijaveliju," in *Dijalektika krize.* English version, "Machiavelli and Machiavellism," in Kosík, *Crisis of Modernity.*

———. "Mluvení a mlčení." Manuscript, 1967.

———. "Naše nynější krize." *Literární listy* (Prague), Apr. 11– May 16, 1968 (p. LL3 in each issue). Excerpts in English appear as "Our Present Crisis" in Oxley, *Czechoslovakia: The Party and the People.* Serbo-Croatian version, "Naša

sadašnja kriza," in *Dijalektika krize;* full English version, "Our Present Crisis," in Kosík, *Crisis of Modernity.*
———. "Nerudovská hádanka." *Plamen* 8 (1961): 70–73. Serbo-Croatian version, "Nerudina zagonetka," in *Dijalektika krize;* English version, "Neruda's Enigma," in Kosík, *Crisis of Modernity.*
———. "Nezastupitelnost národní kultury." *Literární noviny* (Prague) 1967, p. 1. Serbo-Croatian version, "Nezamenljivost narodne kulture," in *Dijalektika krize.* English version, "The Irreplaceable Nature of National Culture," in Kosík, *Crisis of Modernity.*
———. "O cenzuře a ideologii." *Divadelní noviny,* Mar. 26, 1969. English version, "On Censorship and Ideology," in Kosík, *Crisis of Modernity.*
———. "O české otázce." *Literární listy* (Prague) 12 (1969): L9. Serbo-Croatian version in *Dijalektika krize.* English version, "On the Czech Question," in Kosík, *Crisis of Modernity.*
———. "O Havlíčkove demokratismu." Manuscript, 1969.
———. "O pravdě a strachu ze slov." Discussion held at Charles University in Prague, June 1968. Manuscript.
———. "O smíchu." Supplement to a roundtable discussion. Discussion in the editorial office of *Plamen* on June 5, 1969, in which the following persons participated: František Červinka, Iva Janžarova, Miloš Kopecký, Milan Morávek, Ivan Vyskočil. The discussion was entitled: "Laughter and Liberation." It was led by the unforgettable František Červinka, who opened with the sentence "Humor is a very important matter and an important problem." The record of this discussion was never published because in June 1969 the publication of *Plamen* was forbidden. Manuscript 1969. English version, "On Laughter," in Kosík, *Crisis of Modernity.*
———. "Praha má další autobusové nádraží." *Plamen* (Aug. 1961).
———. "Přeludy a socialismus." *Literární noviny* (Prague), Mar. 9, 16, 1957.
———. "Řeč se vysmívá." Manuscript, 1969.
———. "Rozum a svědomí." *Literární listy* (Prague), Mar. 1, 1968. Speech by Kosík at the Fourth Congress of Czechoslovak Writers, which was held June 27–29, 1967 in Pra-

gue. This speech was used to inaugurate the newpaper *Literární listy.* Reprinted in English in Oxley, *Czechoslovakia: The Party and the People.* Serbo-Croatian version, "Razum i savest," in *Dijalektika krize.* Another English version, "Reason and Conscience," in Kosík, *Crisis of Modernity.*

———. "Špatný vtip." Talk given at a Prague youth rally, Jan. 1969. Excerpt from a tape-recording, with some stylistic corrections made by author. Manuscript.

———. "Stujte v poznané pravdě." Talk at a youth rally in Mar. 1968 in Prague. *Tribuna otevřenosti* (Mar. 1968).

———. "Švejk a Bugulma neboli posedlnost násilím." Manuscript, 1969. English version, "Švejk and Bugulma, or, Possession by Force," in Kosík, *Crisis of Modernity.*

———. "Třídy a realná struktura společnosti." *Filosofický časopis* 5 (1958): 721–33.

———. "Váha slov." *Plamen* 4 (1969): 16–17. Serbo-Croatian version, "Težina reči," in *Dijalektika krize.* English version, "The Weight of Words," in Kosík, *Crisis of Modernity.*

———. "Věk predvadivosti." Manuscript, 1967.

———. "Vlast Máchova." Manuscript, 1967.

———. "Zaslepenost uhlířské víry." *Literární noviny* (Prague), (June 1964). English version, "The Blindness of Sheer Faith," in Kosík, *Crisis of Modernity.*

———. "Zitřek je v naších rukou." *Literární noviny* (Prague), (Jan. 4, 1958), pp. 1, 4.

Kusin, Vladimir V. *The Intellectual Origins of the Prague Spring.* Cambridge: University Press, 1971.

Liehm, Antonin J. *The Politics of Culture.* Translated by Peter Kussi. Introduction by J. P. Sartre. New York: Grove Press, 1967.

Lobkowicz, Nikolaus. "Philosophical Revisionism in Post-War Czechoslovakia." *Studies in Soviet Thought* 4 (June 1964): 89–101.

———. Review of *Dialektika konkrétního: Studie o problematice člověka a světa,* by Karel Kosík. *Studies in Soviet Thought* 4 (Sept. 1964): 248–251.

Navrátil, Jan. [Karel Kosík]. "2,000 slov a hystérie." *Plamen* (Aug. 1968). English version, "Two Thousand Words" and "Hysteria," published in Kosík, *Crisis of Modernity.*

———. [Karel Kosík]. "O dělnickych radach—kriticky." *Plamen* (Aug. 1968). English version, "A Word of Caution on Workers' Councils," in Kosík, *Crisis of Modernity*.

Oxley, Andrew, et al. *Czechoslovakia: The Party and the People*. London: Allen Lane; Penguin Press, 1973.

Radio Free Europe Research. "The Positive Hero and Socialist Realism." *Situation Report—Czechoslovakia* 24 (1975): 1–4.

Satterwhite, James. "Marxist Critique and Czechoslovak Reform." Chapter on Czechoslovakia in *The Road to Disillusion*, Ray Taras, ed. Armonk, N.Y.: M. E. Sharpe, 1992.

———. "Philosophy of Man and the Revival of Culture in Czechoslovakia, 1956–1968." *Denver Quarterly* 12, no. 4 (1977).

Schmidt, James. "Praxis and Temporality: Karel Kosík's Political Theory." *Telos* 33 (Fall 1977): 71–84.

Sedlak, J. "Filosofie a dnešek." *Literární noviny* (Prague), Dec. 1, 1956.

———. "K vetši aktivitě na kulturní frontě." *Literární noviny* (Prague), Dec. 23, 1958. Svaz československých spisovatelů. *IV Sjezd Svazu československých spislovatelů: Protokol*. Prague, Czechoslovakia: n.p. 1957.

Sviták, Ivan. *The Czechoslovak Experiment: 1968–1969*. New York: Columbia University Press, 1971.

———. "A Diamond at the Bottom." *Literární noviny* (Prague), Apr. 23 (1966). Translated in RFE Research.

———. "Filosofie a život." *Literární noviny* (Prague), Dec. 29, 1956.

———. "Kafka as Philosopher." *Survey* 59 (Apr. 1966): 36–40.

———. *Lidský smysl kultury*. Prague: Československý spisovatel, 1968.

———. *Man and His World: A Marxian View*. Translated by Jarmila Veltrusky. New York: Dell, 1970; Delta Books, 1970.

———. "Některé přičiny zaostavaní teorii." *Literární noviny* (Prague), Apr. 1, 1956.

Szulc, Tad. *Czechoslovakia Since World War II*. New York: Grosset and Dunlap; paperback edition published by arrangement with Viking Press, 1972.

Teige, Karel. *Jarmark uměni.* Prague: Československý spisovatel, 1964.

――――. *Výbor z dila.* Edited by Jiří Brabec, et al. Foreword by Robert Kalivoda. Vol. 1, *Svět stavby a basně: Studie z dvatcatých let.* Prague: Československý spisovatel, 1966.

――――. *Vyvojove proměny v uměni.* Prague: Nakladatelství československých vytvarných umělců, 1966. Vědecká konference věnovana dilu Franze Kafky. *Franz Kafka.* Liblice, Czechoslovakia: 1963.

Zeleny, Jindřich. "O psuedo-materialistické tendenci v naši filosofii." *Nová mysl* 6 (1959): 580–610.

V. Yugoslavia

For a complete index to the international edition of *Praxis*, the reader is referred to Mihailo Marković and Gajo Petrović, eds., *Praxis: Yugoslav Essays in the Philosophy and Methodology of the Social Sciences.* Also, although many articles appear in both the Yugoslav and international editions, no attempt at cross-reference is made in the following bibliography. Articles in the Yugoslav edition are designated (YE), and those in the international edition (IE).

Bosnjak, Branko. "Ime i pojam praxis." *Praxis* (YE) 1, 1 (Sept.–Oct. 1964).

Bosnjak, Branko and Supek, Rudi, eds. *Humanizam i socijalizam.* 2 vols. Zagrab: Naprijed, 1963.

Carter, April. *Democratic Reform in Yugoslavia.* London: Frances Pinter, 1982.

"Čemu praxis." *Praxis* (YE) 1, 1 (Sept.–Oct. 1964).

Čovek danas. Edited by Miloš Stambolić. Belgrade: Nolit, 1964.

Crocker, David. *Praxis and Democratic Socialism: The Critical Social Theory of Marković and Stojanović.* Sussex: Harvester Press, 1983. Portions appear in *Inquiry*, and in Burke, et al., eds. *Marxism and the Good Society.* London: Cambridge University Press, 1981.

Golubović, Zagorka. "Aktualni problemi marksističke koncepcije društva." *Gledišta* 3, 1960.

――――. Antropološka analiza ljudskih funkcija kulture." *Filosofija* 3/4, 1969.

――――. "Cilj i motivacija kao determinante istorijskih procesa." *Sociologija* 3 (1965).

――――. *Čovek i njegov svet.* Belgrade: Prosveta, 1973.

――――. "Da li imamo jasno definisanu koncepciju socialnog razvoja?" *Filosofija* 3, 1967.

――――. "Jedna značajna humanistička interpretacija Marksa." Review of Erich Fromm's *Marx's Concept of Man.* *Gledišta* 5, 1961.

――――. "Kultura kao most između utopije i realnosti." *Praxis* (YE) 9, 1/2 (1972)

――――. "Mesto antropologije u Marxovoj koncepciji istoriskog materializma." *Praxis* (YE) 4, 3 (1967).

――――. "Mesto teorije otuđenja u Marksovoj humanističkoj filozofiji." *Gledišta* 2, 1963.

――――. "O jednom tumačenju studentskih pokreta i otuđenja." *Filosofija* 4, 1972.

――――. "Pledoaje za antisistem; antiinstitutcionalni marksizam." *Filosofija* 3/4, 1973.

――――. "Problemi savremene tehničke civilizacije: Otuđeni i neotuđeni rad." *Sociologija* 3/4 (1960).

――――. "Putevi i dileme jugoslovenske sociologije." *Filosofija* 1/2, 1968.

――――. "Renesansa autentičnog marksizma u Schaffovoj koncepciji ličnosti." *Filosofija* 3/4, 1968.

――――. "Self-Fulfillment, Equality and Freedom." *Praxis* (IE) 9, 2/3 (1973).

――――. "Socialism and Humanism." *Praxis* (IE) 1, 4 (1965).

――――. "Socialist Ideas and Reality." *Praxis* (IE) 7, 3/4 (1971).

――――. " 'Sociologija ličnosti' i zamke sociologizma." *Filosofija* 1, 1969.

――――. *Stalinizam i socijalizam: Nastanak Stalinizma u ideologiji i praksi Sovjetskog društva,* Filozofske studije. Beograd: Filozofsko Društvo Srbije, 1982.

――――. "The Trends and Dilemmas of Yugoslav Sociology." *Praxis* (IE) 5, 3/4 (1969).

――――. "What Is the Meaning of Alienation?" *Praxis* (IE) 2, 3 (1966).

――――. Why Is Functionalism More Desirable in Present-Day Yugoslavia than Marxism? *Praxis* (IE) 9, 4 (1973).

Grlić, Danko. "Čemu umjetnost." *Praxis* (YE) 3, 2 (1966).

――――. *Contra dogmaticos.* Zagreb: Praxis, 1971.

———. "Dogma ili filozofija." *Praxis* (YE) 2, 3 (1965).

———. "Društvena organizacija i teatar." *Praxis* (YE) 10, 3/4 (1973).

———. "Kreacija i akcija." *Praxis* (YE) 4, 5/6 (1967).

———. "Literarna kritika i marksistička filozofija." *Filosofija* 4, 1979.

———. "Marginalije o problemu nacije." *Praxis* (YE) 3, 3/4 (1971).

———. "Neki problemi morala kod Friedericha Nietzschea." *Pogledi* 12 (1953).

———. "Neki temeljni problemi suvremene estetike." *Praxis* (YE) 7, 3 (1970).

———. "O nekim filozofskim aspektima Krležinog djela." *Sociologija* 5 (1963).

———. "Postoji li građanska i socijalistička umjetnost?" *Praxis* (YE) 10, 5/6 (1973).

———. "Revolucija i teror." *Praxis* (YE) 7, 5/6 (1970).

———. "Smisao angažiranosti u filozofiji." *Praxis* (YE) 4, 4 (1967).

———. "Smisao ili besmisao povijesti." *Praxis* (YE) 2, 6 (1965).

Gruenwald, Oskar. "Humanism and Marxism: The Yugoslav Perspective." Ph.D diss., Claremont Graduate School and University Center, 1972.

Horvat, Branko, et al., eds. *Self-Governing Socialism*. 2 vols. White Plains, N.Y.: International Arts and Sciences Press, Inc., 1975.

Johnson, A. Ross. "The Dynamics of Communist Ideological Change in Yugoslavia, 1945–1953." Ph.D diss., Columbia University, 1967.

Jugoslovensko udruženje za filozofiju. *Neki problemi teorije odraza: Referati i diskisija na IV stručnom sastanku udruženja; Bled, Nov. 10–11, 1960: n.p., 1961.

Kangrga, Milan *Čovjek i svijet*. Razlog biblioteka, no. 85. Zagreb: Sveučilišna biblioteka liber, 1975.

———. *Etički problem u djelu Karla Marksa*. Zagreb: Naprijed, 1963.

———. Etički smisao socijalizma." *Naše teme* 1, 1957.

———. *Etika i sloboda*. Zagreb: Naprijed, 1966.

———. "Fenomenologija ideološko-političkog nastupanja jugoslavenske sredne klase." *Praxis* (YE) 8, 3/4 (1971).

———. "Filozofe, šta misliš?" *Praxis* (YE) 1, 1 (1964).

———. "Hegel i Marx." *Pregled* 11/12, 1961.
———. "Hegel—metafizika ili revolucija." *Praxis* (YE) 7, 5/6 (1970).
———. "Marxov pojam otuđenja." *Pregled* 4, 1961.
———. "O utopijskom karakteru povijesnoga." *Praxis* (YE) 6, 5/6 (1969).
———. "Politička i socijalna revolucija." *Filosofija* 3, 1967.
———. "Povijesnost i mogučnost." *Praxis* (YE) 2, 6 (1965).
———. "Povijest i tradicija." *Praxis* (YE) 5, 4 (1968).
———. "Praksa i kritika." *Praxis* (YE) 2, 2 (1965).
———. "Problem ideologije." *Pogledi* 11 (1953).
———. "*Razmišlenja o etici*. Zagreb: Praxis, 1970.
———. "Smisao Marxove filozofije." *Praxis* (YE) 4, 3 (1967).
———. "*Smisao povijesnog*. Razlog biblioteka, no. 39. Zagreb: 1970.
———. "Socijalizam i etika." *Praxis* (YE) 3, 4 (1966).
———. "Suvremenost Marxove filozofije." *Naše teme* 2, 1958.
Krešić, Andrija. *Dijalektika politike*. Sarajevo: Veselin Maslesa, 1968.
———. "Ekonomska vrijednost i etička vrijednost." *Praxis* (YE) 3, 4 (1966).
———. *Kraljevstvo božje i komunizam*. Beograd: IMRP, 1975.
———. "Marksistička i apstraktno-materialistička dijalektika." Afterword to A. Deborin, *Uvod u filozofiju dijalektičkog materializma*. Sarajevo: Veselin Maslesa, 1960.
———. "Nenasilje kao ljudski način opstanka." *Praxis* (YE) 7, 1/2 (1970).
———. *Političko društvo i politička mitologija; Prilog kritici "kulta licnosti"*. Belgrade: Vuk Karadžić, Zodiak, 1968.
———. "The Proletariat and Socialism in the Works of Marx and in the World Today," *Praxis* (IE) 5, 3/4 (1969).
———. "Socializam kao pitanje istorije." *Praxis* (YE) 2, 1 (1965).
Kurtz, Paul and Svetozar Stojanović. *Tolerance and Revolution: A Marxist–Non-Marxist Humanist Dialog*. Contemporary Philosophical Themes. Belgrade: Philosophical Society of Serbia, 1970.
Kuvačić, Ivan. "The Basis and Prospects of the Radical Right." *Praxis* (IE) 8, 3/4 (1972).
———. "Contemporary Forms of Mental Violence." *Praxis* (IE) 6, 1/2 (1970).

———. "Ideologija srednje klase." *Praxis* (YE) 9, 3/4 (1972).

———. "Kultura i politika." *Praxis* (YE) 7, 3 (1970).

———. "Marksizam i funkcializam." *Sociologija* 1: (1965).

———. "Marxova analiza građanskog društva i teorija konvergencije." *Praxis* (YE) 10, 5/6 (1973).

———. "Masovne komunikacije i savremeno društvo." *Sociologija* 10, 4 (1968).

———. "Naučno-teknički progres i humanizam." *Praxis* (YE) 6, 1/2 (1969).

———. "O perspektivama razvoja naše sociologije." *Sociologija* 8 (1966).

———. "O rutinizaciji života." *Praxis* (YE) 2, 4/5 (1965).

———. " 'Postindustrial Society' and Freedom." *Praxis* (IE) 9, 2/3 (1973).

———. "Postoji li kriza u sociologiji?" *Praxis* (YE) 11, 3-5 (1974).

———. "The Rebellion Against the Institutions of the Affluent Society." *Praxis* (IE) 4, 3/4 (1968).

———. "Spontanost i organizacija." *Praxis* (YE) 9, 1/2 (1972).

Marko, Kurt. "Marxismus aus Yugoslavien: Ein Literaturbericht." *Östereichische Ost-Hefte* 3, 1971.

Marković, Mihailo. "Basic Issues of Self-Management." *Praxis* (IE) 10, 1/2 (1974).

———. "Cause and Goal in History." *Praxis* (IE) 2, 1/2 (1966).

———. "The Concept of Revolution." *Praxis* (IE) 5, 1/2 (1969).

———. *The Contemporary Marx.* European Socialist Thought series, no. 3. London: Spokesman Books, 1974.

———. "Critical Social Theory in Marx." *Praxis* (IE) 6, 3/4 (1970).

———. "Dijalektika kao metoda kritičkog mišljenja." *Filosofija* 4, 1970.

———. "Economism or the Humanization of Economics?" *Praxis* (IE) 6, 3/4 (1970).

———. "Entfremdung und Selbstverwaltung." In *Folgen einer Theorie: Essays uber 'Das Kapital' von Karl Marx.* Edited by Ernst Theodore Mohl. Frankfurt: Suhrkamp Verlag, 1967.

———. *From Affluence to Praxis: Philosophy and Social Criticism.* Ann Arbor: University of Michigan Press, Ann Arbor Paperbacks, 1974.

———. "Gramsci on the Unity of Philosophy and Politics." *Praxis* (IE) 3, 3 (1967).

————. "Historical Praxis as the Ground of Morality." In *Humanist Ethics*. Edited by Morris Storer. Buffalo: Prometheus Books, 1980.

————. "Human Nature and Social Development." In *Contemporary East-European Philosophy*, vol. 1. Edited by Edward D'Angelo. Bridgeport, Conn.: Spartacus Books.

————. *Humanizam i dijalektika*. Biblioteka današnji svet. Belgrade: Prosveta, 1967.

————. "Jednakost i sloboda." *Praxis* (YE) 10, 1/2 (1973).

————. "Marks i naučna kritička misao." *Filosofija* 3/4, 1968.

————. *Marksizam, dogmatizam i skepticizam*. Radnički Univerzitet: Dialektički materializm. Series ed. M. Marković. Belgrade: Rad, 1958.

————. "Marksova dijalektika i humanizam danas." *Gledišta* 1, 1964.

————. "Marxist Humanism and Ethics." *Inquiry* 6, 1963.

————. "Nasilje i samoostvarenje čoveka." *Filosofija* 3, 1972.

————. "O mestu i ulozi društvenih nauka u našem društvu." *Praxis* (YE) 2, 2 (1965).

————. "Opšti metodološki problemi društvenih nauka u našoj zemlji." *Sociologija* 2 (1965).

————. "Osnovi dijalektičko-humanističke teorije istine." *Praxis* 2, 2 (1965).

————. "The Possibilities for Radical Humanism." In *In the Name of Life: Essays in Honor of Erich Fromm*. Edited by Bernard Landis and Edward S. Tauber. New York: Holt, Rinehart and Winston, 1971.

————. "The Problem of Reification and the 'Verstehen-Erklarung' Controversy." *Acta Sociologica* (Copenhagen) 15.1 (1972).

————. *Revizija filozofskih osnova Marksizma u Sovetskom savezu*. Biblioteka savremene filozofije. Belgrade: Srpsko Filozofško Društvo, 1952.

————. "Samoupravljanje i efikasnost." *Praxis* (YE) 10, 5/6 (1973).

————. "Socialism and Self-Management." *Praxis* (IE) 1, 2/3 (1965).

————. "Struktura moći u jugoslovenskom društvu." *Praxis* (YE) 8.6 (1971).

————. "Uslovi i mogučnosti usmeravanja društvenog razvoja u socializmu." *Praxis* (YE) 2, 4/5 (1965).

————, and Cohen, Robert S. *Yugoslavia: The Rise and Fall of Socialist Humanism; A History of the Praxis Group.* Nottingham: Spokesman Books, 1975.

————, and Petrović, Gajo, eds. *Praxis: Yugoslav Essays in the Philosophy and Methodology of the Social Sciences.* Boston Studies in the Philosophy of Science, vol. 36. Synthese Library, vol. 134. Dordrecht, Holland: D. Reidel, 1979. Selections from *Praxis,* Yugoslav Edition, 1965–1974.

Marks i savremenost, vols. 1, 2, 3. Belgrade: Institut za izučavanje radničkog pokreta and Institut društvenih nauka, 1963, 1964, 1966.

Pešić—see Golubović.

Petrović, Gajo. "Dialectical Materialism and the Philosophy of Karl Marx." *Praxis* (IE) 2, 3 (1966).

————. "The Development and Essence of Marx's Thought." *Praxis* (IE) 4, 3/4 (1968).

————. "Dvije knjige o sovjetskoj filozofiji." *Pogledi* 8 (1953).

————. "Filozofija i revolucija." *Praxis* (YE) 6, 1/2 (1969).

————. "Filozofija u SSSR-u od oktobarske revolucije do 1938g." 1 and 2. *Pogledi* 2 (1952); 3 (1953).

————. "Filozofska i sociološka relevantnost Marxova pojma otuđenja." *Praxis* 3, 4 (1966).

————. *Filozofski pogledi G. U. Plehanova.* Zagreb: Kultura, 1957.

————. "Humanism and Revolution." In *In the Name of Life: Essays in Honor of Erich Fromm.* Edited by Bernard Landis and Edward S. Tauber. New York: Holt, Rinehart and Winston, 1971.

————. "Kultura između elite i masa." *Praxis* (YE) 8, 6 (1971).

————. "Man as Economic Animal and Man as Praxis." *Inquiry* 6, 1963.

————. *Marx in the Mid-Twentieth Century.* Garden City, N.Y.: Doubleday & Co., Anchor Books, 1967.

————. "Marxova filozofija." *Praxis* (YE) 2, 4/5 (1965).

————. *Mišlenje revolucije.* Biblioteka naprijed. Zagreb: Naprijed, 1978.

————. *Mogučnost čoveka.* Biblioteka razloga, no. 30. Zagreb: Studentski centar sveučilišta, 1969.

————. "Philosophy and Socialism." *Praxis* (IE) 3, 4 (1967).

————. "Povijest i klasna svest." *Praxis* (YE) 11, 3–5 (1974).

————. "Smisao i mognćnost stvaralaštva." *Praxis* (YE) 4, 5/6 (1967).

Plotzker, Herman J. "Contemporary Yugoslav Marxism: A Study in the Meaning of a Critical Humanism." Ph.D diss., New York University, 1978.

Popov, Nebojša. "Naučna istina i istina jedne politike." *Praxis* (YE) 11, 1/2 (1974).

————. "Oblici i karakter društvenih sukoba." *Praxis* (YE) 8, 3/4 (1971).

————. "Prologomena za sociološko istraživanje društvenih sukoba." Foreword to *Jun-Lipanj, 1968: Dokumenti.* Special issue of *Praxis,* 1969.

————. "Sociologija i ideologija." *Praxis* (YE) 9, 3/4 (1972).

————. "Strajkovi u savremenom jugoslovenskom društvu." *Sociologija* 4 (1969).

Rus, Veljko. "Institutionalization of the Revolutionary Movement." *Praxis* (IE) 3, 2 (1967).

————. "Moć i struktura moći u jugoslovenskim preduzečima." *Sociologija* 2 (1970).

————. "Odgovornost u našim radnim organizacijama." *Sociologija* 3 (1969).

————. "Participatirna i reprezentativna demokratija." *Praxis* (YE) 8, 5 (1971).

————. "Self-Management Egalitarianism and Social Differentiation." *Praxis* (IE) 6, 1/2 (1970).

Rusinow, Dennison. *The Yugoslav Experiment, 1948–1974.* Published for the Royal Institute for International Affairs. Berkeley and Los Angeles: University of California Press, 1978.

Rutten, Ursula. "Marxismus als Gesellschaftskritik: Die *Praxis* Gruppe in Jugoslawien—Grenzen und Möglichkeiten." Ph.D diss., Rheinisch-Westfalische Technische Hochschule, Aachen, 1976.

Sher, Gerson, ed. *Marxist Humanism and Praxis.* Buffalo: Prometheus Books, 1978.

————. *Praxis: Marxist Criticism and Dissent in Socialist Yugoslavia.* Bloomington: Indiana University Press, 1977.

Smisao i perspektive socializma: Zbornik. Special Issue of *Praxis.* Edited by Danilo Pejović and Gajo Petrović. Zagreb: Croatian Philosophical Society, 1965.

Stojanović, Svetozar. *Between Ideals and Reality: A Critique of Socialism and its Future.* Translated by Gerson S. Sher. New York: Oxford University Press, 1973.

————. "Contemporary Yugoslavian Philosophy." *Ethics* 76 (July 1966).

————. "Freedom and Democracy in Socialism." *Praxis* (IE) 1, 2/3 (1965).

————. *In Search of Democracy in Socialism: History and Party Consciousness.* Translated by Gerson S. Sher. Buffalo: Prometheus Books, 1981.

————. "The June Student Movement and Social Revolution in Yugoslavia." *Praxis* (IE) 6, 3/4 (1970).

————. "Prospects of the Socialist Revolution in the Present Time." *Praxis* (YE) 5, 1/2 (1969).

————. "Šta je kritika." *Gledišta* 2, (1964).

Stojanović, Svetozar, and Svetlana Knjazeva-Adamović, eds. *Problemi filozofije marksizma.* Politička škola. Belgrade: Rad, 1967.

Supek, Rudi S. R. "Aktualnost Hegelove i Lenjinove misli." *Praxis* (YE) 7, 5/6 (1970).

————. "Čemu, nastalom, sada još i ovaj marksizam." *Praxis* (YE) 9, 3/4 (1972).

————. *Egzistencijalizam i dekadencija.* Zagreb: Matica Hrvatska, 1950.

————. "Etičke antinomije revolucionarne egzistencije." *Praxis* (YE) 2, 1 (1965).

————. *Humanistička inteligencija i politika.* Biblioteka razlog, no. 45. Zagreb: 1971.

————. *Imamo li sociologiju i gdje je ona?" *Praxis* (YE) 1, 2 (1964).

————. "Još jednom o alternativi: Stalinistički pozitivizam ili stvaralački marksizam." *Praxis* (YE) 2, 6 (1965).

————. "Jugoslavensko samoupravljanje pred europskim forumom." *Praxis* (YE) 7, 3 (1970).

————. "Književnost i psihoanaliza." *Pogledi* 1 (1952).

————. "Kultura i socijalističko samoupravljanje." *Pogledi* 3 (1954).

————. "Marx i revolucija." *Praxis* (YE) 6, 1/2 (1969).

————. "Materijalni, socijalni i personalni osnovi socijalističke kulture." *Pogledi* 4 (1953).

———. Nacija i nacionalna kultura." *Praxis* (YE) 2, 3 (1965).
———. *Participacija, radnička kontrola i samoupravljanje.*
Zagreb: Naprijed, 1974.
———. "Partija i inteligencija." *Praxis* (YE) 2, 3 (1965).
———. "Plehanov je vidio točno." *Pogledi* 9/10 (1953).
———. "Policija, birokracija i struktura staljinizma." *Praxis*
(YE) 6, 3/4 (1969).
———. "Politika stare i nove radničke klase." *Sociologija* 1
(1975).
———. "Psihologija nacija i nacionalizama." *Filosofija* 3 (1967).
———. "Sociologija i marksizam." *Sociologija* 1 (1969).
———. *Sociologija i socializam.* Biblioteka Gledišta. Zagreb:
Znanje, 1966.
———. "Some Contradictions and Insufficiencies of Yugoslav
Self-Managing Socialism." *Praxis* (IE) 7, 3/4 (1971).
———. "Sudbina proizvođačke zajednice." *Praxis* (YE) 2, 1
(1965).
———. "Teorija otuđenja i sociologija." *Sociologija* 1/2 (1964).
———. "Zašto kod nas nema borbe mišlenja?" *Pogledi* 12
(1953).
———. "Značaj teorije otuđenja za socialistički humanizam."
Pregled 1, 1953.
Tadić, Ljubomir. "Autoritet i autoritarno mišljenje." *Filosofija*
1/2 (1968).
———. "Autoritet i osporavanje." Manuscript that was to have
been published in 1975 in Zagreb but was refused publi-
cation because of political pressure.
———. "Birokratija—poštvarena organizacija." *Praxis* (YE) 4,
5/6 (1967).
———. "Diferenciranje pojma demokratije." *Praxis* (YE) 10, 1/2
(1973).
———. "Filozofija i ideologija." *Filosofija* 1, 1970.
———. "Inteligencija u socializmu." *Filosofija* 1/2, 1967.
———. "The Limits Set to Human Freedom by Private Prop-
erty." *Praxis* (IE) 9, 1 (1973).
———. "Moć, elite, i demokracja." *Praxis* (YE) 7, 1/2 (1970).
———. "Nacionalizam i internacionalizam." *Filosofija* 3, 1967.
———. "O suvislosti jedne odbrane birokratije." *Praxis* (YE) 2,
4/5 (1965).
———. "Prirodno pravo i socijalna utopija." *Praxis* (YE) 3, 3
(1966).

―――. "Socialistička revolucija i politička vlast." *Praxis* (YE) 6, 1/2 (1969).

―――. "Stvarnost, utopija i anarhija." *Filosofija* 2/3, 1971.

―――. "Uz problem društvene jednakosti." *Praxis* (YE) 3, 4 (1966).

Vranicki, Predrag. "Aktualnost marksove misli." *Praxis* (YE) 4, 3 (1967).

―――. "Antonio Gramsci i smisao socijalizma." *Praxis* (YE) 4, 4 (1967).

―――. "Antropološki element materialističkog shavačanja historije." *Praxis* (YE) 4, 4 (1967).

―――. *Čovek i historija.* Biblioteka logos. Sarajevo: Veselin Maslesa, 1966.

―――. "Država i partija u socijalizmu." *Praxis* (YE) 4, 5/6 (1967).

―――. "Engels i filozofija." *Praxis* (YE) 3, 1 (1966).

―――. "Filosofija u našem vremenu." *Filosofija* 1/2, 1968.

―――. *Filozovske studije i kritike.* Belgrade: Kultura, 1957.

―――. "Građanski svijet i socijalizam." *Praxis* (YE) 10, 5/6 (1973).

―――. *Historija marksizma.* 2 vols. 2d ed., rev. and enl. Zagreb: Naprijed, 1971.

―――. "Jedna diskusija o dialektici." *Praxis* (YE) 1, 2 (1964).

―――. "Marksizam u Čehoslovačkoj." *Praxis* (YE) 7, 4 (1970).

―――. *Misaoni razvitak Karla Marxa.* 2d ed. Zagreb: Matica Hrvatska, 1963.

―――. "Moral i historija." *Praxis* (YE) 8, 6 (1971).

―――. "Nekoliko misli o humanitetu u teoriji i historijskoj praksi." *Praxis* (YE) 2, 6 (1965).

―――. "O koegzistenciji." *Praxis* (YE) 1, 1 (1964).

―――. "On the Problem of Praxis." *Praxis* (IE) 1, 1 (1965).

―――. "O nekim problemima odnosa u komunizmu." *Praxis* (YE) 2, 4/5 (1965).

―――. *O problemu opčeg, posebnog i pojedinačnog kod klasika marksizma.* Belgrade: Kultura, 1952.

―――. "Socialism and the Problem of Alienation." *Praxis* (IE) 1, 2/3 (1965).

―――. "Socijalizam i kriza." *Praxis* (YE) 8, 3/4 (1971).

―――. "Socijalizam i nacionalno pitanje." *Praxis* (YE) 5, 4 (1968).

Životić, Miladin. *Čovek i vrednosti.* Biblioteka današnji svet, no. 7. Belgrade: Prosveta, 1969.

———. "The Dialectics of Nature and the Authenticity of Dialectics." *Praxis* (IE) 3, 2 (1967).

———. "The End of the Ideals or of Ideology?" *Praxis* (IE) 3/4 (1969).

———. "Hajdegerova kritika metafizike." *Filosofija* 3/4, 1968.

———. "Is Equality a Moral Value in Our Society?" *Praxis* (IE) 2, 4 (1966).

———. "Istina i njena konkretnost." *Praxis* (YE) 2, 2 (1965).

———. "Nekoliko teza o destruktivnoj, konformističkoj i stvaralačkoj ličnosti." *Praxis* (YE) 3, 4 (1966).

———. "O aktualizaciji istorije." *Praxis* (YE) 2, 6 (1965).

———. *O ideologiji.* Radnički univerzitet: Dijalektički materijalizam. Belgrade: Rad, 1958.

———. "Socialism and Mass Culture." *Praxis* (IE) 1, 2/3 (1965).

———. "Socijalistički humanizam i jugoslovenska filozofija." *Filosofija* 1/2, 1968.

———. "Za naučnu interpretaciju i tačnu interpretaciju." *Gledišta* 3, 1963.

INDEX

Alienation, 61, 83, 104, 109, 182–84, 204nn124, 126; and freedom, 40, 47, 53; and needs, 93–94, 99; and "world of appearances," 50, 53, 54, 203n102

Baczko, Bronisław, 17, 18, 19, 68–69, 183–84; and critique of Stalinism, 22, 25; and discussion of freedom, 46–55, 61; and discussion of needs, 59; and philosophy, 28–32, 65
Bahro, Rudolf, 195n2
Bauman, Zygmunt, 17, 18, 19, 191, 197n10; and community, 53; and critique of bureaucracy, 20, 21; and human nature, 55–57, 183, 204n126; and philosophy, 22–26, 28, 65, 215n147; and sociology, 23–24, 32–36, 67–68; and utopia, 69–70
Berlin Conference on Freedom, 78, 201n68, 208n17
Bernstein, Eduard, 6, 175, 195n3
Bielińska, Maria. See Hirszowicz, Maria

Camus, Albert, 69, 146
"Care," 146, 154–55, 199n32
Charter 77, 191

Club of the Crooked Circle (Klub krzywego koła), 13, 197n1
Community, 53–54, 91, 94, 107, 111, 183–84, 204n118; and "everyday life," 118–19, 121–23; and freedom, 40; and orthodoxy, 37–38; and the Praxis group, 221n13
CPSU (Communist Party of the Soviet Union), Twentieth Congress of, 13, 73, 78–79, 130, 178
Czechoslovak Writers' Union, 132–33, 136, 151

Dialectical materialism, 29, 178
Dilthey, W., 69
Dubrovnik Conference on "Man Today," 136

Engels, Friedrich, 100
Epistemology, 9, 57–58, 60, 138, 143, 150, 199n33
Existentialism, 135, 144

Fehér, Ferenc, 74–75; and art, 109–10; and needs, 114–17
Frankfurt School, 10, 36, 175

Gomułka, W., 14
Gramsci, Antonio, 30, 88, 174, 204n129

253

Márkus, György, 74, 75; and
human essence, 81–83, 182,
203n103, 209nn25, 27, 210n42,
212n94
Márkus, Maria, 74, 75; and community, 122–23; and freedom,
107; and needs, 114; and sociology, 113, 126–28, 214n147

Nagy, Imre, 72–73
"Need," 81, 83–86, 88–96, 98–
107, 113–19, 122, 124, 126;
human needs, 49, 59–60, 82,
93–94, 99, 104, 107, 115–16,
182–83; radical needs, 99–106,
114–15, 118, 182
New Course, 71, 77
New Economic Mechanism
(NEM), 74
Novomesky, Laco, 133
Novotny, Antonin, 131, 132, 133

Pareto, Antonio, 35, 200n54
Petöfi Circle, 73, 78
Petrović, Gajo, 180, 182
Phenomenology, 135, 152
Pogledi, 187
Polis, 63
Polish October, 6, 17, 45
Prague Spring, 172, 187, 191,
202n87
"Praxis," 149–50, 153, 157, 170,
183, 209n25; as human cre-
ative activity, 40, 48, 83, 135,
142–45, 163, 166, 180, 182;

philosophy of, 80, 85; *Praxis*
(journal), 180, 184–85,
212n103, 241; and work,
160–61
PZPR (Polish United Workers'
Party), 18

Rákosi, Matyas, 71–73, 76
Revisionism, 7, 15, 128, 186, 191,
206n164; philosophical, 7, 16–
17, 19, 57, 67, 70, 188, 190, 192
Rousseau, J. J., 49–55, 156, 184

Sartre, J. P., 69
Schaff, Adam, 221n23
Sik, Ota, 133
Slánsky (Rudolf) Trials, 132
Slovak Journalists' Union, 133
Slovak Writers' Union, 132
Solidarity, 191
Spinoza, 68
Stojanović, Svetozar, 190, 196n6,
212n103, 220n5
Svitak, Ivan, 132, 145–46; and
art, 163–68; and ideology, 151–
52; and philosophy, 134–36,
139–41, 173, 199n29

Tito, Josip Broz, 177, 188
"Totality," 184–85

Utopia, 44, 50

Vajda, Mihaly, 74, 75, 84, 97, 127,
201n71
Vranicki, Predrag, 180, 220n5

Weber, Max, 86–88, 112, 209n35

PITT SERIES IN

RUSSIAN AND
EAST EUROPEAN STUDIES

Jonathan Harris, Editor